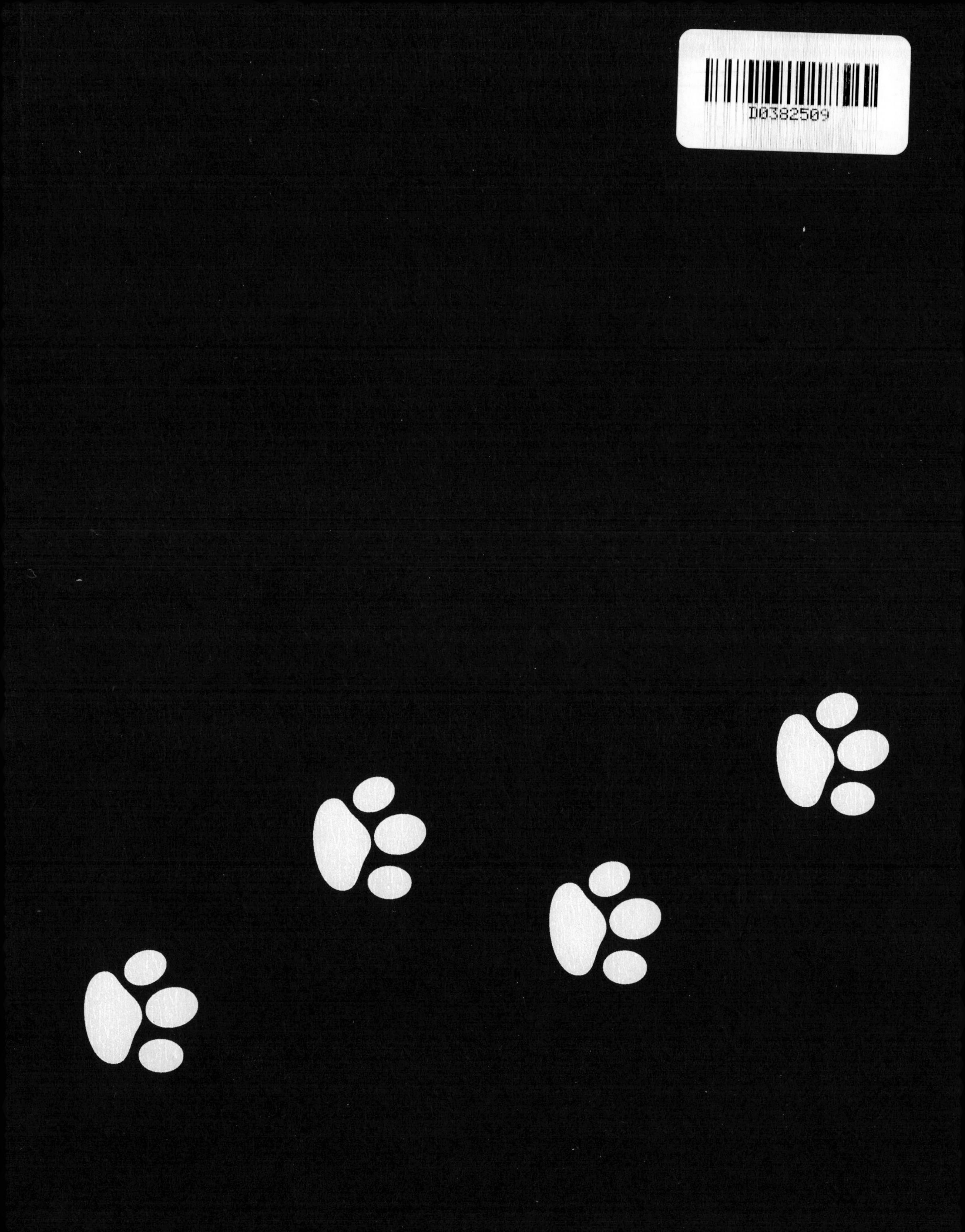

THE NITTANY LION

An Illustrated Tale

Jackie R. Esposito and Steven L. Herb

THE NITTANY LION

An Illustrated Tale

Foreword

by

Joe and Sue Paterno

The Pennsylvania State University Press
University Park, Pennsylvania

Library of Congress Cataloging-in-Publication Data

Esposito, Jackie R.
The Nittany Lion : an illustrated tale /
Jackie R. Esposito and Steven L. Herb ;
foreword by Joe and Sue Paterno.
p. cm.
Includes bibliographical references (p.) and index.
ISBN 0-271-01588-8 (alk. paper)
1. Pennsylvania State University—Mascots—History.
2. Statues—Pennsylvania—University Park—History.
3. Lions. I. Herb, Steven. II. Title.
GV691.P4E76 1997
796.332'64'0974853—dc21 97-1836
CIP

Printed in the United States of America
Published by The Pennsylvania State University Press,
University Park, PA 16802–1003

It is the policy of The Pennsylvania State University Press to use acid-free paper for the first printing of all clothbound books. Publications on uncoated stock satisfy the minimum requirements of American National Standard for Information Sciences—Permanence of Paper for Printed Library Materials, ANSI Z39.48–1992.

To the loves of my life,
Emily and Bridget, who named their first cat "Nittany Lion"
after seeing Tim Durant perform at the Homecoming Parade in 1991,
and
David, for his vision.

JE

To Sara, with love,
I present these two additional and very important Nittany Lion facts:
We met just 1,000 feet from the Shrine,
and married 100 feet closer.

SH

To the Paterno Libraries Endowment,
a most worthy cause in honor of the family of two extraordinary people,
Joe and Sue Paterno,
to which the authors have assigned a significant
portion of the royalties earned from this book.

Contents

Foreword

The Nittany Lion Shrine is the majestic symbol of a proud University. For years, students, alums, and fans have had their pictures taken on it, children have climbed all over it, and all Penn Staters have identified their experiences at Dear Old State with it.

The Nittany Lion has a special significance and an individual meaning for every Penn Stater. That significance is difficult for people who have never been to Penn State to understand, but it is easily recognized by those who have studied, worked, or lived here, or even visited once or twice. That undefined something makes Penn Staters smile when they hear the expression "Happy Valley." They know the significance behind that often-used psychological description for State College and Penn State—it's true! Not every person, not every day, but generally this valley we inhabit is happy. The people who live and work and study here are caring people who have made a commitment to their local community and to the University they share, to make Happy Valley a region true to its name. The Nittany Lion captures that commitment to the region, that shared enthusiasm for Penn State that brings us all together.

The Nittany Lion became a part of our lives soon after we arrived at Penn State. From his first day as an assistant coach for Rip Engle in 1950, Joe saw the Shrine every morning on his way to his Rec Hall office. In 1959, Sue lived across from the Shrine in McKee Hall, where seeing Mr. Warneke's creation every day made it natural for her to identify this "stately Nittany Lion" with her wonderful experiences in college.

The Shrine is more than just another location on campus dedicated to some tradition or another: it is the embodiment of what we believe Penn State represents. First and foremost, anyone who has looked into those big eyes knows that it is one smart lion—having, of course, studied at the land-grant university he protects. He is powerful, yet not overbearing; regal, yet not snobbish. The Nittany Lion Shrine symbolizes Penn State's past accomplishments while reflecting its hopeful future, which is the key to Penn State's success in all its academic and athletic endeavors. A great university must simultaneously represent what it has been and promise what it will be. No school symbol does that better than Penn State's Nittany Lion.

The authors of *The Nittany Lion* have used our University Archives in Pattee Library to find most of the facts presented in this history of Penn State's admired symbol. Readers will find that this fascinating history of the Nittany Lion is also a history of the University, of presidents and students, of sports teams and athletes, of mischief-makers and heroes. It is a well-told "tale" that is sure to make every Penn Stater proud.

Over the years, memories of college days at Penn State may grow dim, but not the emotions and excitement that surround the Nittany Lion. It is more than just a symbol; it has become whatever Penn State is to each one of us who holds this great University close to our hearts.

Joe and Sue Paterno

Introduction

Every College has a legend
Passed on from year to year
To which they pledge allegiance
And always cherish dear;
But of all the honored idols,
There's but one that stands the test,
It's the stately Nittany Lion,
The symbol of our best.

—James Leyden, Class of 1914

A university of Penn State's reputation and size is represented by thousands of images and millions of words, but to most "Penn Staters" there are only two images necessary to capture the essence of Penn State—the Mascot and the Shrine—and only two words needed to name both: the **Nittany Lion.**

Penn State's Mascot is a burst of enthusiasm in a lion suit running and tumbling and flying through the air. The sporting crowd is in his hands (or paws) as he asks for and receives its collective voice in extolling the virtues of Penn State's athletic teams. It is the Nittany Lion who acts the way we wish we could, when we are so excited about winning we'd like to jump out of our seats and onto the court, or to float all the way to the rim of Beaver Stadium on a wave of fans' fingertips. The Lion often reminds us to laugh, and during frightening moments he reminds 95,000 people to exhale in unison. The Lion also helps us with the losses, by always recognizing the importance of every team's effort and every crowd's contribution. The Lion Mascot represents what is best about school spirit at this University—the enthusiasm, the joy, and the loyalty. The Nittany Lion Mascot symbolizes the heart of Penn State.

The other image is as still as the Mascot is active. For more than half a century it has been vigilantly watching over its corner of the University Park campus. The sun has beaten down unmercifully on its head while it has borne patiently the pats of a million hands. The rain, sleet, hail, and other winter delights we watch from inside have marked its back with wear, as have the pants and legs of a million riders. Over the years, it has been hugged, kissed, and stroked

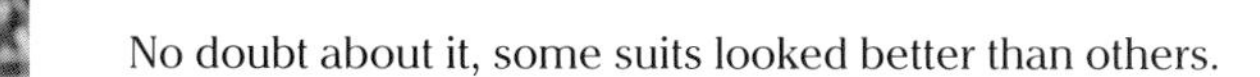

No doubt about it, some suits looked better than others.

The Nittany Lion Shrine in its full glory.

Sample of Nittany Lion Licensing, 1996.

by countless friends, and a few enemies have drawn, painted, and otherwise defaced it. It has been photographed more than any Penn State or State College landmark, more than all the presidents of the University combined, perhaps more than any single President of the United States. The Nittany Lion Shrine has withstood all with a dignity that is abundantly evident in a first glimpse of the sculpture.

Of all the scores of delightful attractions Penn State holds, a visit to the University is not complete without a pilgrimage to the famous lion sculpture across from Rec Hall. The Shrine represents the solid traditions of the University—the history, the campus, and the students. The Nittany Lion Shrine symbolizes the soul of Penn State.

This book tells the story of the Nittany Lion from its birth to the present day. It is a collection of tales interwoven. One is about a Penn State baseball player and a boast he made at Princeton University one cold April morning long ago. Another is the story of the last Pennsylvania mountain lion, who now lives in Pattee Library on Penn State's University Park campus. It is the tale of a campus humor magazine's call for a guardian spirit for Penn State. It is the legend of Nita-nee, the Indian princess. It is the story of the gift of the Class of 1940 and of the wonderful sculptor who turned a 13-ton block of limestone into a Penn State icon. It is also the story of three dozen students and one gymnastics coach who, with the donning of a head and a suit, transformed themselves from ordinary humans into the legendary Nittany Lion.

Even on the Mascot's occasional day off, or in a corner of the campus far from the Shrine, it is not hard to locate the image of the Nittany Lion at Penn State University. One can find the Lion on nearly every conceivable souvenir and in every manner of publication, except one. The Nittany Lion has been mentioned in countless books, in magazine and newspaper articles, in athletic program guides, and in other University publications, but this marks the first time a book has been devoted exclusively to Penn State's treasured symbol. The Nittany Lion is long overdue for a touch of historical devotion.

The Baseball Season of 1904

H. D. Mason

THE SEASON OF 1904, on the whole, was an eminently successful one, since out of sixteen college games, eleven were victories, and such rivals as Princeton, W. & J., Dickinson, F. & M., West Virginia, Fordham, Bloomsburg, Gettysburg, and Mt. St. Mary's were decisively defeated. Out of five games played with such strong professional clubs as Williamsport, Altoona, and Watsontown, the latter easily beaten, while all three Williamsport games were exceedingly close ones. At the opening of the season the prospects were very unfavorable for a winning nine, since the graduation of '03 left but three 'Varsity men in college, viz: Captain Elder, First-baseman Ray, and Pitcher McIlveen. In addition to this difficulty

1

Creating a Mascot

The Boast at Princeton

The Nittany Lion was born on a bitter cold April day in 1904—but not in Happy Valley, where he reigns as king. His life began where many of Penn State's sports teams have faced their toughest hurdles—on the road.

The Penn State baseball team awoke that blustery Wednesday morning about to face their strongest opponent of the season. Expectations had not been high for a team that returned only three varsity players to the diamond, and after an opening-game win over Bellefonte Academy at home the eastern road trip was proving difficult. The men from State were shut out by West Point (1–0) on April 16th and by Manhattan College (6–0) on the 18th, all but wiping out any joy they had obtained by beating Bloomsburg Normal in their first contest on the road.

Penn State's baseball team, 1904. The uniformed player immediately in front of the student manager (in white cap, top row, far right) is "Joe" Mason.

A hard-fought one-run victory at Fordham University the day before had brightened their spirits, and now it was April 20, the final game of the eastern leg of the season—and that meant Princeton. Penn State had beaten Fordham and held their own at West Point, but the Princeton baseball team was tough to beat anywhere, and on their own field they were formidable. The Pennsylvania State College nine were tired from all that train travel and looking forward to returning home, but first they had to face the Princeton Tigers.

It is hard to gauge just how certain the Princeton nine were of winning the game that day, but during a morning tour of campus for the Penn State team, a couple of tour guides couldn't resist a pre-game boast. Third Baseman Harrison "Joe" Mason remembered it this way four decades later at the dedication of the Nittany Lion Shrine:

> As you students well know, sophomores are generally pretty cocky chaps, and when these two escorted us into their beautiful gymnasium, they stopped us in front of a splendid mounted figure of a Bengal tiger. One chap spoke up: "See our emblem, the Princeton Tiger, the fiercest beast of them all." An idea came to me, and I replied, "Well, up at Penn State we have Mount Nittany right on our campus, where rules the Nittany Mountain Lion, who has never been beaten in a fair fight. So, Princeton Tiger, look out!"

Realistically, there was far more truth in the boast of the Princeton sophomores regarding the prowess of their Tiger than in Freshman Joe Mason's wishful retort about a nonexistent mountain lion mascot, but sometimes life does imitate art, even when art is a tall tale. In a stunning upset, Penn State beat Princeton 8–1 that afternoon. The box score showed Joe Mason at his usual third-base position. He threw out three men on ground balls and caught two fly balls or line drives. He scored a run, had one hit, and made one error. No mention is made of the remarkable achievement he set into motion that morning at the Princeton gym. Before he graduated in the spring of 1907, Joe Mason would transform his spur-of-the-moment boast into the Nittany Lion Mascot, one of the nation's most recognized and respected symbols of school spirit.

The Princeton baseball team, 1904.

The Princeton Tiger.

STATE.	R.	H.	O.	A.	E.
Mason, 3d.	1	1	2	3	1
Kilmer, c.	2	1	3	5	0
Ray, 1st	1	2	14	1	2
McIlveen, p.	1	1	1	5	0
Moorhead, m.	1	1	1	0	0
Haverstick, l.	1	2	1	0	0
Elder, s. s.	1	0	1	3	1
Forkum, 2d.	0	2	4	4	1
Thompson, r.	0	0	0	1	0
Total	8	10	27	22	5

PRINCETON.	R.	H.	O.	A.	E.
Davis, r.	0	0	0	0	0
Cosgrove, m.	0	0	3	0	0
Underhill, l.	0	1	3	0	0
Furnell, 3d.	1	1	2	2	1
Bard, 1st.	0	1	12	0	1
Cooney, 1st.	0	0	1	0	0
Wells, 2d.	0	1	2	1	0
Sat'waite, s. s.	0	0	0	2	1
Reid, c.	0	0	4	2	0
Stevens, p.	0	0	0	8	0
Doyle, p.	0	0	0	1	0
Total	1	4	27	16	3

State	0	0	0	5	0	0	3	0	0	—8
Princeton	0	0	0	0	0	0	1	0	0	—1

Two Base hits—Wells, Haverstick, 2; Elder, Thompson, Reid. Stolen base—Thompson. Struck out—By McIlveen, 3; by Doyle, 1; Stevens, 1. Bases on balls—Davis, Moorhead, 2; Underhill. Hit by pitched ball—Elder, McIlveen, Davis. Time of game—1:55. Umpire—Goldeaux.

Box score, Penn State vs. Princeton, April 20, 1904.

Harrison Denning "Joe" Mason.

A Love of Baseball

Harrison Denning Mason Jr. was a quiet, unassuming young man—except when he played baseball. Harry Mason loved baseball, and he was very good at it. At 5 feet, 11 inches and only 150 pounds, his physical presence was not imposing, yet his skill at the game was easily observed on any diamond he graced. At the turn of the century Harry Mason was one of Western Pennsylvania's best baseball players, but it was not likely that anyone would have learned of his talent from Mason himself. On the field he could chatter with the best of them, and off the field he would talk up the terrific

The Mason Family, c. 1912. *Bottom row, left to right:* Ella McCargo Mason, Harrison Denning Sr., Harrison Jr., Earle. *Top row, left to right:* Charles, Dean, Dale, and David.

exploits of his fellow players, but he was not one to blow his own horn. Hundreds of newspaper clippings of Harry Mason's various teams' accomplishments from 1901 to 1912 show nary an underline of his name, although he was one of the best players on every squad and many of his teams won championships. What's even more remarkable is that Harry Mason wrote many of the stories for a number of Western Pennsylvania newspapers and never once sang his own praises. While the adjectives flowed for his teammates, he simply reported a hit or a run for himself.

Growing up in Pittsburgh, Harrison Jr. was the eldest of six sons born to Harrison Denning Mason and Ella McCargo. Harrison Sr. was a purchasing agent for the Allegheny Railroad by day, but at night he was a poet, an essayist, and the coach of a burgeoning baseball squad where every player seemed to be named Mason.

Harry was born on December 19, 1879. Two verses excerpted from a Mason Sr. poem appearing in the *Parker (Pa.) Weekly Phoenix*, reveal a father's love for his toddler son:

Issuing from out the embers
Comes a laughing little boy;
He has seen but two Decembers
Life to him is all a joy.

He is mine—this little fairy,
With cheeks of red and eyes of blue;
With his step and motion airy,
With his face so fair and true—

(Pittsburgh, January 22, 1883)

In addition to his writing, Harrison Denning Mason Sr. loved the game of baseball. He had played semi-pro ball as a catcher back in the days when the catcher stood far enough behind the plate to catch the ball on one hop. His intense fondness for baseball was passed along to all six of his sons. About the time Harry Jr. reached full adulthood, in that last summer before the century turned over, the six Mason boys with their three girl cousins from next door could knock off any other neighborhood baseball nine.

Harry Mason Jr. also picked up his father's love for words. Harry's college scrapbook is largely devoted to the game they both loved, but every few pages a quote from Mark Twain appears between box scores, or the obituary of Jules Verne is squeezed between two successful team outings. Both baseball and writing would play a part in Harry Mason's pursuit of the Nittany Lion, but it was baseball alone that turned him from Harry to Joe.

A Handful of Harrys

There is no record of why Harry Mason decided to go to college in the autumn of 1903, but it is certainly likely that he foresaw the distinct advantages a college degree would bring. There is also no record of why he chose to attend the Pennsylvania State College, but it is highly probable that he knew they could use a third baseman. He heard that from someone in a position to know—Harry McIlveen, who had just finished his freshman year on the varsity baseball team.

"Lefty," "Irish," "Mac," "Mal," "Harry"—the many names of Henry McIlveen.

Score by Innings	1	2	3	4	5	6	7	8	9	
Windsors	1	1	0	3	0	0	0	8	0	- 13
Leetsdale	0	0	2	0	0	0	1	0	2	- 5

Date - July 13, 1901
Place - Leetsdale
Attendance - 400
Scorer - [illegible]
Rooters - [illegible] Kirk, Cole, Mason, McCauley
Substitutes - Stauffer, Chipley, Cassidy
Batteries - Blakely and Fisher, Small and Mortimer
Passed Balls - Mortimer
Wild Pitches - Small 1
Struck Out - By Blakely 5 By Small 6
Bases on Balls - Off Blakely 4 Off Small 4
Sacrifice Hits - Bell, Lewis
Stolen Bases - [illegible]
Hit by Pitched Ball - Mason, Jackson 2, Bell, Hohan, Blakely, [illegible]
Innings by each Pitcher - Blakely 9, Small 8, Lewis 1
Two Base Hits - Fisher, Jackson, [illegible]
Three Base Hits - Mortimer, Leight
Home Runs - x
Double Plays - [illegible] to Stacey
Triple Plays - x
Time of Game - 2:00
Umpire - McCauley

Windsors: Mason - 3; McIlveen - M; Fisher - C; Mooar - 1; Jackson - SS; Jenner - 2; Bell - L; Hohan - R; Blakely - P
Totals: 33 13 14 27 13 1 1 12 4 6 6

Leetsdale: Mortimer C; Copeland SS; Stacey 1; Maratta 3; Lewis M; Weber 2; Leight L; Bauman R; Small P.
Totals: 5 7 27 8 1 1 1 4 2 5

Keeping Score: Windsor vs. Leetsdale, July 13, 1901. McIlveen and Mason are listed as players (from Mason scrapbook).

Mason and McIlveen were already the best of friends. Between 1895 and 1901 they had played more than 150 baseball games together for an amateur baseball club, the Windsor Rough Riders, and at Penn State they would share the diamond for three highly successful seasons. McIlveen would captain the Penn State baseball team in 1906—his fourth and last year of college eligibility under new rules that limited college play to four years in any sport. Mason followed his friend as team captain the next season, but in the fall of 1903, when Harry Mason arrived at Penn State, even the 1904 baseball season seemed ages away. Mason was about to become a college man and to face the challenges that being a college man entailed. He may not have known it that fall, but Harry Mason was also about to give his heart to Dear Old State.

The Track House exterior.

The Track House interior.

Harry "Sticks" Haverstick.

Harry Mason faced one of his biggest adjustments to college life early in his first year at school, when he took up residence with roommate Harry McIlveen in the newly completed Track House. The problem became evident when they met additional roommates Harry Hoyt Haverstick and Harry Yoder. When somebody would yell "Hey Harry" from below, all four of them would jump. The Harrys decided they all needed new names, and new names they received. Harrison Denning Mason Jr. had already taken one step from his formal name when he became Harry as a boy. In the fall of 1903, this 23-year-old freshman took one more step and forever became "Joe" Mason to his friends.

In the spring of 1904, the fans of Penn State baseball would find out what many fans in Pittsburgh already knew—there would be a talented freshman starting at third base. His name was Mason, and to use the lingo of the time, he was full of ginger.

A stoopful of former Track House "Harrys."

Dear Old State

In 1859 the first class entered Farmers' High School, as Penn State was known at its founding in 1855, and the fiftieth anniversary of that founding would be celebrated during Mason's years at Penn State. Joe Mason became a student during a time of great change at the Pennsylvania State College. It had grown from a tiny agricultural school in the middle of nowhere to a true representative of the purpose of the Morrill Land-Grant Act signed into law by President Abraham Lincoln:

> The endowment, support, and maintenance of at least one college where the leading object shall be, without excluding other scientific and classical studies and including military tactics, to teach such branches of learning as are related to agriculture and the mechanic arts, in such manner as the legislatures of the states may respectively prescribe, in order to promote the liberal and practical education of the industrial classes in the several pursuits and professions of life.

Old Main, c. 1860.

A large measure of Penn State's success at the turn of the century could be attributed to its president, George Washington Atherton, who was nearing the end of his term (and his life) when Mason enrolled in 1903. Although there were many achievements in Penn State's first twenty-five years, the ups were largely overshadowed by the downs—until the arrival of President Atherton in 1882. Wayland Dunaway recorded in the *History of The Pennsylvania State College*:

> When [Atherton] began, the foundations of the College were shaky and its prospects far from bright. . . . There were divisions among the Trustees and the faculty, the morale of the institution was low, and its reputation unsavory. . . . The attitude of the public toward the school was critical, not to say hostile. The Legislature had never accorded to it due recognition, nor taken seriously its covenant with the Federal Government to support it; no appropriations had been made for maintenance, and but few for other purposes. It was everywhere the object of misunderstanding and

> prejudice. The physical plant was inadequate and unattractive, practically all the activities of the institution being carried on in one gloomy-looking building unsuited to its purposes. . . . The College had no library worth mentioning, no regular chaplain, and no suitable living accommodations for the faculty or the women students. Almost everything dear to the hearts of students was lacking; there were no fraternities, no organized athletics, no student publications, no dancing or other amusements, no cadet band or other musical organizations, and sad to relate, not even college colors or college song, or college yell. Furthermore, the place in which the College was located was a struggling village of about a hundred people, without churches, without a public school, and without civic improvements.

At his inaugural ceremonies in 1883, President Atherton stated: "The conclusive fact remains that the vast majority of those who pursue advanced degrees, do so with a utilitarian aim. . . . Their primary purpose is not the cultivation of their minds, however desirable that may be, but the acquirement of a means of livelihood; and the call for that kind of education is steadily increasing, with the development of our vast material wealth." Although not by any means prepared to abandon the "cultivation of the mind," President Atherton understood the land-grant mission of Penn State and the crucial role of the land-grant college in higher education. Dunaway continued:

> The Atherton Era was a turning point in the history of the College—the beginning of a forward movement which gathered momentum with each passing year. It marked the transition from a period of drifting and experiment to one with a sound and enlightened policy, well understood and clearly defined. Its guiding principles, based on a true interpretation of the Morrill Act, were to go far toward shaping College policy for all time to come. . . . The faculty increased from 17 to 66; the student body, from 87 to 800. The physical plant underwent a complete change: Old Main was renovated and a dozen major buildings, besides a number of professors' residences and other minor buildings, were erected. The courses of study were increased in number, broadened and liberalized. The technical courses were greatly expanded, and the work in the liberal arts was developed. Everywhere were seen evidences of a strong, growing institution, with high morale, increasing prestige, and a promising outlook.

In *Penn State: An Illustrated History*, Michael Bezilla commented more guardedly: "It would be an exaggeration to say that by the time of Atherton's death, Penn State had become one of the nation's leading institutions of higher learning. Even among Pennsylvania schools, its reputation was not outstanding. Yet the College had kept pace with the progress made by most other land-grant schools, and this in itself was no mean accomplishment, given the multitude of problems it confronted."

Main drive

Carnegie Library

Armory

Ladies' Cottage

Engineering Building

Botanical Gardens

The campus of the Pennsylvania State College, c. 1904.

A rare photo of President George Atherton as a young man.

When President Atherton died on July 26, 1906, and was interred beside Schwab Auditorium on the Penn State campus, Benjamin Gill, Dean of the School of Language and Literature, remarked in his eulogy that Atherton "saw from the first not the college that was, but the college that was to be."

School Spirit

In the autumn of 1903, when Joe Mason arrived, Penn State's future looked bright. President Atherton was still in fairly good health, new buildings were springing up through the generosity of the legislature and such men as Charles Schwab and Andrew Carnegie, and school spirit was strong.

The "blue and white," or, as they were often called in those days, the "white and blue," had become the school colors in 1890. They had replaced the highly interesting "pink and black," which the student-run football squad had picked in 1887. While the black had remained black, the pink tended to fade to white in the wash.

The Pennsylvania State College was about to embark on an athletic thrill ride that its student body would long remember. As memories of sports stars from the 1890s were fading, some twentieth-century athletes were about to carry the football and baseball teams to new heights. Some of their names would be as colorful as their exploits—William T. "Mother" Dunn,* "Hi" Henry, Cy "Wrong Way" Cyphers, "Sticks" Haverstick, and "Irish" or "Lefty" or

* So named by an upperclassman who saw the very large Dunn leading his fellow freshmen across campus one day and said, "There goes Mother Dunn leading his chickens," according to Penn State football historian extraordinaire Ridge Riley.

Penn State's 1889 football team on a break from the game in their pink and black uniforms!

"Mal" McIlveen (depending on whether it was football season or baseball season or a couple of former "Harrys" sitting around the Track House). Others were never quite as famous on the field, but worked behind the scenes, making the name of Penn State ring out in the collegiate sports world whenever they could.

In addition to his baseball talent, Joe Mason wielded another weapon on behalf of Penn State's growing athletic reputation—his pen. When Walter Camp of Yale chose "Mother" Dunn for his highly coveted and Ivy League dominated All-America Football Team in 1906, Penn State fans were delighted. Mother Dunn never credited this honor to his

William T. "Mother" Dunn, Penn State's First All-American (1st Team).

Mason on the job, wearing his "State" sweater. (Photo with inscription from Mason Scrapbook)

Harrison Denning "Joe" Mason Jr.

Biographical Particulars

Born: December 19, 1879, Pittsburgh, Pennsylvania.

Father: Harrison Denning Mason, purchasing agent for the Allegheny Railroad.

Mother: Ella McCargo.

Early education: Allegheny High School, Elders Ridge Academy.

College: Pennsylvania State College, B.S. in Mining Engineering in 1907, M.S. in Mining Engineering in 1913.

Marriage: To Blanche Odell Frye on April 20, 1914.

Children: John Denning Mason, a son. A daughter, Mary Jane Mason, died as a result of a prescribed overdose of asthma medication at age 8, in 1926.

Career: Semi-professional baseball player, coal miner, and mining engineer specializing in mine safety and mine rescue. During his four years of service in the U.S. Bureau of Mines, attended "33 mine disasters and [wore] the breathing apparatus at 16 disasters." Formed the Mines Safety Appliance Company with fellow Penn Staters George Deike and Jack Ryan in 1915 and left in 1924. Served as secretary-treasurer of the Coal Mining Institute, where management and labor worked together to solve problems. Worked for the Pennsylvania Department of Highways at the time of his death.

Died: October 9, 1948, of a heart attack at his home in Ebensburg, Pennsylvania.

own performance in the single game at Yale where Camp saw him play. He gave the credit to the man who had been promoting his exploits for years—Joe Mason. In his dispatches to the Tri-State News Bureau in Pittsburgh, which found their way into papers all over Western Pennsylvania and beyond, Joe Mason gave Mother Dunn the exposure his talents deserved.

Penn State's bulldog enjoying a big taste of Princeton's Tiger.

School Symbols

One year after Joe Mason's boast at Princeton, the 1905 Penn State baseball nine were even better than the previous year's team. McIlveen won 9 and lost 0 as their left-handed ace. He also led all batters with a .481 average. Mason was one of three other players who batted better than .300. They won fifteen games and lost only three. For the second year in succession, the college yearbook, *La Vie*, began its baseball section with a cartoon picture of the Princeton Tiger as a tasty morsel for a bulldog labeled "State." Actually, it was only the tail of the famous Princeton Tiger hanging from the bulldog's mouth, and this time sporting tags labeled '04 *and* '05. Penn State had performed the miracle at Princeton once again, this time by a score of 8–6. The State bulldog, growling, said, "This flavor is decidedly fine." The bulldog may have been labeled "State," but it was not a Penn State mascot in any formal, or even informal, sense. It had been adopted (borrowed from a Philadelphia newspaper), rumor had it, to guard the Ladies' Cottage, being the tenacious creature that it was.

From the beginning, Penn State students occasionally adopted symbols to suit specific purposes. There was certainly no shortage of traditions and class associations and nicknames and rituals, but an "all school" symbol, a true school mascot, had been elusive. The Nittany Lion existed only in the anniversary of a clever retort. For the second straight year, the two campus tour guides at Princeton, now juniors, likely regretted their part of that exchange.

In addition to the always present "Dear Old State" ideal and several larger-than-life faculty members (Professor George "Swampy" Pond, for example), when Joe Mason enrolled at Penn State there were perhaps three additional symbols on campus that served in the absence of an all-school mascot. One was Coaly, the old mule who had hauled stone for the building of Old Main back in 1857. Coaly had belonged to the family of Piersol Lytle, who had moved to

"Old Coaly" in retirement.

Central Pennsylvania in 1855. Coaly did his job so well, the story goes, that he was purchased by the Farmers' High School for the amazing and highly unlikely price of $190. From 1857 to 1893 Coaly worked on campus and some surrounding farms. Thanks to his good nature and a record of service unequaled by any Penn State human at the time, the old mule became a campus pet.

When Coaly died, his skeleton continued to serve in an honored capacity. During Mason's years, his bones were in a wildlife museum on campus. Although the skeleton spent some time in storage in the 1930s and 1940s, Coaly's permanent place in Penn State history was ensured by the founding of the Penn State Coaly Society in 1951. This honorary society recognizes outstanding students in agriculture. The society's motto is a tribute both to a hardworking Penn State mule and to the ideals of a Penn State education: "A first-rate man is defined not by his birth but according to his services." Coaly's skeleton stands proudly in a display case in the Agricultural Administration Building on the Penn State University Park campus.

Andy Lytle, Penn State's "perennial freshman"—and a Halftime Tribute to him.

The second symbol emerged in the early 1900s in the person of Andy Lytle, one of Piersol's nine children. As an 11-year-old youngster, Lytle too had worked on the construction of Old Main with the family mule, Coaly. As the years went by, he gained the distinction of being the last person who had been present at the start of the Farmers' High School, the last person who had helped to build Penn State's oldest and most respected building.

It also didn't hurt that Andy Lytle was one of Penn State's greatest sports boosters. For years he attended every home football game, and most games on the road as well. He could also be found cheering at most of Penn State's other sporting events on campus. The students rightly recognized the hero that Andy Lytle had become and began to acknowledge his presence with great fanfare. One of Andy's nicknames was "the perennial freshman," and one of his self-chosen duties was to greet each incoming class with "You're the best darn bunch of freshmen I've ever seen!" On October 11, 1924, the student body observed "Andy Lytle Day" and carried the elderly freshman across campus to the football field to the cheers of his many fans. Andy died on January 16, 1928.

The third symbol was probably the least recognized as such at the time. It was the only one of the three that never walked among the students on campus, but Joe Mason walked past this symbol on his way to class or baseball practice nearly every day. The stuffed lion in the display case in Old Main led an ordinary lion's life when he walked the Pennsylvania mountains, but the life he led after he died was another story.

2

The Last Pennsylvania Mountain Lion

Samuel Brush

At the end of November in 1856, three years before the first students gazed on the rather forlorn campus of what was then the Farmers' High School, and twenty-three years before Joe Mason was born, Samuel Brush of Brushville shot a mountain lion. Even in 1856 that was quite a big deal in Susquehanna County. The local papers all ran stories about the incident. The once-plentiful animal had become all but extinct, and few people living at the time had ever hunted or seen one. As the years went by, the aging hunters who did remember were sounding more like storytellers than historians.

When Sam heard that a couple of boys had discovered some unusually large catlike tracks, he was highly skeptical that they belonged to anything out of the ordinary, until he came upon them.

Samuel Brush.

> Sam was surprised when he saw the tracks. He had little time to ponder though, as the dogs picked up the tracks and soon gave voice. The tempo of the dog's baying changed and Sam knew that they had jumped the animal. The beast stood momentarily at bay against a ledge on the southeast side of the valley. Sam could hear the dog's excited baying mingled with their yelps of pain and he knew that this was no ordinary animal.
>
> The animal broke and, with the dogs in hot pursuit, came down across the valley in front of Sam. Any questions Sam might have had were answered, suddenly, for here was an adult mountain lion. We can only imagine the thoughts that raced through Sam's mind in those brief seconds.
>
> As the lion came across in front of him, Sam shot and knew not whether he hit or missed. In a short distance the lion treed and the dogs clamored at the tree trunk. In the tall tree the lion was not an easy target, but at least it was a still one. How many times Sam shot and reloaded the old muzzle-loader we will never know.
>
> One version says that the seventh and fatal shot hit beneath the lion's ear and that the lion fell from the tree dead. Another says that on the third shot the lion fell from the tree motally [*sic*] wounded and that in its death throes tore one of the dogs to pieces. Regardless of the detail, we know for sure, that here . . . the last known mountain lion of Susquehanna County was killed.

Don Stearns wrote those words in the *Montrose Independent* (New Milford) in 1966, based on old newspaper accounts and interviews with Samuel Brush's descendants. In those few

SUSQUEHANNA COUNTY'S LAST MOUNTAIN LION

(Photo reproduced by John Wilcox)

Mountain lions were once common in Susq. County. Sometimes called "panthers," "caugars," or 'catamounts," they hunted the hills and valleys of the region. Don Stearns of New Milford, who has made a study of the mountain lion, has written a series of articles about this animal which will appear in this newspaper. The first installment follows. The above shows a picture of the lion which Mr. Stearns has in his office in New Milford. The muzzle-loading rifle in the picture was used by Sam Brush to shoot the lion pictured above. It is the property of Morton Brush, Brushville, a grandson of Sam.

By Don Stearns

When the first settlers began to trickle into Susquehanna County, in the 1780's and 1790's, they found the area well populated with mountain lions. The lion was native to this region and for untold time had hunted these hills and valleys.

Each ridge had its den of lions beneath some overhanging ledge

lean, winter months when the lion was gaunt from hunger.

The lion ranged far and hunted a vast area, and the nightly, half-human cry of the lion, echoing down from the ridges, chilled the heart of many a pioneer. No curfew was needed to call in the children at nightfall and the dog curled close to the cabin door.

manent settler where New Milford Borough now lies, trapped a complete den of lions from a ledge along the northeast line of the present Borough.

The mountain lion, because of his nature, was doomed to extinction in this region. He could not stand against the rapid pace of settlement and the advance of

County, between New Milford and Susquehanna, there lies an undefined section known as the Highlands. This section is well south of the Susquehanna River partly in New Milford, Great Bend, Jackson and Oakland Townships. State Game Land No. 35 now lies on part of these Highlands.

Though most of the virgin timber in the county had been cut by 1860, this section had hardly been touched. It held dense stands of virgin hemlock, which were to fall a few years later when the tanning industry was at its peak. Settlement here was sparse and the country was rugged and wild.

In the very early days of settlement, before the Highlands were settled, a road had been cut through them. This road ran from New Milford to the Harmony Settlement on the Susquehanna River now known as Lanesboro. It is known as the "Old Harmony Road" and the part from New Milford to Cam[p] Susquehanna is still traversab[le] by auto.

The section that ran from Ca[mp] Susquehanna along the hills above the headwaters of Mitchell Creek, over to the present Camp Res Mor and on down to Brushville has long since been abandoned and the time-weathered imprint of its course is discernible only [to] the experienced eye.

Two small boys were walk[ing] down this abandoned section [of] the Old Harmony Road, this ce[rtain] winter morning, on their way [to] the small settlement at Brushvil[le]. They came upon some tracks in the snow which puzzled them. Definitely they were the tracks of a cat. The boys knew that there were bobcats in this section and had seen many of their tracks, but these tracks were much too large for any bobcat of which they had ever heard of or dreamed.

They sensed that there was something here beyond their comprehension and felt a warning tingle of fear. Without much hesitation, they scurried on down the road to Brushville to look for Sam Brush

The tempo of the dog's baying their yelps of pain and he knew

that this was no ordinary animal.

The animal broke and, with the dogs in hot pursuit, came down across the valley in front of Sam. Any questions Sam might have had were answered, suddenly. For here was an actual, live, extra large, adult mountain lion. We can only imagine the thoughts that raced through Sam's mind in those brief seconds.

As the lion came across in front of him, Sam shot and knew not whether he hit or missed. In a short distance the lion treed and the dogs clamored at the tree trunk. In the tall tree the lion was not an easy target, but at least it was a still one. How many times Sam shot and reloaded the old muzzle-loader we will never know.

One version says that the seventh and fatal shot hit beneath the lion's ear and that the lion fell from the tree dead Another says that on the third shot the lion fell from the tree motally wounded and that in its death throes tore one of the dogs to pieces. Regardless of the detail, we know for sure, that here and then the last known mountain lion of Susquehanna County was killed.

Though history gives us few detailed facts, the year of this incident can, quite accurately, be placed between 1857 and 1859. Weston, in his "History of Brooklyn, Susquehanna County", published in 1889, says: "The panther ...

from western Pennsylvania, where the lion still existed in very limited numbers? This is feasible. But, if so, why had he left there? Being an old, male lion, had he been driven out and replaced by a younger male? Or the sentimentalist might like to think that he had been driven from these Highlands those many years before and had now come home to die!

Why was this lion alone? The fact that he was alone would tend to prove that he was an old and outcast lion. No tracks nor trace of another lion were ever seen and we can rest assured that, after the shooting, the Highlands area and that whole section of the country were thoroughly hunted.

Sam Brush took the dead lion home and bringing the carcas into the little settlement of Brushville created a bit of excitement. He skinned the lion out and left the pelt intact for mounting. Doctor Latham Smith, a medical doctor in New Milford who evidently had acquired the skills of taxidermy, mounted the pelt for Sam. The subsequent history of this mounted specimen is so intriguing that, though it be anticlimatic, it should be included in the history of Susquehana County's last mountain lion.

The mounted lion specimen was kept in Sam Brush's home in Brushville. It was exhibited at gatherings and was an excellent conversation piece. For a time it was outranked only by the Starrucca Viaduct and even outranked the diggings of Joseph Smith. All of

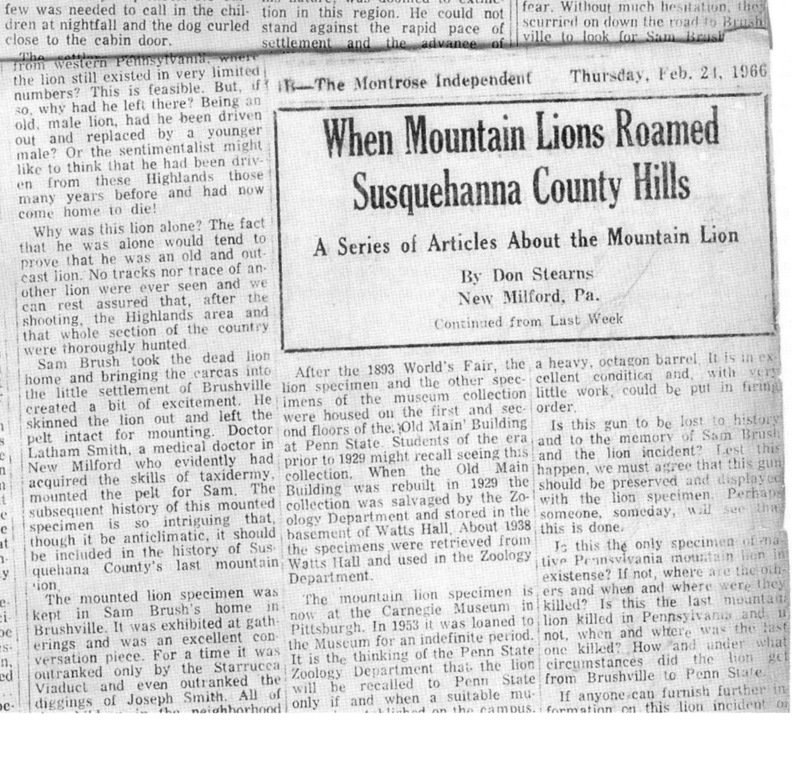

The Montrose Independent — Thursday, Feb. 24, 1966

When Mountain Lions Roamed Susquehanna County Hills

A Series of Articles About the Mountain Lion

By Don Stearns
New Milford, Pa.

Continued from Last Week

After the 1893 World's Fair, the lion specimen and the other specimens of the museum collection were housed on the first and second floors of the 'Old Main' Building at Penn State. Students of the era prior to 1929 might recall seeing this collection. When the Old Main Building was rebuilt in 1929 the collection was salvaged by the Zoology Department and stored in the basement of Watts Hall. About 1938 the specimens were retrieved from Watts Hall and used in the Zoology Department.

The mountain lion specimen is now at the Carnegie Museum in Pittsburgh. In 1953 it was loaned to the Museum for an indefinite period. It is the thinking of the Penn State Zoology Department that the lion will be recalled to Penn State only if and when a suitable mu-

a heavy, octagon barrel. It is in excellent condition and, with very little work, could be put in firing order.

Is this gun to be lost to history and to the memory of Sam Brush and the lion incident? Lest this happen, we must agree that this gun should be preserved and displayed with the lion specimen. Perhaps someone, someday, will see that this is done.

Is this the only specimen of native Pennsylvania mountain lion in existense? If not, where are the others and when and where were they killed? Is this the last mountain lion killed in Pennsylvania and, if not, when and where was the last one killed? How and under what circumstances did the lion get from Brushville to Penn State.

If anyone can furnish further information on this lion incident or

Clippings from Don Stearns's article in the *Montrose Independent*.

The Brush Lion, a.k.a. The Original Nittany Lion.

sentences it is easy to see that a "story" was being told, a story that tempts the reader to wonder about the differentiation between fact and fancy that day in 1856. Certainly Don Stearns told a story. He took some newspaper accounts that were already reporting news items as tales and retold those, but there is one thing about this mountain lion that was absolutely true in 1856 and is still true today: The animal Samuel Brush shot that day, the animal Don Stearns described more than a century later, was "no ordinary animal."

It may not have been the largest of its kind or the oldest or the strongest, but this lion was one of the last to roam the forests of Pennsylvania. And since its death it has traveled to Chicago, resided in Pittsburgh, and visited Harrisburg. It has done something no other Pennsylvania mountain lion has managed to do—survive. Today, this last Pennsylvania mountain lion resides in a specially created display case in Pattee Library on the University Park campus of Penn State.

The short trip from Ferguson Building to Pattee Library is likely the last this traveling treasure will ever make.

"Felis concolor"

The Pennsylvania mountain lion has a history fraught with controversy. The first problem arises over what to call this king of Pennsylvania cats. Is it a mountain lion or a puma or a catamount or a cougar or a panther or the settlers' version of a panther—a "painter"? Apparently all those names have been used interchangeably to describe the same animal. The descendants of Samuel Brush have always thought of the stuffed and mounted prize of their great-grandfather as a panther—the Brush panther.

Even scientists have not always agreed on a name. Most mammal specialists have used the widely accepted scientific name, *Felis concolor,** but renowned naturalist Samuel Rhoads took issue with *concolor* in his 1903 text, *Mammals of Pennsylvania and New Jersey*: "As this binomial was given by Linnaeus to a Brazilian specimen, and North American specimens had proved to differ from those of South America in some degree, the modern naturalist became restive."

Pennsylvania folklorist Henry Shoemaker didn't need to read that comment twice. Always on the lookout for anything that made the animals or trees or legends of Pennsylvania unique, Shoemaker adopted Rhoads's advice and called the lion *Felis couguar* in his 1914 book, *The Pennsylvania Lion or Panther: A Narrative of Our Grandest Game Animal*. He included a description of the animal from *Cougar de Pennsylvanie* by Georges Buffon: "It is low on its legs, has a longer tail than the Western puma; it is described as five feet six inches in length, tail two feet six inches; height before, one foot nine inches; behind one foot ten inches." Shoemaker's interviews with old hunters and witnesses to recently deceased panthers** helped him come up with his own description:

> Body, long, slim, head large (averaging eight inches in mature specimens, wide in proportion to length); legs strong, short; tail, long and tufted at end; color greyish about the eyes; hairs within the ears grey, slightly tinged with yellow, exterior of ears blackish; those portions of the lips which support the whiskers, black; the remaining portion of the lip pale chocolate; throat, grey; beneath the neck pale yellow. General color, reddish in Potter county, shading from a dull gray to a slate further South in the State.

A second controversy surrounding the mountain lion's past had to do with its temperament. Rhoads wrote:

> The character of the cougar is eminently cowardly, sneaking, thievish, but often courageous when with young. When starved, it is emboldened to follow and (very

* To further complicate matters, the second edition of *Mammal Species of the World: A Taxonomic and Geographic Reference*, edited by Don E. Wilson and DeeAnn M. Reeder (1993), has called for a genus switch from *Felis concolor* to *Puma concolor*.

** The measurements of mounted animals do not reflect the animal's true size because for mounting the skin was often stretched to boost the ego of the hunter!

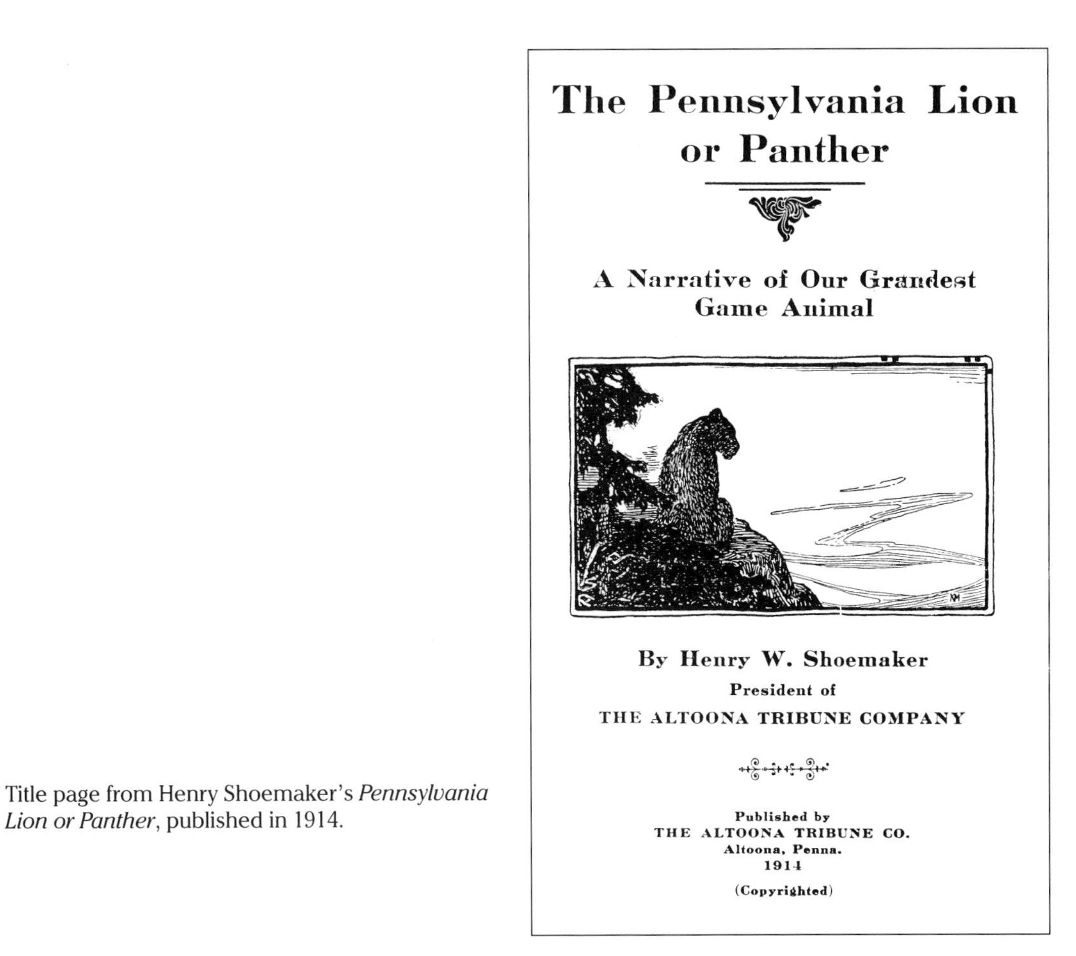

The Pennsylvania Lion or Panther

A Narrative of Our Grandest Game Animal

By Henry W. Shoemaker
President of
THE ALTOONA TRIBUNE COMPANY

Published by
THE ALTOONA TRIBUNE CO.
Altoona, Penna.
1914

(Copyrighted)

Title page from Henry Shoemaker's *Pennsylvania Lion or Panther*, published in 1914.

> rarely) attack a man. It may be fenced off when wounded by the courageous use of a stick or gun barrel, but sometimes leaps upon its assailant. It never seems to realize its power of offense or defense, and a well-trained cur will inspire it with terror and quickly tree it.

Henry Shoemaker did not like to have any native Pennsylvania animal described as cowardly or, on the other end of the continuum, as a threat to people. According to Shoemaker, that was simply a misunderstanding based on one of the panther's more unusual attributes. "From the earlest [*sic*] times the Pennsylvania lion or panther has been unjustly feared. The first Swedish settlers on the Delaware hunted it unmercifully. They could not but believe that an animal which howled so hideously at night must be a destroyer of human life."

The nighttime cry of the lion was the one thing everyone agreed about—it was bone-chilling. Most people who heard it never wanted to hear it ever again. "Half-animal, half-human" (or more often, half-*child*) were the words used to describe the terrible wail that made people clutch their children closer in the night and that firmly convinced the children of Irish immigrants in northern Pennsylvania that the banshees had come to America. In a

Joseph Trimble Rothrock, founder of the Forestry Commission of Pennsylvania.

letter to Henry Shoemaker, Dr. J. T. Rothrock, founder of the Forestry Commission of Pennsylvania, recalled the one time he had heard the cry many years before:

> That panther cry—I have often asked myself how I could describe it and failed to satisfy the inquiry, though I think I have at this very minute a somewhat clear remembrance of it. It would not be an adequate reply if I said it sounded like the wail of a child seeking something, a cry, distinct, half inquiry and half in temper. There was something human in it, though unmistakably wild, clear and piercing. And yet I do not know how to make a more satisfactory reply, except to say that the cry seemed to be in all its tones about a minute long. I heard it one evening in Treaster Valley repeated so often that I could recognize it as coming from an animal moving along the rocky slope of the mountain where no child could have been at that hour, and was told by those residents in the region, "Oh, it's the *painter's* cry."

A terrible cry does not necessarily a wicked beast make, according to Henry Shoemaker. He decried all the pages that had been written in natural histories describing the animal's unpleasant characteristics, where not a word had been said in its favor. Shoemaker claimed he wasn't attempting to make the Pennsylvania lion grander or greater than its relatives in other parts of the country. He simply believed it *was* bigger, and had a noble nature.

A Lion at College

Twenty-five years after Sam Brush shot his lion, it was still with the Brush family. The few indigenous live lions remaining could only be found in Centre, Clearfield, and Mifflin Counties, but the Brush children still had their own stuffed specimen to ride and wrestle and occasionally use to frighten some unsuspecting visiting youth. The Brush Lion probably faced its toughest years, alive or dead, with the Brush children!

The lion had been mounted by Dr. Latham Avery Smith Jr., a prominent New Milford doctor who had evidently also acquired some excellent skills in taxidermy. The continuing existence of his work provides ample evidence of his skill with dead animals. Edwin Bell of Albright College cites an 1887 history of Susquehanna County that reports Dr. Smith was "the premier of the Susquehanna County medical fraternity," testimony that his medical skills extended to live humans as well.

By the early 1890s, the mountain lions of Pennsylvania had dwindled to a handful and teetered on the brink of extinction. The last bounty paid for a panther in Centre County was recorded in 1886, and the last reported kill was in 1893 by a James Moore. Coincidentally, 1893 also proved to be a remarkable year in the "afterlife" of the Brush Lion. It finally broke free of the escapades of the neighborhood children when George Friant of Scranton and Dr. B. H. Warren, the state ornithologist, persuaded Mr. Brush "to give the specimen to State College, Bellefonte, Pa., for the sake of its preservation." Friant's account documents the lion's arrival

THE PANTHER.

In former times the Panther was present in all parts of Pennsylvania, but now, if the animal is found here at all, and I very much doubt the species' presence in our State, it is certainly restricted to a very few of the most inaccessible mountain sections. The bounty records of Centre county for 1886 shows money was given for a "panther" killed there in that year. Mr. Rhoads quotes the following from Mr. Seth Nelson: "There may be one or two yet in Clearfield county; but the Askey boys and I killed two, two years ago (1891)." Mr. Rhoads, also on the authority of Mr. Seth Nelson, makes reference to a Panther taken in 1893 by the Long boys on "big run of Beech Creek."

The last bounty paid for a panther in Centre County is recorded in Pearson's *Diseases and Enemies of Poultry*.

at Penn State in 1893, states that it was cleaned and remounted in anticipation of another trip, and indirectly proves that Penn State's geographic location wasn't exactly well known.

The trip the Brush Lion took later that year was to the World's Columbian Exposition in Chicago, where people now showed their affection by looking and reading, rather than wrestling and riding. The Brush Lion was part of an exhibit in the Anthropology Building entitled "A Collection of Birds and Mammals, Collected and Mounted by Dr. B. H. Warren, State Ornithologist, West Chester." The *Catalogue of the Exhibits of the State of Pennsylvania* stated: "Probably no similar exhibit on the grounds elicits so much attention and commendation as this."

When the Brush Lion returned from Chicago, it was to new quarters in the wildlife museum started by President Atherton and located in Old Main. The lion measured 7 feet, 9 inches in

The Brush Lion, in the midst of the foliage, at the World's Columbian Exposition.

Penn State at the World's Columbian Exposition, Chicago, 1893

A short distance away from the Brush Lion, in the Liberal Arts Building, The Pennsylvania State College Experiment Station was also exhibiting some items at the World's Columbian Exposition: a collection of chemical preparations, an exhibit of the Chautauqua course of home reading in agriculture, plans for the improvement of a dairy farm, an exhibit of garden tools, and ninety-five varieties of wood native to Centre County collected by Mr. Samuel Brugger. One other Pennsylvania item making the trip to Chicago gives some indication of the importance the Exposition held for Pennsylvania and its people: The Liberty Bell was one of the Brush Lion's fellow exhibits.

length, was 30 inches high at the shoulders, and had weighed 147 pounds when it was shot. Its mouth was drawn back in the ferocious growl Dr. Smith had chosen for it decades earlier.

Not much is known about the Brush Lion's early years at Penn State, but occasional notes confirm its presence. *The Free Lance*, Penn State's first student newspaper, ran a brief mention under its "College Miscellany" section in November 1902: "Measurements and plaster casts of the teeth of the panther in our museum have been made for Dr. Samuel N. Roades [*sic*], of the Philadelphia Academy of Natural Sciences, who is preparing a book upon the 'Mammals of Pennsylvania and New Jersey.' "

Whoever was supposed to send the measurements to Dr. Rhoads must have responded too late, because Rhoads reported in his book: "I have written without success to obtain a

The Old Main Museum, c. 1904.

description of the Pa. panther in State College museum." That Old Main museum at Penn State was where Joe Mason first saw the Brush Lion in the autumn of 1903. The lion stayed in the wildlife museum until 1929, when, in preparation for Old Main's renovation, it was taken to the basement of Watts Hall along with one of its fellow exhibits whose star also seemed to be fading: Coaly the mule.

The Zoology Department took over the Brush Lion in about 1938 and began to use it in class instruction. Edwin Bell remembers the "large spectacular mount" standing out clearly from among its fellow mammals in the basement of the Agriculture Education Building when he was a student at Penn State from 1948 to 1950.

An Extended Visit

In 1953 two former curators of the Carnegie Museum in Pittsburgh visited Penn State's Wildlife Management Professor Pennoyer English and asked if they could borrow the Brush Lion for a year, for an exhibit of exterminated animals. Dean Lyman Jackson of the School of Agriculture, and S. K. Hostetter, Comptroller of the College, gave permission, specifying that the lion (also known as PSC 1–14562) would be on loan for one year, that the Carnegie Museum was to bear the expenses of transportation, and that the museum was to return the specimen in better

The Carnegie Museum of Natural History, a "temporary" residence of Penn State's Nittany Lion for nearly forty years.

The Nittany Lion Mascot demonstrates the correct way to do push-ups for his apparently stunned ancestor.

condition than it was received. The Brush Lion was about to prove once more that it was "no ordinary animal." It would be away from Penn State for the next forty years.

The one-year exhibit, entitled "Deadline for Wildlife," stretched to eighteen years, and when it finally came down the Brush Lion went into storage at the Carnegie's taxidermy lab, awaiting its long overdue restoration. But the lion outlasted the taxidermy lab—which was dissolved in 1979—and was returned to the museum's mammals section. "By that time," wrote Suzanne B. McLaren of the Carnegie, "no one was around who knew the history of the specimen. Eventually, I stumbled onto a small file regarding the loan." McLaren contacted Professor George Kelly, who was in charge of the wildlife museum at Penn State at that time, and he recommended that the Carnegie hold on to the specimen until Penn State had facilities that were better suited for long-term maintenance. So, with Penn State's permission, the Brush Lion spent the years 1980–81 at the William Penn Museum in Harrisburg as part of a display entitled "Extinction and Endangerments." John Schreffler, a preparator for natural science in

The face that inspired fear in many of Pennsylvania's residents and admiration from one fast-talking Penn State third baseman.

Brush Lion, a.k.a. the Brush Panther and the Original Nittany Lion

Biographical Particulars

Born: Late 1840s, Susquehanna County, Pennsylvania.

Father: Unknown.

Mother: Unknown.

Early education: Largely self-taught.

College: Attended Pennsylvania State College 1893–1929.

Marriage: Unknown.

Children: Unknown.

Career: Served as children's play toy, 1860?–90. Worked as instructor in the Zoology Department at Penn State College, 1938–53; visiting instructor at Carnegie Museum in Pittsburgh, 1953–71. Often spent long periods in seclusion between teaching assignments (1929–38; 1971–80; 1981–93). Visiting instructor at William Penn Museum, Harrisburg, 1980–81. Lion Emeritus at Penn State, 1993 to present.

Died: While minding his own business on November 30, 1856, of severe trauma caused by Samuel Brush's musket, near Brushville, Pennsylvania.

Reborn: About 1856, thanks to Dr. Latham Avery Smith, taxidermist.

Richard Yahner and the Original Nittany Lion.

the Exhibits Department, recalls the lion arriving at the State Museum in rough shape with one ear detached, the tail in three pieces, and the head hanging precariously on a broken neck. Beginning in 1981 it was returned to the Carnegie for one more decade of storage.

The interest of Don Stearns (Class of 1933) in Susquehanna County's history probably saved the Brush Lion from a permanent home in Pittsburgh. In his role as chairman of the New Milford Township and Borough Historical Committee, Stearns tracked down how the lion got to the Carnegie Museum in 1953 and what it had been doing since 1893 at Penn State. He already knew the Brush part of the story. Stearns helped to reestablish the relationship between Penn State and the Brush Lion in his series of four newspaper articles in the *Montrose Independent* in February 1966.

In the mid-1980s, Edwin Bell (Class of 1950) also helped to maintain Penn State's contact with the Brush Lion when his research on Pennsylvania mountain lions led him to the long-term loan at the Carnegie and to a renewed fascination with this remarkable specimen he had first encountered as an undergraduate.

In 1992, Penn State Wildlife Conservation Professor Rich Yahner was talking with his friend Duane Schlitter, curator of mammals at the Carnegie Museum of Natural History, when Schlitter caught him off guard by asking, "When do you want your lion back?" Yahner thought Schlitter was kidding, until he heard the whole story. In December of that year, Yahner saw the lion for the first time at a Pittsburgh warehouse for old specimens, and a long overdue homecoming was planned. In 1993, graduate students Carolyn Mahan and Brad Ross traveled

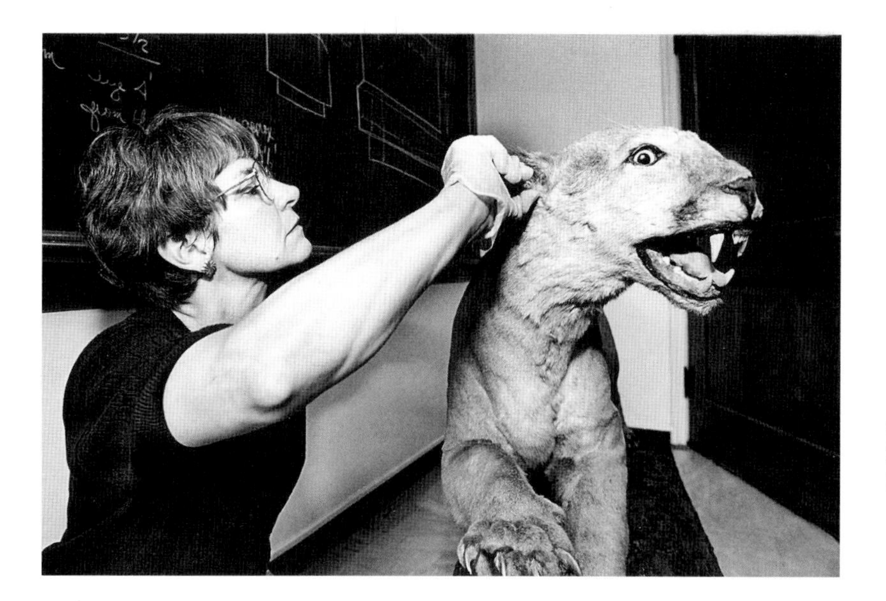

Conservator Catherine Hawkes works to repair the Original Nittany Lion.

The Original Nittany Lion Restoration Committee: *Bottom row, left to right:* Tom Laird, Nittany Lion Mascot Nick Indeglio, Richard Yahner. *Top row, left to right:* Stacie Bird, Jackie Esposito, Carolyn Mahan, Steven Herb, Shirley Davis, Richard Kipp.

to Pittsburgh to bring the lion home, exactly forty years after it had departed for a one-year field trip to the Carnegie.

The work to restore the lion was undertaken by Catherine Hawkes, one of the half-dozen remaining wildlife conservators in North and South America, and a fund was established to aid in the cost of the restoration. In its restored state, the Brush Lion provides a remarkable number of opportunities. In addition to its role as an interesting example of 1850s taxidermy, the Brush Lion, with its skull and some of its teeth as well as the skin intact, is the most complete specimen of Pennsylvania's *Felis concolor* (or *Puma concolor!*) in existence.*

A freak train accident that occurred in 1942 is the reason the Brush Lion is one of the very few specimens in existence. Edward A. Goldman at the National Museum of Natural History in Washington was conducting research for a publication about cougars that he was co-authoring with Stanley P. Young. He arranged to borrow all the specimens of eastern cougars or mountain lions the Carnegie Museum owned—every skull, tooth, and skin. The train accident that occurred between Pittsburgh and Washington seemed to affect only the car containing the lions, which burst into flames, destroying all the specimens. From that day forward, museums would never again ship or share entire collections of any species.

Research using biochemical analysis or computer-assisted tomography may allow the Brush Lion to finally help answer one of the oldest questions regarding the Pennsylvania mountain lion, a question for which Pennsylvania advocate Henry Shoemaker suspected he already knew the answer: Was the Pennsylvania mountain lion a distinct and unique subspecies?

Duane Schlitter states that the Brush Lion "is as unique and significant to the history of the Commonwealth as is William Penn's original deed to Penn's Forest." In Happy Valley, the last Pennsylvania mountain lion often goes by another name, which honors its incredible longevity and attachment to the University. Alive when Penn State was founded in 1855, and residing in Old Main the year of Joe Mason's boast at Princeton, the Brush Lion is now often called the Original Nittany Lion.

* A 1994 X-ray of the lion confirmed the presence of the intact skull George Friant had reported to Samuel Rhoads in 1903.

The Lemon

A Squirt of Astringent Juice for Everybody in State College

PRICE TEN CENTIMOS

3

The Lion in *The Lemon* and Other Mysterious Places

A Squirt of Astringent Juice

Spring 1906 found Penn State's baseball team once more high atop the mountain of a victorious season. For the third straight year, Princeton fell to visiting State, but this time by a score of 1–0. Penn State managed only one hit off the Princeton pitchers, but Captain McIlveen's twirling held Princeton to the same, as the men of State kept all from crossing home plate that day, except for one of their own. That summer, as he had many summers before, Joe Mason toured the eastern United States playing semi-professional baseball.

It was a tumultuous time for the men and women of Penn State when they returned to campus in the autumn of Joe Mason's senior year. President Atherton's death in July left a void that would take sixteen months for the Trustees to fill. For half the life of their college, Atherton had been president, and now everyone at Penn State—the Board, the faculty, and the students—were anxiously poised to see what would happen.

That fall, one small group of students meeting in secret decided that Penn State had some needs they might be able to meet. They had an idea that just might reduce the pomposity of some faculty members, increase the school spirit of some students, hasten the search for a new president, and deliver a touch of self-deprecating humor to the whole College. The editor of Penn State's first humor magazine, *The Lemon*, would finally have the forum he needed to promote an idea that had been on his mind since he was a freshman—the creation of a school mascot.

The first issue of *The Lemon: A Squirt of Astringent Juice for Everybody in State College* hit the newsstands on December 14, 1906, for the cost of "10 Centimos." "Published Semi-monthly for the Edification and Acidulation of All Those Who Need the Juice—Do You?" was the header above a masthead where everyone had the middle name "Lemon" and the last name "Ade."

Loaded with references to Penn State and State College, *The Lemon* was probably difficult to fully understand even a year or two after its publication, as customs changed, private

In Duplicate.

Burlington Base Ball Association

(INDEPENDENT)

PLAYER'S CONTRACT.

THE Burlington Base Ball Association of Burlington, Chittenden County, State of Vermont, party of the first part, does hereby engage for the season of 1906 as a member of its playing team Mr H. W. Mason of State College, State of Pa., of the second part, to play on its said team the position of 3rd Base or any other position that may be deemed advisable by the management, and also agrees to pay said H. W. Mason a monthly salary of One hundred & Seventy-five dollars and in addition to said salary, to pay necessary travelling expenses when away from Burlington playing games, from the time said party of the second part reports at Burlington, Vermont, in a fit condition to play ball, and until released by said Association, said salary to be paid on the first and fifteenth of each month.

The playing season is expected to open on or about the 21st day of June, 1906, and continue for about ten weeks.

The said party of the second part hereby agrees and binds himself to accept the above situation with said party of the first part and also to accept the terms herein set forth; to be governed while in the employ of said party of the first part, by the rules and regulations of said Association; to report for duty at the said City of Burlington, Vermont, when required so to do, after receiving proper notice; while in the employ of the said party of the first part to refrain from the use of intoxicating liquors of all kinds; to use every care and precaution to keep himself in a fit condition, physically and mentally, to play good ball whenever called upon; to leave with the Treasurer of said party of the first part twenty-five per cent of his salary, as security for the performance of this contract on his part, all of said sum so received to be paid by the party of the first part to said party of the second part at the expiration of the base ball season, providing the terms of this agreement have been complied with by said party of the second part; to comply promptly with all of the requirements, orders and requests of said Association by its team manager when on duty, at home or abroad, and to refrain upon all occasions from rowdyism and any conduct not becoming to a gentleman.

Dated at Burlington, Vt. this 18th day of April 1906.

Not valid unless signed by the President and Secretary of the Association.

F. K. Milne President. Burlington Base Ball Association, Party of the first part.

[illegible] Secretary. H. W. Mason Jr. Party of the second part.

"Joe" Mason's 1906 baseball contract with the Burlington, Vermont, semi-pro team (from Mason scrapbook).

THE LEMON

PUBLISHED SEMI-MONTHLY FOR THE EDIFICATION AND ACIDULATION of ALL THOSE WHO NEED THE JUICE—DO YOU?

BOARD OF ACIDULATION

Editor-in-Chief - -	George (Lemon) Ade
City Editor - - -	Gus (Lemon) Ade
Railroad Editor - -	Parker (Lemon) Ade
Muck-Rake Editor - -	Reginald (Lemon) Ade
Society Editor - - -	Mae (Lemon) Ade
Sporting Editor - - -	Albert (Lemon) Ade
General Squirt - -	Circus (Lemon) Ade
Your Uncle Gus and Your Anty Bellum } - -	General Wise Guys

GENERAL OFFICES

Lemon Producing Co.,

Floor 13, Room 2323 NITTANY BLOCK

PRICE - - - TEN CENTIMOS

The Lemon masthead.

General James Beaver.

jokes faded, and the objects of jokes graduated or sought employment elsewhere. It is likely, however, that at the time of publication the students, faculty, and administration had no difficulty recognizing themselves or their habits. Some of the articles poked fun at the location of State College and the trials and tribulations of travel to and from Bellefonte. Others deflated faculty and administrative practices of the day. And as with any satirical publication, the humor was mixed with a good deal of truth.

The second issue of *The Lemon* asked whether students were attending the Pennsylvania State College or Beaver University—a jab at General (and former Governor) James Beaver, who was acting president. "Squirt No. 3," as the issues were named, contained a biographical spoof of Andrew Tuscarora Lytle, Ph.D., under the heading "Who's Who in State Colic," and in a section entitled "What Our Critics Are Saying," fictional comments were attributed to the locally famous: "Mother" Dunn and Professor I. Thornton Osmond, among others.

The Call for a Guardian Spirit

In the St. Patrick's Day issue (Squirt 6) of *The Lemon*, dated March 17, 1907, an editorial entitled "Do We Still Sleep?" by Gus (Lemon) Ade is the first known written case for the adoption of the Nittany Mountain Lion as the school symbol:

> Every College the world over of any consequence has a College Emblem of some kind,—all but The Pennsylvania State College. Our Institution, we think, is of some consequence, and from Present Prospects in ten years from to-day "Penn State" will be among the Favorites in the Higher Education Trot,—at least We are willing to bank about 100 to 1 on this Sure Thing! But, Turn, Ye, now, gentle reader, and peruse the Epic on Our Back Cover! Have you read it?—Alright then, We will now Proceed.
>
> What do You Say? Why not get for State College, Our College, the Best in all the Menagerie of College Pets.—Our College is the Best of all,—Then why not Select for ours, The King of Beasts,—The Lion!!
>
> Dignified, courageous, magnificent, "The Lion" allegorically represents all that Our College Spirit should be So why not "The Nittany Mountain Lion?" Prithee, gentlemen, why not,—if there's anything Finer on the Market, why Trot it Out, but in the name of Common-sense, Out with Some good Idea, for surely "Pennsylvania State" is big and strong and loyal enough to decide on some permanent Guardian of this kind!—The Lions which now guard the entrance to our Campus are a move in the right direction.—Step into Princeton's splendid Gymnasium and see there [*sic*] mounted figure of the stately, inspiring Tiger, who stands guard over the stairway! Why cannot State have a kingly, all-conquering Lion, as the eternal Sentinal [*sic*] in the Entrance to our Auditorium. This is Something the Class Funds of '08 or '09 can easily purchase, after the decision is made as to our College's Guardian Spirit.

The "Epic" that Mason asked all *Lemon* readers to peruse had been inadvertently left off the back cover when Squirt 6 went to press, due to "St. Patrick getting his dates mixed during the celebration."

In Squirt 7, under the title "Do We Want the Best?" Mason asked readers if there was any reason why the King of Beasts—the lion—couldn't be adopted as the guardian spirit of Pennsylvania State College and replied that there was no earthly reason.

> So let's get busy and adopt the "Old Nittany Mountain Lion," for Ours before somebody else steps in ahead of us. Just now we can be the only College in the Land with this Noble Pet for our very own, and it's about time "Penn State" owned such an emblem, as per our Strong Argument in our last *Lemon*. If there are any better Beasts in Noah's aggregation, please give us the High Sign, but meanwhile let us deside [*sic*] to get Busy.

Joe Mason's poetic plea finally appeared just two weeks later than intended and nearly three years following his prophetic boast at Princeton:

> Yale she loves her ancient Bulldog,
> Princeton has her Tiger cruel,
> Dickinson her brawny Mastiff
> West Point claims the Army Mule.
> Pennsylvania is the Quaker,
> Michigan the Wolverine,
> But where is Old Penn State?
> Oh! we're sorry to relate
> She still sleeps 'neath the shade of Nittany!
>
> Your Uncle Gus

Penn State's baseball team, 1907. "Joe" Mason, Captain, is in the second row, third uniformed player from the left.

The Final Innings

Captain Joe Mason began his final baseball season two weeks later. The talented Penn State nine had some excellent new pitchers to help fill the void left by McIlveen's departure, and as with any team having Joe Mason at third, everybody played with incredible enthusiasm. Because of his modesty in his dual role as player/historian, little about Mason's baseball exploits at Penn State exists, but a sportswriter's description of Captain Mason's alter ego, Captain Root, and Root's influence on one summer's championship team captures what Penn State fans had now been witnessing for four seasons:

> It was Captain Root who organized this strong line-up of players, and it has been to a large extent the spirit of fight that results from his leadership that brought the victories.
>
> Captain Root plays third base. . . . Off the field [he] is a mild-mannered young fellow, of shy bearing, whose quiet voice would indicate him timid rather than

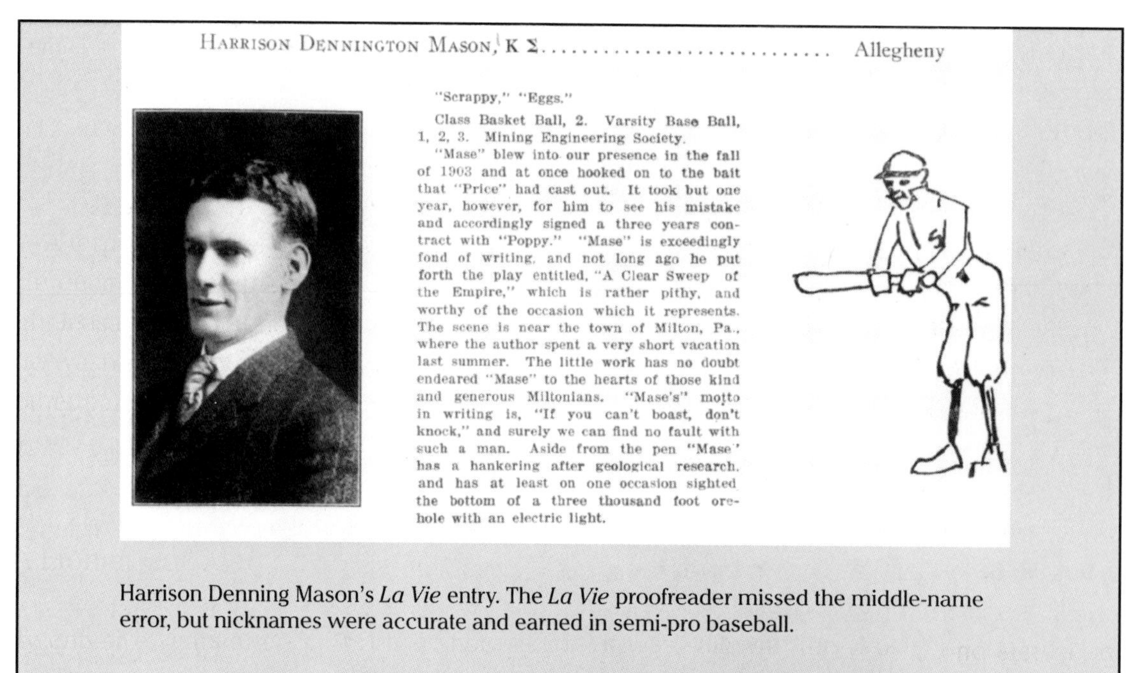

HARRISON DENNINGTON MASON, K Σ.............................. Allegheny

"Scrappy," "Eggs."

Class Basket Ball, 2. Varsity Base Ball, 1, 2, 3. Mining Engineering Society.

"Mase" blew into our presence in the fall of 1903 and at once hooked on to the bait that "Price" had cast out. It took but one year, however, for him to see his mistake and accordingly signed a three years contract with "Poppy." "Mase" is exceedingly fond of writing, and not long ago he put forth the play entitled, "A Clear Sweep of the Empire," which is rather pithy, and worthy of the occasion which it represents. The scene is near the town of Milton, Pa., where the author spent a very short vacation last summer. The little work has no doubt endeared "Mase" to the hearts of those kind and generous Miltonians. "Mase's" motto in writing is, "If you can't boast, don't knock," and surely we can find no fault with such a man. Aside from the pen "Mase" has a hankering after geological research, and has at least on one occasion sighted the bottom of a three thousand foot ore-hole with an electric light.

Harrison Denning Mason's *La Vie* entry. The *La Vie* proofreader missed the middle-name error, but nicknames were accurate and earned in semi-pro baseball.

The Many Names of Harrison Denning Mason Jr.

In a time rich with nicknames, the writer of the "Do We Still Sleep?" piece may have placed second behind his best friend Mal McIlveen, but Mason's record of "assumed names while a Penn State student" likely stands to this day. As editor of *The Lemon*, he went by "Gus (Lemon) Ade." Playing summer semi-pro ball, he was always "Harry" or "Joe," but seldom "Mason." The most often used last names were "Root" and "Eggner," the latter leading to one of his *La Vie* nicknames, "Eggs." His other *La Vie* nickname came from his style of play: "Scrappy."

> aggressive. But on the field behold a transformation! Here is a leader who is battling all the time.
>
> He coaches from the sidelines, he coaches from his position, he talks on the bench. The very last ounce of baseball that is in his men he is striving to get out of them. Every point of batting, fielding, baserunning, pitching, catching, he watches with a never-wearying eye, and his men have become such hard finishers that they are never so dangerous as during the closing innings of a game, no matter how far they may be behind.

Penn State lost only three games during Captain Mason's last season, but one of those losses probably hurt more than the other two. For the first time since Mason had enrolled, the baseball team lost to Princeton, by a score of 2–1. Joe Mason ended his Penn State baseball career that spring having played every inning of every game for his entire four years.

Ma and Pa

The lions Joe Mason referred to in *The Lemon*'s "Do We Still Sleep?" editorial sat atop the new stone pillars on either side of the Allen Street entrance to campus. Stories through the years occasionally mention that the lions came from the same Chicago Exposition of 1893 visited by the Brush Lion. The truth is they had just arrived at Penn State fresh from their appearance as part of the Pennsylvania Mines Exhibit at the St. Louis World's Fair of 1904, and they had brought their pillars with them.

The two African lions stood about 45 inches high, each holding a shield supported at the base by a small keystone. Mason's mention of the alabaster lions in 1907 is one of the earliest known print references, but "Ma" Lion and "Pa" Lion became quite famous over the next ten years. Pa had acquired his name from the abbreviation for "Pennsylvania" appearing on the keystone at his feet. The nickname "Ma" for the other was likely a gift to Pa from the students who guessed what he would have wanted had he been granted one wish.

Mason's promotion of the Nittany Lion mascot helped these two early lions receive a good many pats on the head, but in those days rubbing the lion for luck featured an act of true agility—one had to climb a stone column to get close enough.

In 1916, when some work on the gate commenced, Ma and Pa were removed and "stored in a safe place," as the *Daily Collegian* delicately put it in a 1956 article. Rog Alexander was quoting another *Collegian* article from 1917 that had attempted to locate Ma and Pa but could not. Apparently, lions had been disappearing from Penn State long before the Brush Lion took its forty-year field trip to Pittsburgh!

Alexander reported that the two Lions remained missing for thirty-nine years, until he tracked them to the home of retired Penn State employee George W. Campbell in Petersburg.

Lions at the St. Louis World's Fair, 1904.

"Ma" and "Pa" greet students as they enter the College.

A rare photograph of Pa (or Ma) showing the view students had as they were departing campus for lunch in State College.

Spirit Week of 1926 was a load of fun for the students who dragged whatever wasn't nailed down on campus to Co-op Corner, the intersection of College Avenue and Allen Street, a site for plenty of mischief over the years. Note the silent alabaster visitor by the lamppost at the far left.

George Campbell and his son Clifton "Joe" Campbell, who had been a Penn State student at the time, recalled finding them on a University rubbish heap and taking them home in about 1917. By the time the *Collegian* article was written in 1956, Pa (or perhaps Ma?) had completely disintegrated and the surviving lion was missing ears, tail, and part of the shield, according to Rog Alexander. It stood guard over a backyard woodshed.

Rog Alexander's sources for the story are unknown, but one key player in the history of Ma and Pa does not recall being interviewed back in 1956 by any reporter. But Joe Campbell, born in 1903, does remember a particular day nearly four decades earlier. He thinks he was about 16 years old the day he found the Lions. He liked to hunt groundhogs and rats down by the sinkhole in the woods between Fox Hollow and College Avenue. Penn State's only use for that area at the time was as a massive rubbish heap. Amid the lesser debris, Joe Campbell found the remnants of a treasure—the pieces of Ma and Pa. He recognized them at once as the Lions that had stood atop the Allen Street gate for many years. One was broken into too many small sections to save, he recalls, but the other had one salvageable section—a fairly intact head with one large hole in the back.

The surviving head sat in Joe's parents' yard near Whipple Dam until the mid-1950s, when he sold it to his friend Hubert Koch for $10. Joe Campbell didn't care about making money on the statue. He had only two requirements: that Hubie always preserve and care for the Lion and that he never give it back to the College that threw it away.

Hubie Koch lived in State College from 1913 until his death in 1974. Sometime after his death, Hubie's widow, Ethel, wrote: "Hubie grew up as the Community grew. A graduate of the Pennsylvania State College in 1930 in Industrial Education, [he was] a business man with a great sense of the past and a great hope for the future of the Community." Koch turned that love of the past and his boyhood passion for photography into a lifelong habit of collecting early State College memorabilia and photographs.

When Hubie Koch bought Ma or Pa from Joe Campbell, he repaired the head and mounted it on a stand by running two long bolts through the top of the head, where he attached a strong wooden handle by rope. Hanging behind the Lion's head and unseen from the front, Hubie used the handle to transport the old Lion to and from talks and slide shows he gave around the community. Ethel Koch remembers many older alumni being delighted by her husband's presentations, especially when they had one more chance to rub their old Lion's head for luck.

So, one head survives, and one is disintegrated or smashed. Pa is gone and Ma lives on. Or maybe it is Pa who remains part of the Koch Collection with his mouth and lips painted red many years ago. Or could there be one other possibility? Could Ma have escaped the rubbish heap before Joe Campbell arrived that day in 1919? He remembers pieces of two Lions, but a photograph from 1926 creates the tantalizing possibility that a Lion is still on the loose.

Some of the high jinks of Penn State students were unlikely to please State College residents during Spirit Week of May 1926 (a precursor to Spring Week in later years). Activities that year

"Old Nittany."

included a tug-of-war, a pushball scrap, the burning of class dinks, and the moving-up dance. A Spirit Week 1926 photograph, depicting what is often mistaken for preparation for one of the many downtown bonfires, actually shows the concluding activity of the Pajama Parade, where students grabbed anything not nailed down on campus and deposited said items in the middle of College Avenue and Allen Street, also known as Co-op Corner.

By the lamppost in this well-known photograph sits a mysterious onlooker gazing nostalgically across the street at her (or his!) former home. How could a smashed Lion appear intact on College Avenue seven to ten years after it was destroyed? Perhaps somewhere in Centre County there remains an elderly Lion on the lam.

Old Nittany

Mason's case for the Nittany Lion bore immediate results in that spring of 1907. In Squirt 8 under the title "Old Nittany—Our Lion!" gossip columnist "Aunty Bellum" reported:

Horrible Disclosures!!!

Yielding to the horrific abjurations and unceasing clamor for essentially correct information, the Lemon hereby gives the long-waiting and impatient public the only authentic information as to who done it. The following list of the Lemon staff is unfallaciously correct and forms the greatest "scoop" known to modern journalism:

Editor-in-Chief .... Joe Mason

Business Manager............. Bill Slater

Financial Manager and Society Reporter .... Bull German

Literary Editor and Spring Poet..... .... F. E. Wilber

Dramatic Critic and Sporting Reporter.. .... Baul Reece

Assigned from the Pinkerton staff..... .... Schnitz Snyder

Hack Writer and Editor of the "Squeezer" .... Mussie Mussina

War-correspondent (absent on furlough) .... Easy Evans

3

The Lemon, Squirt 13, the "Horrible Disclosures," in which "Joe" Mason is identified as the editor.

Emblem of the Lion's Paw Honor Society, founded in 1908.

The 1910 version of the Nittany Lion.

> [The] idea of adopting the King of the Beasts for our College Emblem is very pleasing to the members of the present Junior Class, and . . . in their coming *La Vie*, a beginning will be given to "Old Nittany"—Penn State's guardian Mountain Lion. And as the years roll by the veneration will increase for this guardian spirit of our College.

Indeed, the Class of 1908 did feature the Lion prominently in their *La Vie*, both inside and embossed on the cover. Along with a poem entitled "Old Nittany," there was a tribute of the same name that alluded to the "Lemonite" who first heard the Lion's roar. The dedication ended with "May we all hail thee with one loud roar. Long live, 'Leo,' 'King of the living' 'Old Nittany.' "

So half a century after its founding, Penn State finally had its symbol. In print, it was usually mentioned that the Nittany Lion was a mountain lion, implying at least that it was a lion indigenous to Pennsylvania, but for the next three decades the Nittany Lion had a decidedly African appearance. This may have started with Mason's own comment that Ma and Pa were "a move in the right direction," followed by the Class of 1908's use of the name "Leo" and the depiction of Old Nittany as a king of beasts who had never set foot in any Pennsylvania forest. Whatever the cause for its shaggy mane, the acceptance of the Lion as a symbol was rapid by college tradition standards and welcomed by nearly everyone associated with Penn State.

The Lemon ended its run with a number of interesting lists. Readers finally learned who was who among the large (Lemon) Ade family, with Joe Mason pegged as editor-in-chief. Perhaps not trusting the memories of their readers, *Lemon* staffers also included a summary of "What the Lemon Advocates." Some of the items on the list were followed by "We have it now!" Number 6 was a "typical guardian spirit for our college—'the Old Nittany Lion'—we will have it soon."

Toward the end of Squirt 13, *The Lemon* answered its own question, "Has the Lemon done any good?" with another question: "Would Old Penn State have found her Lion without the assistance of the Lemon?" The answer was probably no.

"Nittany" and "Lion" began to appear together, and in connection with Penn State, throughout the campus. In 1908 the Lion's Paw, a senior honor society, was formed. In 1914, Jimmie Leyden wrote the music and lyrics of his song "The Nittany Lion." At the five-year reunion of the Class of 1910, forty class members "costumed as jesters and accompanied by a band and a life-like 'Nittany Lion' . . . cavorted through the streets of the village to the delight of the early morning crowd."

Even though the Nittany Lion was obviously catching on, there seemed to be room for discussion. In a letter to folklorist Henry Shoemaker dated December 31, 1914, Richard Ernest, then head of the Department of Fine and Industrial Arts at Penn State, wrote:

> I am a great admirer of your books and read them all so far, I am at the same time just now interested in a matter in which I want to turn to you as an authority, and I sincerely hope that you can help us out with the information wanted so very much.

THE PENNSYLVANIA STATE COLLEGE
STATE COLLEGE, PA.

DEPARTMENT OF INDUSTRIAL ART AND DESIGN

December, 31st, 14.

Mr Henry W. Shoemaker,

Author,

My dear Sir.

I am a great admirer of your books and read them all so far, I am at the same time just now interested in a matter in which I want to turn to you as an authority, and I sincerely hope that yu can help us out with the information wanted so very much.

It is this: The college here with its nearly 3000 students mostly boys want to adopt an emblem, something like Harvard has in its Tiger.

I have suggested that they use an Indian and have Painted for them an Indian which I called Chief "Nittany" from the name of the Mountain by the same name here. I have put into the design as background this mountain and some of the scenery here, to gether with the old Pine tree the historic one near Boalsburg under which it is said the Indians used to trade with the whites.

I am wondering if you have any history of the name "Nittany" its first origin and wether there is any history of Chief Nittany that can be gotten at. If so would you be good enough to give me the information for the boys, so that we can found our Emblem on something tangible, it may be that I have overlooked or not seen yet all that you have written and you may have already imortalised that name or Mountain or Indian. Perhaps you can also give us the meaning of the word.

I will be very gradeful to you for any help in this matter and I am Sure that the many boys here will also feel grateful to you.

So thanking you in advance for anything that yu can do for us. I am

Very sincerely yours,
Richard Ernest.
Head Dept of Fine & Ind Arts.

Letter from Richard Ernest to Henry Shoemaker, December 31, 1914.

> It is this: The college here with its nearly 3000 students mostly boys want [*sic*] to adopt an emblem, something like Harvard has its Tiger [*sic*]. I have suggested that they use an Indian and have Painted for them an Indian which I called Chief "Nittany" from the name of the Mountain by the same name here. . . . I am wondering if you have any history of the name "Nittany" its first origin and wether [*sic*] there is any history of Chief Nittany that can be gotten at.

Richard Ernest's information regarding Harvard's emblem may have missed the mark, but his question about the origin of "Nittany" was posed to just the right man.

4

The Legends and the Mountain

Nita-nee and the Creation of Mount Nittany

Henry Shoemaker was delighted to find someone interested in collecting and preserving the old legends and folklore of the Central Pennsylvania mountains. He replied to Professor Ernest's request in a letter dated just four days later:

> As I have no authorities to draw from, and one old settler's version is as reliable as another's, I cannot say that no Indian chief gave his name to Mount Nittany, though I have never heard of a chief of that name. It is my belief that the name is feminine for the following reasons. I will copy herewith from my note book a legend told me by an old farm laborer who was working near State College in the summer of 1912, when I met him, who claimed to have spent his boyhood near the foot of Nittany Mountain.

Henry Shoemaker as a young man.

Henry Wharton Shoemaker

Biographical Particulars

Born: February 4, 1880, New York City.

Father: Henry F. Shoemaker, railroad financier.

Mother: Blanche Quiggle Shoemaker.

Early education: Private tutors and Dr. E. D. Lyons's Classical School.

College: Attended Columbia University but did not graduate.

Honorary doctorates: Juniata College, 1917; Franklin and Marshall College, 1924.

Marriage: To Beatrice Barclay in 1907; to Mabelle Ord in 1913.

Children: Henry Francis Shoemaker, a son with his first wife.

Career: Railroad; diplomatic posts in Costa Rica, Portugal, and Berlin; banking. Writing career began when "The Legend of Penn's Cave" first appeared in 1903. Newspaper publisher beginning in 1905, owning at least one newspaper through 1950, including the *Jersey Shore Herald*, the *Bradford Record*, the *Reading Times*, the *Altoona Tribune* (all of Pennsylvania), and the *Bridgeport Telegram* (Connecticut). National Guard, 1907; served in the U.S. Army during World War I. Wrote and published many collections of Pennsylvania legends, reminiscences, travel pieces, and speeches on Pennsylvania history. Ambassador to Bulgaria, 1930–33. Member of the Pennsylvania Historical Commission, 1915–30; the Pennsylvania State Forest Commission, 1918–30; the State Geographic Board, 1924–30. Chairman of the Pennsylvania Historical Commission, 1923–30 and 1936–40. State Archivist, 1937–48; Pennsylvania's first State Folklorist and director of the Folklore Division of the Pennsylvania Historical Museum Commission, 1948–56. Director of the Pennsylvania State Museum, 1939–40.

Died: July 15, 1958, of a heart attack in Williamsport, Pennsylvania.

Shoemaker's *Juniata Memories: Legends Collected in Central Pennsylvania.*

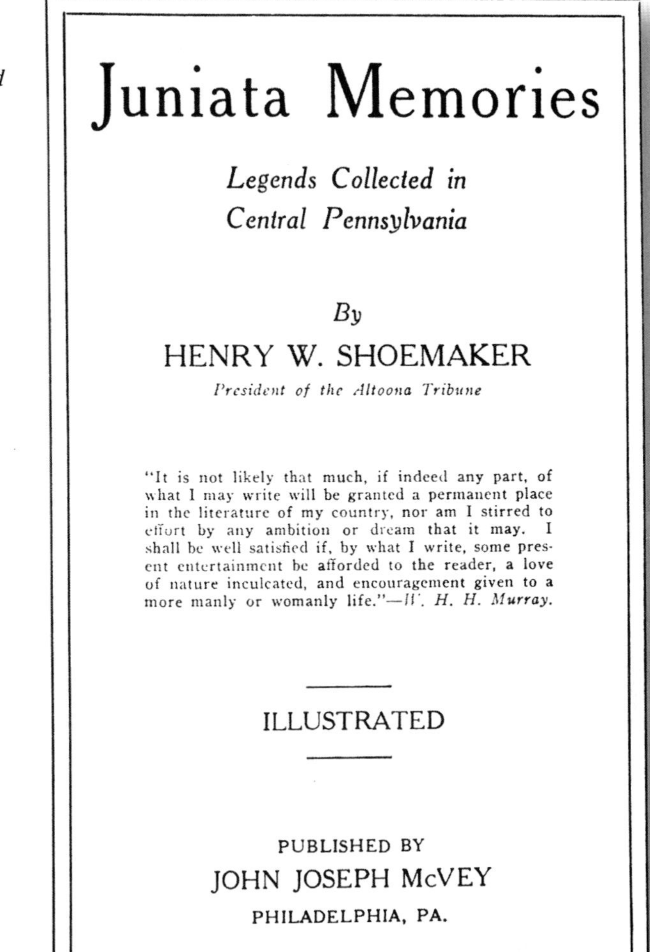
Juniata Memories

Legends Collected in Central Pennsylvania

By

HENRY W. SHOEMAKER

President of the Altoona Tribune

"It is not likely that much, if indeed any part, of what I may write will be granted a permanent place in the literature of my country, nor am I stirred to effort by any ambition or dream that it may. I shall be well satisfied if, by what I write, some present entertainment be afforded to the reader, a love of nature inculcated, and encouragement given to a more manly or womanly life."—*W. H. H. Murray.*

ILLUSTRATED

PUBLISHED BY

JOHN JOSEPH McVEY

PHILADELPHIA, PA.

Shoemaker's letter version of the creation of Mount Nittany, "named for a saintly Indian maiden, Nita-nee, who lived several thousand years ago," predates the first published edition of the legend in his book *Juniata Memories* by a full year. The translation of "Nita-nee," according to Shoemaker, was "The Kindly Spirit Who Tempers the Winds from the Valley."

The legend itself was attributed to an elderly Seneca—Jake Faddy—who would travel around trading his well-told tales for a place to stay or a warm meal. The legend begins:

> Of all his stories, by odds his favorite one dealt with the Indian maiden, Nita-nee, for whom the fruitful Nittany Valley and the towering Nittany Mountain are named. This Indian girl was born on the banks of the lovely Juniata, not far from the present town of Newton Hamilton, the daughter of a powerful chief. It was in the early days of the world, when the physical aspect of Nature could be changed over night by a fiat from the Gitchie-Manitto or Great Spirit. It was therefore in the age of great and wonderful things, before a rigid world produced beings whose lives followed grooves as tight and permanent as the gullies and ridges.

When Nita-nee was young there had been a great war between her tribe and the Indians from the south who coveted the beautiful land that Nita-nee's people called home. Nita-nee's father, Chun-Eh-Hoe, fought the war valiantly, as did all his people, but the southern tribes prevailed and drove Chun-Eh-Hoe northward to the Seven Mountains and beyond. Chun-Eh-Hoe was humiliated in his defeat. His once-dark hair turned pure white, and he never ventured out in daylight again. He died not many years after his defeat, and his eldest child, Nita-nee, assumed leadership of the tribe until such time as her younger brother, Wo-Wi-Na-Pe, would be old enough to assume his rightful leadership role.

Nita-nee was a peace-loving leader and had no wish to avenge her tribe's defeat, but in time the southern tribes began to move farther north again, killing innocent people in their path and forcing others to flee. Following the death of her brother and mother, Nita-nee was chosen queen, and as queen she put aside her natural inclination and led her strong army southward, sweeping "down to the settlements of the southern Indians, butchering every one of them. They pressed onward to the Bear Meadows, and to the slopes of Bald Top and Tussey Knob. There they gave up the population to fire and sword."

After some time passed, the Indians to the south mistook Nita-nee's reluctance to press her advantage farther south as cowardice rather than a return to her peaceful inclinations. Their miscalculation led to a final defeat at the hands of the reluctant warrior queen. Following the victory, Nita-nee disbanded her armies and encouraged all to return to their peaceful avocations.

> Under her there was no nobility, all were on a common level of dignified citizenship. Every Indian in her realm had a task, not one that he was born to follow, but the one which appealed to him mostly, and therefore the task at which he was most successful. Women also had their work, apart from domestic life in this ideal democracy of ancient days. Suffrage was universal to both sexes over twenty years of age, but as there were no official positions, no public trusts, a political class could not come into existence and the queen, as long as she was cunning and able, had the unanimous support of her people.

In those days there was no range of mountains where the Nittany chain now stands, and the wind that blew down from the Seven Mountains and across the plains was cruel and cold. "Only the strong and the brave could cope with these killing blasts, so intense and so different from the calming zephyrs of the Juniata." As queen Nita-nee returned home, many of her people came out of their settlements to greet her and present gifts. When Nita-nee neared the place of her childhood memories, an aged Indian couple approached and addressed their queen:

> We are very old. The winters of more than a century have passed over our heads. Our sons and our grandsons were killed fighting bravely under your immortal sire, Chun-Eh-Hoe. We have had to struggle on by ourselves as best we could ever since. We are about to set out a crop of corn, which we need badly. For the past three years the north wind had destroyed our crop every time it appeared; the seeds which we plan

Mount Nittany.

> to put in the earth this year are the last we've got. Really we should have kept them for food, but we hoped that the future would treat us more generously. We would like a wind-break built along the northern side of our corn patch; we are too feeble to go to the forests and cut and carry the poles. Will not our most kindly queen have someone assist us?

Many warriors volunteered so quickly that the task was performed in what seemed to the old couple to be miracle time. They fell on their knees in gratitude to their kind queen, who promised to return one day soon to share corn from their harvest. More than the victory in war, this simple act of beneficence had a profound effect on Nita-nee.

> [This] smoothing of rough pathways for the weak or oppressed helped her resolve more than ever to dedicate her life to the benefiting of her subjects. No love affair had come into her life, she would use her great love-nature to put brightness into unhappy souls about her. . . . And thus in broad unselfishness and generosity of thought and

deed the great queen's life was spent, making her pathway through her realm radiant with sunshine.

And when she came to die, after a full century of life, she requested that her body be laid to rest in the royal forest, in the center of the valley whose people she loved and served so well. Her funeral cortege, which included every person in the plains and valleys, a vast assemblage, shook with a common grief. It would be hard to find a successor like her, a pure soul so deeply animated with true godliness.

And it came to pass that on the night when she was buried beneath a modest mound covered with cedar boughs, and the vast funeral party had dispersed, a terrific storm arose, greater than even the oldest person could remember. The blackness of the night was intense, the roar and rumbling heard made every being fear that the end of the world had come. It was a night of intense terror, of horror. But at dawn, the tempest abated, only a gentle breeze remained, a golden sunlight overspread the scene, and great was the wonder thereof! In the center of the vast plain where Nita-nee had been laid away stood a mound-like mountain, a towering, sylvan giant covered with dense groves of cedar and pine. And as it stood there, eternal, it tempered and broke the breezes from the north, promising a new prosperity, a greater tranquillity, to the peaceful dwellers in the vale that has since been called John Penn's Valley, after the grandson of William Penn.

A miracle, a sign of approval from the Great Spirit, had happened during the night to forever keep alive the memory of Nita-nee, who had tempered the winds from the cornpatch of the aged, helpless couple years before. And the dwellers in the valleys adjacent to Mount Nittany awoke to a greater pride in themselves . . . since they were the special objects of celestial notice.

And the name of Nita-nee was the favorite cognomen for Indian maidens, and has been borne by many of saintly and useful life ever since.

Nita-nee in *La Vie*

Professor Ernest seemed pleased that Henry Shoemaker had corresponded with him so quickly, but he was not necessarily thrilled with the news that "Nittany" originated with a woman, Nita-nee. Ernest did promise an eventual artistic rendering of Nita-nee for Shoemaker to see, yet his search for a male emblem was still evident. In a letter dated January 28, 1915, he wrote: "I have painted the Indian Chief 'Woapalanee,' the chief Bald Eagle who was the leading chief in Centre co and it is up to the boys now to adopt him. If it is and is done in Post cards will send you one. I shall also paint a little later Nittany the maiden and see what they think of her."

Henry Shoemaker's legend of Nita-nee and the creation of Mount Nittany became part of Penn State's history when the 1916 *La Vie* ran its own version. In the *La Vie* retelling of the

The Legend of the Valley

A LONG, bright, ribbon of gold, blending, graying, into the deep blue of a twilight sky, set atop of a mountain line, rugged, irregular; the breath of a night wind, soft, uncertain, rustling faintly across the broad expanse of tree tops; a thread of shining white in the valley just below her, all this Nittany saw and was thankful. Many were the moons and long, since her warrior went out to battle. Many were the flocks of wild geese that had flown northward and southward above her, and still, he had not returned. Manitou, Manitou the Mighty, was cruel, and yet—the south wind grew bolder and kissed her brown cheek, withered now and old; the dying light in the west lingered on her face, kindled answering lights in her eyes,—another day was gone.

Down in the valley, lived an old warrior and his squaw. Weak, feeble, scarcely able to grind the corn or gather the berries which were their food, they lived alone, the remnant of a people once great and powerful. Frequently it had happened that just when the maize they had planted with so much labor was ready to reap, then the north wind had come, bending the oak trees in his strong fingers, and had wrested it from them so that in the long winter there was little to eat. And this Indian maid, since she was good and kind, had come down from her hilltop into the valley when all was dark, and had built a shield for them against the northwind, a barrier that even his strong fingers could not break. The old people saw with wonder the thing that she had done, and called her Nittany, which means "wind breaker."

Then a great sickness came upon her and she died, and the old warrior and his squaw mourned her, and all who had known her mourned her; called her pious, called her good. And they built a mound over the place where she lay that her resting place might be remembered. Then in the night came the Great Spirit with thunderings and lightnings; the earth shook, great trees came crashing down and the people were sore afraid. After a time, the thunders grew duller and duller, the lightnings flashed less and less often, and peace, dark, silent, brooded over the valley. When the dawn came, the first pale light of morning, the people came forth and marveled; for in the place where they had builded the mound, now rose a great mountain. And they called it Nittany in honor of her who was called pious and good.

The snows of many winters had lain on the valley, many summers had come and gone. A new people had come up from the southward and had taken possession of the land. Men with white faces had come from the eastward. There arose among this new people a great warrior chief named Woap-a-lanne, whom the men with white faces called Bald Eagle. He lived in this same broad valley, and he extended his hunting grounds far to the northward. Brave was he and led his warriors to victory, and many were the songs that the singers made in honor of his bravery and his daring. Woap-a-lanne loved his brothers with

First page of "The Legend of the Valley."

legend, there is still an old Indian couple having trouble with their corn, they are still shown kindness by Nita-nee (called Nittany), who constructs a "wind-break," and Mount Nittany is still formed from the Indian maid's burial mound, but other elements of Shoemaker's legend are missing, and two new characters appear.

One new character is Nittany's warrior Manitou the Mighty, who never returned from battle. The other, many years later, is the actual Chief "Woap-a-lanne," or Bald Eagle. The legend concludes with a description of "the Great Mother," or Penn State, "[whose] sons went out into the world and worked with the arts she had taught them and brought back to her honor and glory. The world knew them; for in their minds was the gentleness of Nittany, in their hearts, the strength of Woap-a-lanne." It appears that Professor Ernest's "boys" did accept at least a portion of what Henry Shoemaker had told their professor.

Nita-nee's appearance in Shoemaker's *Juniata Memories* and reappearance in Penn State's *La Vie* were not the first times her name had appeared in print. An Indian maiden bearing her name was featured in a popular local legend for more than a decade. The reteller of that first Nita-nee legend was none other than Henry Shoemaker.

Nita-nee and the Legend of Penn's Cave

Henry Wharton Shoemaker was introduced to the legends he would spend his whole lifetime researching and retelling when he was 12 years old on his annual summer visit to his grandmother's home in Clinton County. As he recalled ten years later, the original tale-teller—Isaac Steele—was "an aged Seneca Indian . . . visiting familiar scenes in the West Branch and Bald Eagle Valleys. The venerable man sat on the trunk of a felled apple tree at the corner of the old Quiggle orchard, at McElhattan, and recounted the Legend of Penn's Cave."

The Legend of Penn's Cave tossed about in Shoemaker's mind for more than a decade before he finally committed it to paper. The story appeared for the first time in a Centre Hall newspaper, the *Centre Reporter,* on Thursday, March 12, 1903, on the front page under the headline "The Legend of Penn's Cave: The Story as Told by an Old Seneca Indian in 'Wild Life in Western Pennsylvania,' by H. W. Shoemaker, NY."

Shoemaker's legend grabbed his readers immediately. It began:

> In the days when the West Branch Valley was a trackless wilderness of defiant pines and submissive hemlocks, twenty-five years before the first pioneer had attempted a permanent lodgment beyond Sunbury, a young Pennsylvania Frenchman from Lancaster County, named Malachi Boyer, alone and unaided, pierced the jungle to the point where Bellefonte is now located. . . . A short, stockily built fellow was Malachi Boyer, with unusually prominent black eyes, and black hair that hung in ribbon-like strands over his broad, low forehead.

VOL. LXXVI. CENTRE HALL, PA., THURSDAY, MARCH 12, 1903. NO. 11.

CENTRE COUNTY IN THE CIVIL WAR.

148th Regiment, Pennsylvania Volunteers.

GENERAL REVIEW OF MAJOR AND MINOR EVENTS.

Experiences of the Rank and File—Anecdotes and Observations.

By T. P. Meyer, Sergeant Co. A., 148th Regiment, P. V.

[To be Continued.]

On Jan. 16th one hundred and twenty of us from the 148th P. V. were sent on picket duty to the Rappahannock river. The weather was exceedingly cold; yet at midnight three Johnnie Rebels swam and waded the icy waters of the Rappahannock and surrendered, saying that they had been impressed into the Confederate service, but they had resolved not to fight for secession; that there were some twenty more who had agreed to come with them but failed to be on hand at the appointed hour and they would not wait for them. We made coffee for them and fed them full of crackers and pork, and sent them to the rear to Headquarters.

On Jan. 19th marching orders were again circulated through the entire army to be ready for extended move and next morning the Left Grand Division, under Maj. General Franklin, whose camps were five miles below us began to move by and through our camp, north on all available roads and open fields, presenting a magnificent sight. Endless columns of soldiers with flags and banners; ponton bridge trains; wagon trains, the head and rear extending out of sight lost in woods and hills in the distance; all wagons alike, with white canvas covers; battery after battery of artillery moved laboriously along the muddy roads.

That very evening heavy rains set in and continued all night and next day, rendering the roads absolutely impassable. The roads were canals of liquid mud, axle deep. Just above our camp a heavy field gun stuck in the mud, and twenty-four horses could not, or would not, pull it out; the horses were all taken away. An inch and a half rope one hundred and fifty

THE LEGEND OF PENN'S CAVE.

The Story as Told by an Old Seneca Indian in "Wild Life in Western Pennsylvania" by H. W. Shoemaker, N. Y.

In the days when the West Branch Valley was a trackless wilderness of defiant pines and submissive helmlocks, twenty-five years before the first pioneer had attempted a permanent lodgment beyond Sunbury, a young Pennsylvania Frenchman from Lancaster County, named Malachi Boyer, alone and unaided, pierced the jungle to the point where Bellefonte now stands. The history of his travels has never been written, partly because he had no white companion to observe them, and partly because he himself was unable to write. His very indentity would now be forgotten were it not for traditions of the Indians, with whose lives he became strangely entangled.

A short, stockily built fellow was Malachi Boyer, with unusually prominent black eyes, and black hair that hung in ribbon-like strands over his broad, low forehead. Fearless, yet conciliatory, he escaped a thousand times from Indian cunning and treachery, and as months went by and he penetrated further into the forests he numbered the redskins among his cherished friends.

Why he explored these boundless wilds he could not explain, for it was not in the interest of science, as he scarcely knew of such a thing as geography, and it was not for trading, as he lived by the way. But on he forced his path, ever aloof from his own race, on the alert for the strange scenes which encompassed him day by day.

One beautiful Springtime, there is no one can tell the exact year, found Malachi Boyer camped on the shores of Spring Creek. Near the Mammoth Spring was an Indian camp whose occupants maintained a quasi-intercourse with the pale-faced stranger. Sometimes old Chief O-ko-cho would bring gifts of corn to Malachi, who in turn presented the chieftain with a hunting knife of finest steel. And in this way Malachi came to spend more and more of his time about the Indian camps, only keeping his distance at night and during religious ceremonies.

Old O-ko-cho's chief pride was cen-

some pair meet in the mossy ravines near the camp ground. But this was all clandestine love, for friendly as Indian and white might be in social intercourse, never could a marriage be tolerated, until—there always is a turning point in romance—the black-haired wanderer and the beautiful Nita-nee resolved to spend their lives together, and one moonless night started for the more habitable east. All night long they threaded their silent way, climbing the mountain ridges, gliding through the velvet soiled hemlock glades, and wading, hand in hand, the splashing, resolute torrents. When morning came they breakfasted on dried meat and huckleberries, and bathed their faces in a mineral spring. Until—there always is a turning point in romance—seven tall, stealthy forms, like animated mountain pines, stepped from the gloom and surrounded the eloping couple. Malachi drew a hunting knife, identical with the one he had given to Chief O-ko-cho, and seizing Nita-nee around the waist, stabbed right and left at his would-be captors. The first stroke pierced Hum-kin's heart, and uncomplaining he sank down dying. The six remaining brothers, although all recieved stab wounds, caught Malachi in their combined grasp and disarmed him ; then one brother held sobbing Nita-nee, while the others dragged fighting Malachi across the mountain. That was the last the lovers saw of one another. Below the mountain lay a broad valley, from the center of which rose a circular hillock, and it was to this mound the savage brothers led their victim. As they approached, a yawning cavern met their eyes, filled with greenish limestone water. There is a ledge at the mouth of the cave, about six feet higher than the water, above which the arched roof rises thirty feet, and it was from here they shoved Malachi Boyer into the tide below. He sank for a moment, but when he rose to the surface, commenced to swim. He approached the ledge but the brothers beat him back, so he turned and made

ASSIGNMENT OF MINISTERS.

Central Pennsylvania Body Adjourns when These were Made Known.

The ninth annual meeting of the Central Pennsylvania Conference of the United Evangelical church, in session at Baltimore closed Tuesday night with the announcement of assignments of the ministers to the various stations, a list of which appears below.

YORK DISTRICT.
J. W. Messenger, presiding elder.
York, Grace—J. Hartzler.
Baltimore, Grace—M. A. Kennally.
Shrewsbury—F. H. Foss.
Loganville—J. D. Stover.
East Prospect—E. D. Keen.
Red Lion—C. W. Finkbinder.

CARLISLE DISTRICT.
J. C. Reeser, presiding elder.
Mount Holly Springs—B. Hengst.
Dillsburg—W. W. Rhoads.
Hellam—L. E. Crumbling.
Wrightsville—A. Stapleton.
Marysville—D. L. Kepner.

CENTER DISTRICT.
E. Crumbling, presiding elder.
Altoona—M. I. Jamison.
Bellwood—C. F. Garrett.
Milesburg—W. K. Shultz.
Bellefonte—W. H. Brown.
Howard—D. A. Artman.
Nittany—J. M. Price.
Sugar Valley—A. S. Baumgardner.
Rebersburg—S. Smith.
Centre Hall—J. F. Shultz.
Spring Mills—W. C. Bierley.
Millheim—I. N. Bair.
Millmont—S. Auraud and E. I. Confer.
Mifflinburg—C. C. Mizener.
Buffalo—L. Dice.
New Berlin—S. E. Koontz.
Centerville—N. J. Dubs.
Middleburg—J. Womelsdorf.
McClure—A. D. Gramley.
Port Treverton—H. T. Searle.
Lewistown—N. Young.
Patterson—S. S. Mumey.
Dr. A. E. Gobble, of Albright College, member of New Berlin Quarterly Conference.
George Josephs, member of Lewistown Quarterly Conference.

LEWISBURG DISTRICT.
W. F. Swengel, presiding elder.
Lewisburg—J. W. Thompson.
Milton—J. D. Shortess.
Milton Circuit—J. A. Foss.
Berwick—H. W. Buck.
Nescopeq—D. F. Young.

WILLIAMSPORT DISTRICT.
S. P. Remer, presiding elder.
Williamsport, Newberry—G. W. Currin.
Williamsport, Circuit—J. M. King.
Hughesville—J. J. Lohr.
White Deer—C. H. Goodling and H. C. Walker.
Lock Haven—J. F. Dunlap.
Lock Haven, Circuit—W. N. Wallis.

It was decided that the next conference should convene the first Thurs-

TEACHERS' BILL RECOMMITTED.

Sent Back to the Senate Committee on Judiciary General To Be Amended.

With an inimical Senate determined to harry it to death if its passage was insisted upon without amendments, the friends of the Snyder bill fixing the minimum salary for teachers at $35 a month discreetly outflanked the movement Tuesday and by quick work succeeded in having the bill sent back to the Committee on Judiciary General, where an effort will be made so to amend it that it will meet any objections that are now made to it.

This was not done, however, until it was developed that the opposition had materially strengthened its lines, and that there was some secret force working that the friends were at first unable to locate. Later it was known that the silent force was the Legislative Committee of the State Grange, Patrons of Husbandry, through whose influence resolutions have been adopted in the local granges and sent to the various Senators protesting against fixing the salaries at $35. These protests are printed and in the form of resolutions, and there are hundreds of them to come. Hundreds have already arrived, and they are having their effect.

The resolution referred to is printed in full below. The same was endorsed by nearly every local and County Grange in the State and sent to the State Senator of their district.

We, citizens of Pennsylvania engaged in agriculture, organized into Granges authorized to address your Honorable body, respectfully protest against the passage of the Teachers' Minimum Salary Bill, as it would be a usurpation of the rights of local self government guaranteed under our State Constitution and would establish a precedent in depriving the people locally of the right of "Home Rule" for which the people of the Colonies fought in resenting the exactions of the British crown of "taxation without representation."

The people of the local governments have some rights and qualifications to administer their own affairs, without the right of centralized State interference and in a majority of the counties the salaries paid teachers are commensurate with the resources of the counties, and where teachers have had the requisite qualifications the salaries have been raised to meet the qualifications and in many instances exceed that named in this bill. Should the Legislature pass this bill it will deprive a number of townships of the ability to keep open the schools the requisite number of months required by law owing to want of resource-

TOWN AND COUNTY NEWS.

HAPPENINGS OF LOCAL INTEREST FROM ALL PARTS.

The Manns will erect a large department store at Mill Hall.

Christ Keller, of Penn Hall, was a caller Saturday to renew the Reporter.

H. W. Petrikin, Esq., is the first Democrat who was ever elected burgess of Huntingdon.

Miss Virna Emerick, daughter of Mr. and Mrs. G. H. Emerick, of near town, visited Bellefonte last week.

Miss Katie Keller, who for the past few months had been at Munson and Osceola, returned home a few days ago.

Mrs. John A. Slack and Miss Blanche Durst, both of Potters Mills, visited in Bellefonte the latter part of last week.

Under the head of Child Training, in the April Delineator, are a number of valuable suggestions for keeping the house pure.

The engagement is announced of C. M. Parrish and Miss Rose Fox, of Bellefonte, their marriage to take place in the near future.

Prof. H. F. Bitner, of the Millersville Normal School, Monday attended the funeral of his uncle, George L. Derr, at Laurelton.

Miss Flora Love, Friday of last week went to Watsontown where she was the guest of Mrs. Foster, wife of Rev. W. K. Foster, until Monday.

Wm. Brooks, of Linden Hall, was a pleasant caller Tuesday. He is planning out his spring campaign on the farm and is anxious for an early spring.

District Attorney N. B. Spangler and Attorney Thomas Sexton will move their office to Crider's Exchange, recently occupied by W. E. Gray, Esq., deceased.

Ellis Horner, of near Pleasant Gap, will become a citizen of Bellefonte, where he will be employed at the furnace. His sons have also secured employment.

J. B. Shuman, of State College, was considerably injured by being struck by a wagon to which a runaway horse was hitched. He was picked up

The first appearance of "The Legend of Penn's Cave" by Henry Shoemaker, *Centre Reporter*, Centre Hall, Pennsylvania, 1903.

Through an equal mix of bravery, luck, and negotiating skill, Boyer escaped a fair number of ticklish situations in his relationships with the local Indians and before long became quite friendly with most. He often camped near their camps, but he discreetly kept his distance at night and during religious ceremonies. One spring of undetermined year, he renewed his acquaintance with old Chief O-ko-cho and his followers, who were camped by Spring Creek. O-ko-cho may have been proud of his seven sons, but his "Diana-like daughter Nita-nee" had her brothers' guardianship as well as her father's affection.

Malachi Boyer first saw Nita-nee washing a deer skin in the stream and soon found his temporary camp had become a more permanent home. They didn't speak much in the company of others, but the glances they exchanged were probably as telling as any words of love. As friendly as Indian and white might be in social exchange, love and marriage would not be tolerated. Malachi and Nita-nee reached that turning point in romance where nothing else seems very important when compared with the love two people feel for each other. They resolved to spend their lives together, "and one moon-less night started for the more habitable east."

After a night of silent climbing, wading, and walking hand in hand, the lovers had paused in the morning to eat and refresh themselves when the seven tall brothers stepped out from behind the trees. Malachi, one arm around Nita-nee, drew his knife and killed one brother instantly. Although all received wounds, the remaining six eventually prevailed in disarming the struggling fighter. While one brother held his sobbing sister, the remaining five dragged Malachi across the mountain to a cavern, where from the ledge inside the mouth they threw him into the green water below. For seven days Malachi Boyer attempted to climb that ledge from the water, only to be pushed back by the brothers. Each day he retreated to the dry cave to gather what strength remained to attempt escape once more, but hunger and the determination of the brothers combined to defeat him. On the seventh day, "Malachi Boyer breathed his last."

"And after these years those who have heard this legend declare that on the still summer nights an unaccountable echo rings through the cave which sounds like Nita-nee! Nita-nee!"

Nittany Mountain

Shoemaker's 1903 Legend of Penn's Cave provides the first known written mention of the beautiful Indian maiden Nita-nee, but there is no mention of the connection between the maiden's name and the mountain's or valley's phonetic sibling—Nittany. Shoemaker sets his first hearing of the tale in 1892, when he was 12 years old, but admits: "The various Indian names are purely fictitious, as I transcribed the story from memory for the first time a few days ago."

Shoemaker probably spoke the full truth in that introductory statement to the legend in *Wild Life in Western Pennsylvania*, a

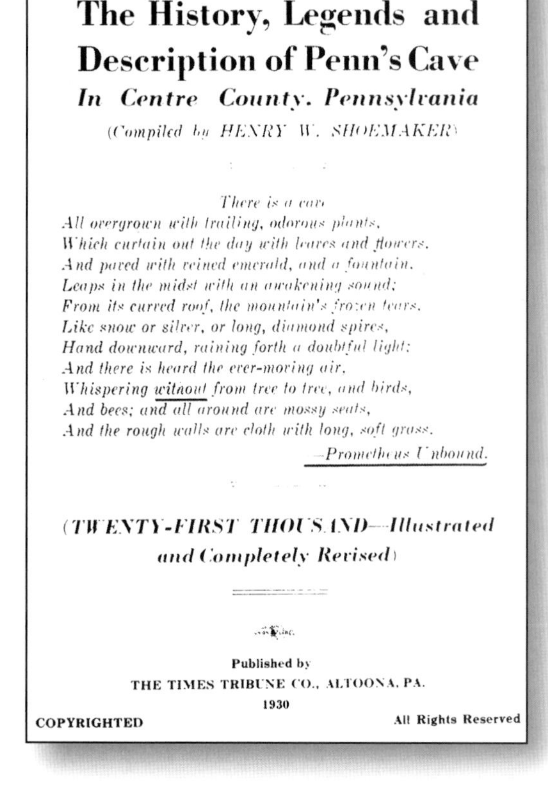
Penn's Grandest Cavern

The History, Legends and Description of Penn's Cave
In Centre County, Pennsylvania
(*Compiled by HENRY W. SHOEMAKER*)

There is a cave
All overgrown with trailing, odorous plants,
Which curtain out the day with leaves and flowers.
And paved with veined emerald, and a fountain.
Leaps in the midst with an awakening sound;
From its curved roof, the mountain's frozen tears.
Like snow or silver, or long, diamond spires,
Hand downward, raining forth a doubtful light:
And there is heard the ever-moving air.
Whispering without from tree to tree, and birds,
And bees; and all around are mossy seats,
And the rough walls are cloth with long, soft grass.
—Prometheus Unbound.

(TWENTY-FIRST THOUSAND—Illustrated and Completely Revised)

Published by
THE TIMES TRIBUNE CO., ALTOONA, PA.
1930

COPYRIGHTED **All Rights Reserved**

Title page for one edition of Shoemaker's *Penn's Cave: Pennsylvania's Grandest Cavern*, 1930.

The entrance to Penn's Cave in early days.

statement he did not repeat in subsequent editions. This was his first book, published long before he established his reputation as keeper of Pennsylvania's legends. He invented the Indian names in "The Legend of Penn's Cave," and he makes no mention that the name of Nita-nee was the single exception to his fabrication. The author's own words point to the most likely relationship between mountain and maiden: Henry Shoemaker used Mount Nittany as the inspiration for the naming of the legendary Nita-nee. A decade later, Shoemaker would supply a legendary connection between the mountain and the maiden in his story of Nita-nee and the Creation of Mount Nittany.

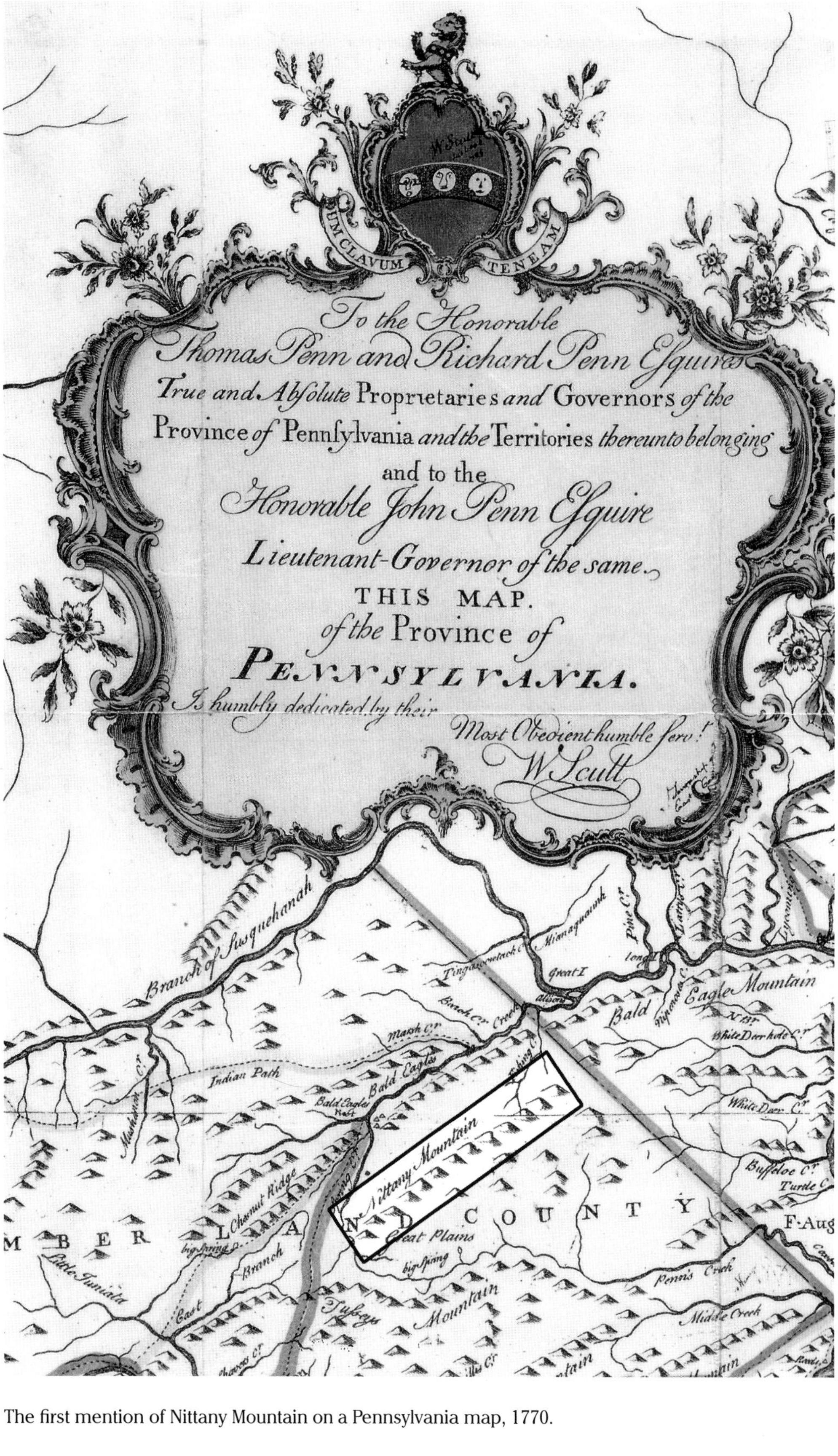

The first mention of Nittany Mountain on a Pennsylvania map, 1770.

The inspiration for Henry Shoemaker's name for the Indian maiden was the same as the inspiration for Joe Mason's boast about the home of a particularly powerful Lion: Mount Nittany. It runs from Lemont to Livonia in Centre County, rising to a height of 2,302 feet just north of Centre Hall. It was pictured but unnamed on the 1759 map whose title also functioned as a dedication: "To the Honourable Thomas Penn and Richard Penn, Esq, True & absolute proprietaries & Governours of the Province of Pennsylvania & Counties of New Castle Kent & Sussex on Delaware, This map of the improved part of the province of Pennsylvania is humbly dedicated by Nicholas Scull."

In his 1883 *History of Centre and Clinton Counties*, John Blair Linn described Nittany Mountain as "the range commencing at Dale's Mills, in College township, and extending down into Buffalo valley, Union County, within six miles of the river; so called as early as 1768." The Scull map of 1770 labels the range "Nittany Mountain," while a version published in 1775 labels the same range "Nittany Ridge."

It is likely that the first peak in that range—the one clearly viewed from Penn State—was the inspiration for the Indians' name for the mountain. It certainly wouldn't be the first or last time that the English-, French-, or German-trained ears of white settlers created their own version of what the Indians actually told them. In *A History of the Indian Villages and Place Names in Pennsylvania*, Dr. George P. Donehoo proposed that Nittany "may be a corruption of *Nekti*, 'single,' and *attin*, 'mountain,' or 'hill,' or it may be a shortening of some other combination of the word *attin*, or *adin*, with some other Indian word."

Nektiattin or Nektiadin? Nita-nee or Nittany? It is unlikely that the two men who helped connect Penn State to "Nittany" and "Lion" would have quibbled over which came first or who inspired what. Born less than fifty days apart, Henry Shoemaker and Joe Mason shared a profound enthusiasm for all things Pennsylvanian.

Henry Shoemaker's Folklore or Fakelore?

Henry Shoemaker addressed the matter of the truth or fiction of his legends often, and it was an area in which he seemed to have difficulty making himself clear to his readers. In his 1911 preface to *Pennsylvania Mountain Stories* (a reissue of *Wild Life in Western Pennsylvania*, the first book to contain "The Legend of Penn's Cave"), he stated: "The query has frequently been made by readers of previous editions of *Pennsylvania Mountain Stories* whether the stories were 'true' or 'made up' by the author. As so many of the tales are devoted to subjects of a more or less supernatural order they cannot very well be true; neither are they of the author's invention." Shoemaker's folklore-collecting practices received a fair amount of criticism in his day, especially for his tendency to go well beyond simply preserving the legends he heard. Some critics since have contended that Shoemaker didn't retell Pennsylvania legends at all, but simply made them up. Don Yoder, in particular, asserted: "I have always found more of Colonel Shoemaker than of Centre County tradition in his stories."

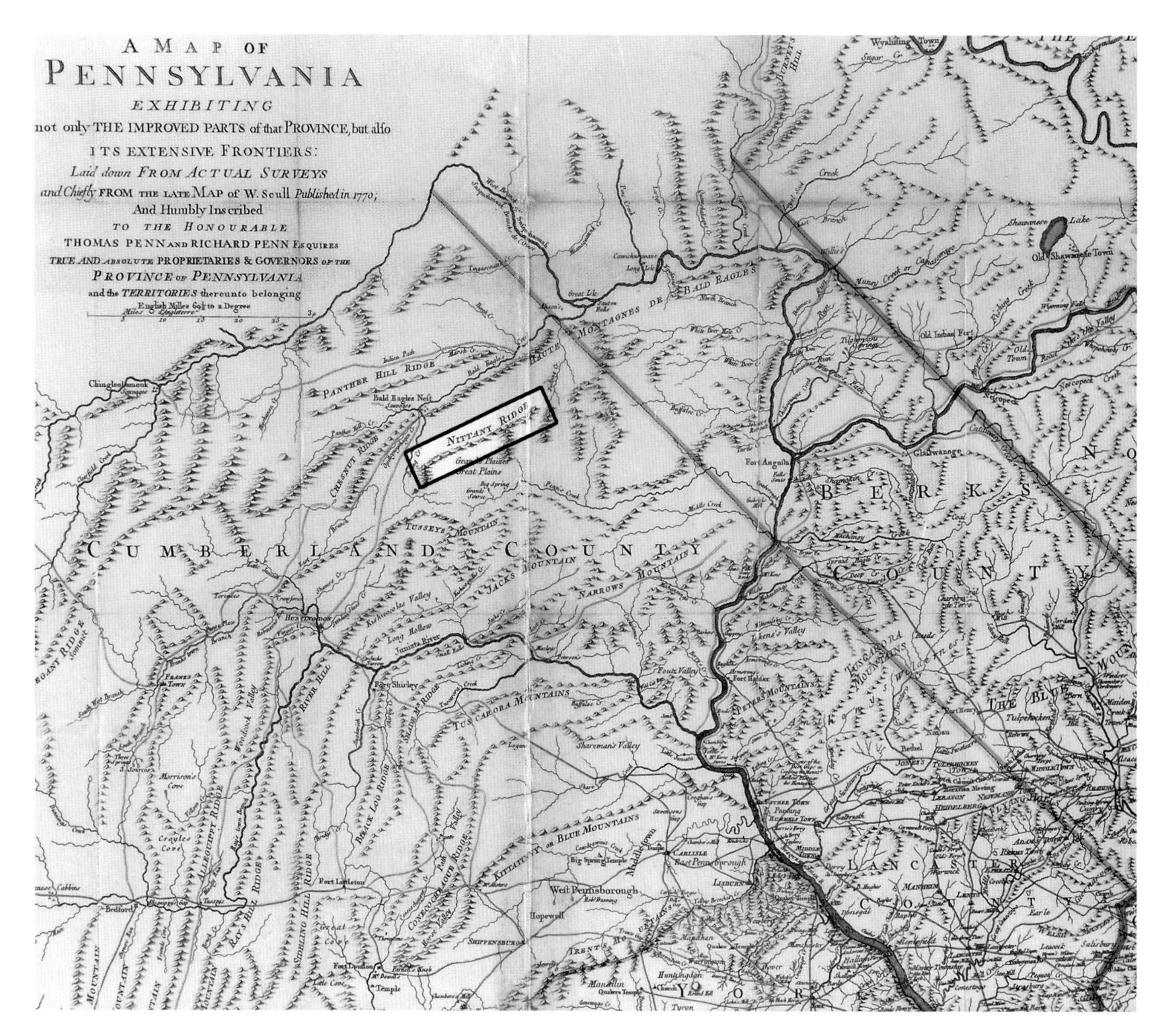

Nittany Ridge, shown on a 1775 map.

From his boyhood on, Henry Shoemaker cherished the Commonwealth of Pennsylvania's natural beauty and lamented the dwindling attention being paid to its preservation. But his lifelong conservation efforts extended well beyond the forests and animals. He also wanted the stories of the early days to be around forever. Through his legends of Nita-nee he accidentally became partners with Joe Mason, Penn State's champion of school spirit and the creator of its eternal symbol, the Nittany Lion. Shoemaker could not have deliberately selected a more natural ally. Thanks to the enduring strength of the Nittany Lion, the legends surrounding the creation of Mount Nittany will likely last as long as the mountain stands.

Mount Nittany from the tower of Old Main.

BEAVER FIELD PICTORIAL
NAVY
PENN STATE
SATURDAY OCTOBER TWENTIETH 1923
OFFICIAL SOUVENIR
PRICE 25 CENTS

5

The Emerging Mascot

The First Lion Mascot

Despite Professor Ernest's efforts to find an alternative, the lion continued to emerge as the Penn State symbol of choice. One even shared top billing in the November 1920 Penn State Players production of a George Bernard Shaw classic. The shaggier of the two title roles in *Androcles and the Lion* was played by Richard Hoffman (Class of 1923), whose menacing portrayal was duly noted by several theater-going members of the athletic department. Forty years later Hoffman recalled how he came to act opposite Androcles and thereby secure the historic Nittany Lion role:

> It was 1919, [a] year after World War I ended, that I became a very green freshman under the blue and white of Penn State. I wasn't very big or very old. When all those 20-plus-year-old brutes came back from France and back to college, Well, I decided

"Nittany Leo I," 1922.

> athletics were not particularly down my alley. They were big and tough, and that's why I went out for Penn State Players. It seemed like dramatics was a lot safer. Survival, then, seemed important.

Richard Holmes Hoffman came to be known as "Nittany Leo I" when he donned the suit and became Penn State's own king of beasts and first Mascot. Hoffman's initial game is unknown, but it was probably the autumn of 1921 that fans first heard the Lion roar. Hoffman recalled:

> Being THE Lion, I necessarily had to roar. . . . Lots of folks have [unique] voices, but few have one like mine. Frankly, it is so low-pitched and so unmusical that it sounds like the noise an old, old bullfrog would make if he had laryngitis and was sitting in an empty rain barrel. . . . It scares people. . . . For three football seasons, I attended every game. With each season my roars grew louder and more terrifying to the opposition. By the time I graduated, I could roar LIKE a Lion—no fooling!

The first photographic evidence of the Nittany Lion raising that unique voice in support of Penn State's eleven was the Penn State–Syracuse game at the Polo Grounds in New York

City on October 28, 1922. There was no mistaking that the Nittany Lion hailed from Africa when it appeared on the football field that Saturday. Hoffman and a similarly suited friend escorted distinguished perennial freshman Andy Lytle onto the football field for a rousing tribute from Andy's Penn State fans, who also witnessed Penn State and Syracuse fight to a scoreless tie.

In addition to being the first Lion Mascot, it seems that Dick Hoffman also started two storytelling traditions continued by most Lions since. The first could be called the "Lion Mascot Game Day Diet Story." This is not, as one might expect, what the Lion had for breakfast on Saturday morning, but rather how effective the game was in removing Lion pounds. During the early sea-

Dick Hoffman, Penn State's first "Man in the Suit."

Andy Lytle and "Nittany Leo I" with a mascot buddy at the Penn State–Syracuse game, New York's Polo Grounds, October 28, 1922.

Mascot Hoffman greets Gifford Pinchot before a marathon speech.

son, Hoffman claimed, it was "hotter than the Mojave inside that lion suit." He added: "I used to sweat off about ten pounds per game."

The second story might be called "Why Being the Lion Mascot Was Not Always Fun." Hoffman had two tales in this category. His first nemesis was not the opposing mascot or even a rabid fan, but rather the athletic manager's bulldog—"a tough little critter with a set of teeth that would do justice to a shark." Playing along with the band at halftime one Saturday, Hoffman's antics aroused the attention of the watchful dog.

> When he spotted the shaggy beast on the 50-yard line, he made a dash for the center of the field, growling and showing his splendid choppers, as he ran. The Nittany Lion, alas, could see only straight ahead. The bulldog chose to attack strictly from the rear. As the lion whirled to evade those dripping jaws, so did the bulldog. Both roared lustily at each other. The crowd went wild. The din only served to urge the bulldog to more splendid efforts. And inside a very dripping, smelly lion suit, one human soul was sweating a pint a minute and wondering and praying—"O Lord! How long is it until the beginning of the second half?"

President and Mrs. John Thomas, c. 1921.

The second tale of woe featured Gifford Pinchot, an even less likely antagonist for the average college mascot. At the time Hoffman shared his memories of being the Lion, he was approaching 60 years old and feeling the effects of stiffening joints, something he jokingly attributed to all those years of walking "on all fours." Modern-day Lions should probably be thankful that somewhere along the way they evolved into a two-legged mascot. Hoffman recalled: "My neck, in particular, is stiff. I still have a picture of Gifford Pinchot, then governor of Pennsylvania, making a speech. It lasted for about two hours. Throughout most of it he relaxed by leaning on the head of a handy Nittany Lion, dutifully seated at his feet. I was inside."

Having no predecessor to guide his performance, Hoffman and the athletic department invented "stunts" for the Lion, most of which seemed more like rules than the skits and antics that would come much later in mascot history. For example, one general rule was: "When you pass President [John] Thomas's box the first time, make a snappy salute, rising from all fours and snapping heels together in military style."

Hoffman completed his bachelor of science degree in natural science with a specialty in industrial chemistry in 1923 and later attended Jefferson Medical College, receiving his M.D. in 1928. He opened a practice in Bellefonte and served the health needs of many Penn State fans, who had no inkling of their doctor's furry former life. In the early 1930s, Hoffman went back to school, this time to receive his pilot's license. During World War II, the Centre County physician served as a surgeon with an air fighter group in Africa and Italy. After the war, Hoffman moved to California to practice endocrinology and became a member of the Outdoor Writers Association of America. It was from one of Hoffman's weekly newspaper columns in California that Katey and Ross Lehman discovered the first Lion's delightful reminiscences. Hoffman died on October 1, 1977, at the age of 74.

The First Nittany Lion Mascot's "Stunts"

1. If the band marches on over the field before the game, the Lion should walk ahead of it, keeping time to music with arms.
2. If the band does not march on the field, keep under cover until it plays its first piece. Then prance around nearby, shimmying, etc.
3. When the SECOND team comes on the field, have someone tip you off, and be waiting at the south end of the field to run through the goal posts and up the field with the team.
4. While the second team is practicing, kicking, etc., make clumsy efforts at catching, kicking the ball, and cut up generally over the field.
5. When the varsity comes on the field, dance around the goal posts after they have gone through, and then head for the sidelines, on the grass in front of the covered stand.
6. When the varsity is practicing, keep off the field. For a few minutes in front of the west stands, cut up with one of the cheerleaders, dancing with him to band music, help lead cheers, etc. Then before the game starts, tour all the way around the field, stopping occasionally to give the audience a snarl or roar, showing full face. Then cut up with cheerleader assistant before east stands.
7. Keep under cover during play, unless you see a good opportunity to do something while time is called out, or between quarters.
8. Between the halves, if the band marches over the field, prance ahead of it, all the way around if possible. Then go through stunts with "keeper"—cheerleader (a clown will be supplied for later games for this purpose).*
9. When the Alma Mater is sung, stand at salute beside song leader on east side of field (new stands).**

* Hoffman's parenthetical comment.
** Again, Hoffman's addition to his own "stunt" list.

"Nittany Leo I" with the 1922 Penn State Building Campaign Goat. The campaign raised more than $2,000,000 for new building construction.

Richard Hoffman started one other Lion tradition more than seventy-five years ago. He performed the role of Mascot with everything he had to give. All the Lions since have known what Hoffman felt the first moment he stepped before a Penn State crowd as the Nittany Lion. Being the Mascot would be a time they would cherish all their lives.

Nittany Reminders from Mason and Shoemaker

The early 1920s also found two old friends of Nittany and Lion with something to say regarding the emerging Penn State symbol. In a letter to the Alumni Association in early 1921, Joe Mason expressed his concern that the current incarnation of the Nittany Lion didn't quite match his original notion. He wrote:

> I note that the newspapers are nowadays referring quite frequently to Penn State's athletes in various branches of sports as "the Nittany Lions." Now before this terminology becomes too common, I believe it well to explain [through] this the medium of the Alumni News to all more recent Penn State men, just how this term originated and what is meant by the same.
>
> Back in 1907 a crowd of us Seniors (1907 men) published during that year a little pamphlet called "the Lemon" taking healthy cracks at all bad practices, as we thought, and praising all that was good in State College Life . . . [and] in an early issue of the Lemon, we sprung the idea that Penn State had no suitable college emblem while almost all our rival institutions had good ones. Therefore we suggested that to top 'em all off, why not adopt the *American Mountain Lion* as the Penn State emblem—remember not the African Lion, nor any other nationality, but the *American Mountain Lion!*

President Edwin E. Sparks.

On October 30, 1922, Henry Shoemaker delivered a speech at the dedication of a historic marker at Centre Furnace, near State College, which he later published as a pamphlet through the Altoona Tribune Press. Penn State President Edwin Sparks was

Centre Furnace before restoration.

among those in attendance for the address, entitled "The Importance of Marking Historic Spots." Shoemaker's penultimate words that day were a reminder of the significance of the Nittany symbol and a call for keeping the Lion hailing from Nittany:

> [The Centre Furnace marker] will serve as a landmark to link the earlier days of this part of Centre County, with its busy, teeming present, the great intense life of State College, and the industry of the olden times. They have one point in common, Old Nittany Mountain looks down on both, impartial in shedding her glories of sunlight and shade. Nittany Mountain is feminine, for she is named not for an Indian chief, but for two beautiful Indian maidens named Nita-nee, one a great war queen of the very long ago, the other a humbler maiden who lived not far from Penn's Cave, and was loved and lost by Malachi Boyer, a Huguenot pioneer from Lancaster County.
>
> And in closing let us say we hear a lot about a so-called Nittany Lion. Do we not mean "Mountain Lion" or panther, for in the old days the panther or Pennsylvania lion, was very much in evidence hereabouts, roaring terribly at night from the mountain tops, answering one another from Tussey Knob, the Bald Top and Mount Nittany. It is the noble supple animal, the Pennsylvania king of beasts, and not the shaggy African man-eater, that should be the patron of courage, force and persistence of our State College youth. If you are not sure of what it looked like, there is a finely mounted specimen in old "College Hall" [none other than the Brush Lion in Old Main].

In addition to the Mason and Shoemaker remarks, two Penn State alumni also made a contribution that helped the Nittany Lion's foothold as a Penn State and a native Pennsylvania

Cougar donated by H. I. "Hickey" Smith.

symbol. H. I. "Hickey" Smith (Class of 1907) and Cuthbert Mather (Class of 1921) went hunting for cougars in Colorado in 1923 and donated the results of their successful hunt to Penn State. These two stuffed mountain lions were placed in Varsity Hall and eventually moved to the newly completed Recreation Hall, where they provided demonstrable evidence that these Nittany Lions were not from Africa. Technically, of course, they were not from Pennsylvania either, but from a species and physical appearance perspective these specimens were a much closer match to their exterminated eastern cousin, the Pennsylvania mountain lion.

The Mascot and the Coach

Nittany Leo I graduated in 1923, and his suit went into storage in Old Main. It wasn't until 1927 that another student was selected to be the Nittany Lion. This time the "Man in the Suit" was Leon DeRoy Skinner, a Pittsburgh native who had enrolled at Penn State in the fall of 1923 at the age of 16. While Skinner was earning his bachelor's degree in dairy husbandry, he worked in the Creamery and was responsible for the cheese-making laboratory.

This second Nittany Lion came by his stint as Mascot in a far more accidental way than his predecessor. In a letter to Lou Bell, Penn State's Public Information Department head, he explained how it happened in the autumn of 1955. "The suit had been stored for a number of years in Old Main and had not been used. One day somebody uncovered it. H. Seymour

Leon Skinner, both in and out of the Suit.

Buck was the head cheerleader. He lived in town and was a friend of mine. Since I was six feet tall and could fill out the suit fairly well, he asked me if I would operate it at the football games. I agreed, and out of storage came the lion. It appeared at about four games."

Unfortunately for Skinner, Penn State lost all four games. "Then came orders from [Coach Hugo] Bezdek, seems as though he was superstitious. He told Buck that every time that g____ d____ lion was on the field State lost and to get that thing off the field fast. Buck relayed the message, and that was the end of the Nittany Lion—African style."

Leon Skinner eventually earned a master's degree in English at Penn State and began working in 1934 at Penn State's School of Forestry in Mont Alto, where he stayed until 1941. For the next twenty-five years, Skinner alternated between teaching and administrative duties at University Park, serving for a time as assistant to College of Liberal Arts Dean Ben Euwema. He retired as Associate Professor of English in April 1967. Thanks to his kind manner and skills in woodworking and the repair of mechanical devices, Skinner was affectionately known as "Mr. Fix-It" in the College Heights community. He died at the age of 67 on June 18, 1973.

Coach Hugo Bezdek. Original Bezdek signature in the left-hand corner.

Coach Bezdek had a strong personality and a love-hate relationship with the players on his team. Some loved him and some hated him, but all played hard. Bezdek's early years as football coach were successful and quite rosy with everyone except, perhaps, the more individualistic players, but by the mid-1920s things were growing sour. A group of Penn State alumni from Pittsburgh had become extremely restless over Penn State's seeming inability to beat the University of Pittsburgh in the early 1920s. "After the 1925 season [and the fourth consecutive loss to Pitt], leaders of the Pittsburgh alumni club formed what they called a

Coach Bezdek and the football team atop Penn State's Mascot.

'College Relations Committee' to determine if and how Bezdek could be relieved of his job. The committee made its recommendation at the annual meeting of the Alumni Association in June 1926," recounted Michael Bezilla in his history of Penn State.

The Pittsburgh alumni were only a part of the atmosphere developing at Penn State that made Bezdek's last ten years at the University quite difficult. Bezdek challenged the ultimate authority of the alumni over control of intercollegiate athletics, and many of those alumni remembered the old days, when students controlled athletics—the days when they were students. Now some alumni wanted more control. Others, including Edward N. "Mike" Sullivan, executive director of the Alumni Association, wanted less "professionalism" and were leading the charge to remove all athletic scholarships, among other benefits for athletes. They were attempting to self-police what they observed, and also what they suspected was coming in a report from a Carnegie Foundation investigation of American college athletics. When eventually published, the report, according to Michael Bezilla, was

Bezdek fondly pets the Lion.

> a carefully researched indictment of the role played by intercollegiate sports, particularly football, at many of the nation's institutions of higher learning. Intercollegiate athletics possessed such great material value for colleges and universities . . . that administrators and alumni frequently resorted to unethical practices and blatant professionalism in order to obtain winning teams. Too much emphasis on intercollegiate competition promoted false values and diverted the interest of students away from the intellectual goals that were supposed to be the main focus of higher education.

The reformers' efforts paid off with support from Penn State President Ralph Hetzel and, remarkably, Coach Bezdek, who had to give up his job as football coach and devote himself solely to the running of the Department of Physical Education, as part of the agreement hammered out between the alumni association and the administration. Perhaps Bezdek saw no other options.

Penn State's decision to drop athletic scholarships was not replicated by more than a few schools, and it was Bezdek himself who began to promote the idea of reinstating athletic scholarships in the mid-1930s. But it was already too late for the former coach. By then, Bezdek had lost the support of President Hetzel and was blamed for Penn State's poor football showing by everyone, on and off campus. Hugo Bezdek was relieved of his administrative duties and left Penn State in 1936.

What drove a football coach who once had posed for a team photo on the "back" of a gigantic lion and could be seen occasionally patting the Lion Mascot on the head to banish the Nittany Lion from all events? In the 1920s, blaming the Lion for bad luck was probably a good enough reason, but it is interesting to note that one prominent member of Penn State's contingent of Pittsburgh alumni was none other than Joe Mason, creator of the school mascot. Was banishing the Lion just about the only response Bezdek could make to send the message to the Pittsburgh alumni that he too could play hardball? Whatever the actual reason, the Nittany Lion Mascot would remain off the playing field for twelve years. It was a disappearance that would seem mild when compared with the eventual sojourn of the Brush Lion, but those who longed for a physical representation of the school symbol missed the Mascot.

Restoring the Mascot

Three years after Bezdek's departure, Carl Schott, Dean of the School of Physical Education and Athletics, asked his new gymnastics coach to bring the Lion Mascot out of its premature retirement. Eugene Wettstone's career as Penn State's gymnastics coach would span nearly four decades and garner international acclaim for Penn State, but as a young man in the autumn of 1939, Wettstone was performing two unusual tasks for a college coach. He was the director (and impresario) of Penn State's newly created Circus and was about to become Penn State's third Nittany Lion Mascot.

That fall the *Collegian* began to solicit money to pay for a new lion suit, and Wettstone was dispatched to New York City to have the suit made. Small fringes of mane would appear now and again over the years, but the Lion was ready to take a huge step toward its rightful Pennsylvania heritage. The Lion was about to go "Nittany" in appearance as well as in name. After an absence of more than a decade, the Nittany Lion would again be rousing the fans at football games and pep rallies. A *Collegian* story on October 10 reported:

> You have a big night ahead of you Friday and we do mean big. Plans for the Student Alumni Pep Rally have been completed and at 7:30 p.m. Friday there will be more action and excitement in Rec Hall than you've ever seen. The Lion's going to be there in all his jungle glory! Clothed in the skin of an honest-to-goodness mountain "varmint" will be one Gene Wettstone (once a gym coach, now his friends claim he has taken to eating raw meat and growling at everybody with true Lion accents). If you've seen Gene at any of the gym meets or at last year's circus, you know that he's going to be a real Nittany Lion and one to be proud of.

The modern era of the Nittany Lion Mascot was about to begin.

Carl Schott, the athletic director responsible for returning the “Man in the Suit” to the field of play.

Eugene Wettstone as he appeared around campus.

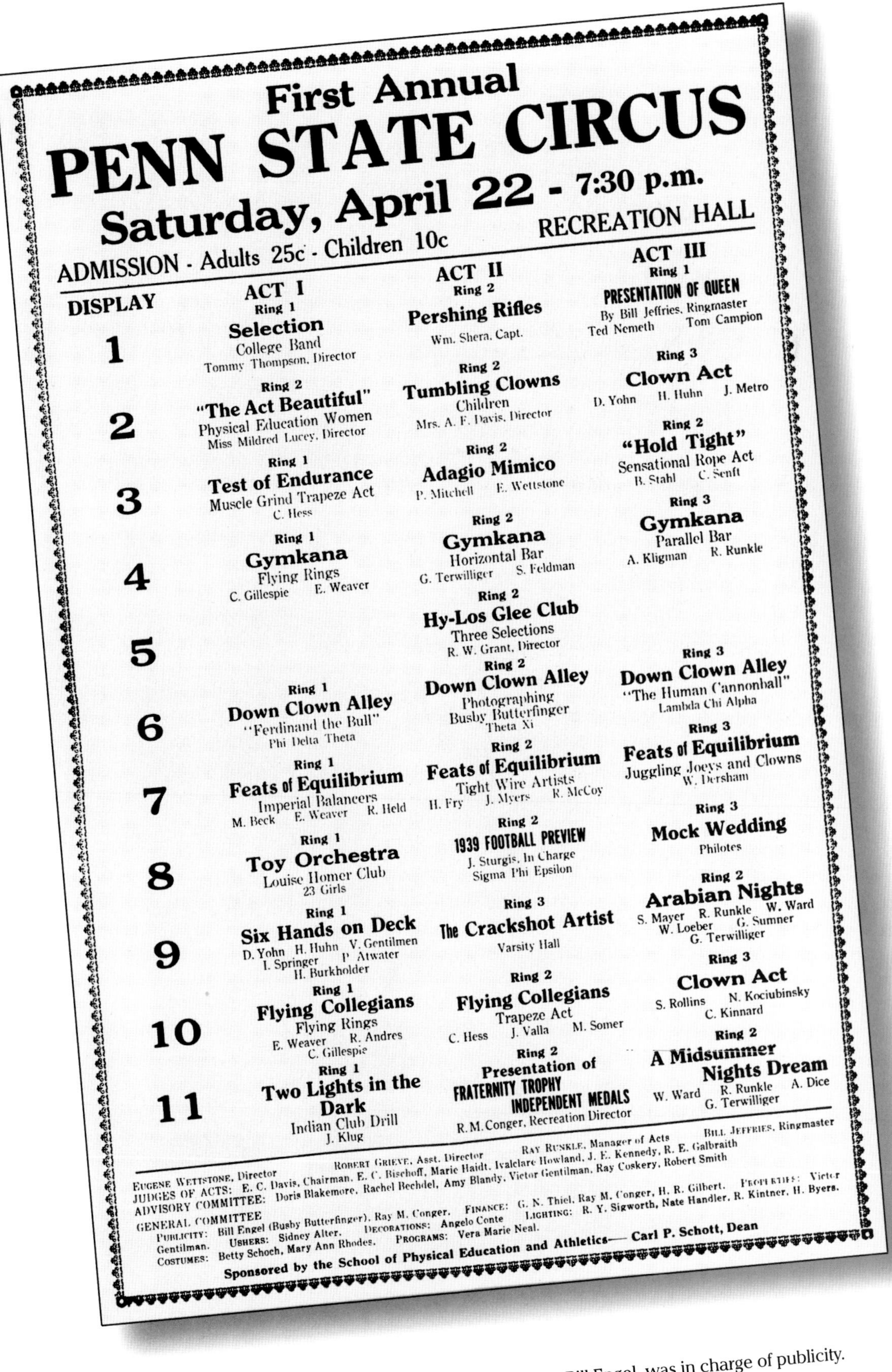

First Annual

PENN STATE CIRCUS

Saturday, April 22 - 7:30 p.m.

RECREATION HALL

ADMISSION - Adults 25c - Children 10c

DISPLAY	ACT I	ACT II	ACT III
1	Ring 1 **Selection** College Band Tommy Thompson, Director	Ring 2 **Pershing Rifles** Wm. Shera, Capt.	Ring 1 **PRESENTATION OF QUEEN** By Bill Jeffries, Ringmaster Ted Nemeth Tom Campion
2	Ring 2 **"The Act Beautiful"** Physical Education Women Miss Mildred Lucey, Director	Ring 2 **Tumbling Clowns** Children Mrs. A. F. Davis, Director	Ring 3 **Clown Act** D. Yohn H. Huhn J. Metro
3	Ring 1 **Test of Endurance** Muscle Grind Trapeze Act C. Hess	Ring 2 **Adagio Mimico** P. Mitchell E. Wettstone	Ring 2 **"Hold Tight"** Sensational Rope Act B. Stahl C. Senft
4	Ring 1 **Gymkana** Flying Rings C. Gillespie E. Weaver	Ring 2 **Gymkana** Horizontal Bar G. Terwilliger S. Feldman	Ring 3 **Gymkana** Parallel Bar A. Kligman R. Runkle
5		Ring 2 **Hy-Los Glee Club** Three Selections R. W. Grant, Director	
6	Ring 1 **Down Clown Alley** "Ferdinand the Bull" Phi Delta Theta	Ring 2 **Down Clown Alley** Photographing Busby Butterfinger Theta Xi	Ring 3 **Down Clown Alley** "The Human Cannonball" Lambda Chi Alpha
7	Ring 1 **Feats of Equilibrium** Imperial Balancers M. Beck E. Weaver R. Held	Ring 2 **Feats of Equilibrium** Tight Wire Artists H. Fry J. Myers R. McCoy	Ring 3 **Feats of Equilibrium** Juggling Joeys and Clowns W. Dersham
8	Ring 1 **Toy Orchestra** Louise Homer Club 23 Girls	Ring 2 **1939 FOOTBALL PREVIEW** J. Sturgis, In Charge Sigma Phi Epsilon	Ring 3 **Mock Wedding** Philotes
9	Ring 1 **Six Hands on Deck** D. Yohn H. Huhn V. Gentilmen I. Springer P. Atwater H. Burkholder	Ring 3 **The Crackshot Artist** Varsity Hall	Ring 2 **Arabian Nights** S. Mayer R. Runkle W. Ward W. Loeber G. Sumner G. Terwilliger
10	Ring 1 **Flying Collegians** Flying Rings E. Weaver R. Andres C. Gillespie	Ring 2 **Flying Collegians** Trapeze Act C. Hess J. Valla M. Somer	Ring 3 **Clown Act** S. Rollins N. Kociubinsky C. Kinnard
11	Ring 1 **Two Lights in the Dark** Indian Club Drill J. Klug	Ring 2 **Presentation of** **FRATERNITY TROPHY** **INDEPENDENT MEDALS** R.M. Conger, Recreation Director	Ring 2 **A Midsummer Nights Dream** W. Ward R. Runkle A. Dice G. Terwilliger

EUGENE WETTSTONE, Director ROBERT GRIEVE, Asst. Director RAY RUNKLE, Manager of Acts BILL JEFFRIES, Ringmaster
JUDGES OF ACTS: E. C. Davis, Chairman, E. C. Bischoff, Marie Haidt, Ivalclare Howland, J. E. Kennedy, R. E. Galbraith
ADVISORY COMMITTEE: Doris Blakemore, Rachel Bechdel, Amy Blandy, Victor Gentilman, Ray Coskery, Robert Smith
GENERAL COMMITTEE
PUBLICITY: Bill Engel (Busby Butterfinger), Ray M. Conger. FINANCE: G. N. Thiel, Ray M. Conger, H. R. Gilbert. PROPERTIES: Victor Gentilman. USHERS: Sidney Alter. DECORATIONS: Angelo Conte LIGHTING: R. Y. Sigworth, Nate Handler, R. Kintner, H. Byers. COSTUMES: Betty Schoch, Mary Ann Rhodes. PROGRAMS: Vera Marie Neal.

Sponsored by the School of Physical Education and Athletics— Carl P. Schott, Dean

Penn State Circus poster, 1939. "Busby Butterfinger," a.k.a. Bill Engel, was in charge of publicity.

The *Collegian* editorial board. This impressive group of student leaders included Bill Engel and Bernie Newman, noted for the Nittany Lion Shrine, and Herbert Nipson, who served as executive editor for *Ebony* magazine. *Left to right:* Emmanuel Roth, Paul Haldeman, Engel, Robert Wilson, Phyllis Gordon, George Schless, Nipson, and Newman.

The same autumn that Coach Wettstone began "eating raw meat," *Collegian* reporter Bernard A. Newman (Class of 1940), with the consent of his editor A. William Engel (Class of 1940), began to promote the idea of a permanent Lion Shrine. Newman had replanted an idea that had been expressed more than thirty years earlier by a student about to graduate from Penn State. In Squirt 12 of *The Lemon,* issued May 29, 1907, Joe Mason made one other wish regarding the emerging mascot: "What a lasting and fitting memorial it would be for some class to place on the centre of the front campus a huge figure of this champion of the forest, 'Old Nittany!' "

PEP
RALLY
BONFIRE
FRI. OCT. 18
7:30 P.M.
Blue Key

A Class Gift

A Safe Place for Bonfires

When Bernard Newman began his *Collegian* campaign for a Nittany Lion Shrine, what he actually had in mind was a place for holding bonfires and pep rallies. The tradition of celebratory (or anticipatory) bonfires was still a strong one in 1939, but there had never been a permanent location for holding them on campus.

One of the most memorable postgame bonfires took place a quarter-century earlier, in the fall of 1914, when Penn State tied Harvard in a well-played football game. The students' collective pleasure at Penn State's showing led to the largest bonfire ever witnessed on campus. The players had returned from Cambridge on Sunday night, and the fire was planned for Monday evening. Newspapers reported the events of the day:

> All day Monday, wagons hauled loads of scrap wood, gathered from miles around, to the drill field between the Armory and the old Beta house [between Willard and Deike

Captain Elgin "Yegg" Tobin.

> buildings today]. The order was to "get anything that isn't nailed down," but much of the "debris" included perfectly serviceable telephone poles, wooden sidewalks, fences, and outhouses. And many wagons, after their final runs, were thrown on, too. Woe to any freshman caught without a piece of wood in his hands—he was sent scurrying off for a contribution.
>
> A crowd estimated at 3,500 assembled at 9 p.m. around the enormous woodpile, over fifty feet high, which had been saturated with five barrels of gasoline. With the football squad in the place of "honor" encircling the wood, Captain Elgin ["Yegg"] Tobin walked forward carrying the torch. He threw on the ignition and was instantly blown off his feet by the gigantic explosion that shook the whole valley, blowing out all the windows in the east side of the Beta house more than a hundred yards away, breaking some windows in Carnegie Library, and knocking down plaster in the president's house.

Captain Tobin was one of the more severely burned students and missed most of the remainder of the season. The students claimed they thought their fire-starting "helper" had been kerosene.

In light of the outcome of that event, it is amazing that the bonfire tradition continued into Newman's generation, but it had. Old photos of State College indicate that even the

One of the many bonfire sites on campus.

middle of the intersection at College Avenue and Allen Street occasionally played host to these migratory conflagrations. In the fall of 1938 the *Collegian* reported that one such College and Allen bonfire had gotten out of hand—the students, not the fire. Under the headline "MOB DAMAGE MAY MOUNT TO $2,000," the *Collegian* reported a pep rally gone awry:

> Swelled by the minute, a hell-bent mob of more than 2,000 students blockaded the streets, wrecked parking meters and kindled a two-story-high bonfire in front of the campus gates at the corner of South Allen Street and College Avenue during a three hour demonstration Tuesday night.
>
> Six parking meters, valued by borough officials at $58 each, were reported ripped off their posts and stolen. Besides, 10 dial faces were smashed, 11 hands broken and 32 glass crystals shattered.

A 20-foot square of brick on College Avenue, which served as the fire bed, was damaged by the intense heat from the fire. Repairs will cost an estimated $90. Several street lights in the Locust Lane sector also were smashed, police said.

Penn State President Ralph Hetzel was concerned enough about preventing a repeated assault on State College that he called a special meeting of the senior class for the following Tuesday and addressed them in Schwab Auditorium. Calling for leadership from the seniors, he expressed regret about the message the riot had sent the public, especially the state legislators. Along with a story about the unusual meeting, the *Collegian* reported highlights of the president's speech in the next issue:

President Ralph D. Hetzel.

> I feel—I know—it's exceedingly harmful to the College when things such as that [Tuesday's mob demonstration] occur. . . . Even a thousand football victories can't offset such a demonstration of a lack of control, such a demonstration of an element of viciousness. You [seniors] can lead in the establishment of an attitude on the part of all students that will be respected, an attitude that will be fused throughout the entire student body. Soon we must ask the Legislature for a 50 per cent increase in the school's appropriation from the state. . . . We must ask for six and a half millions for operations during the next two years. I must meet these people, request this money, meet their criticism. I must explain student action.

In addition to making a plea to the seniors, President Hetzel took an additional step that did not depend on the riot-preventing abilities of the Class of 1939. He invited *Collegian* reporter Bernard Newman to his office for tea one Friday afternoon in late autumn 1938 and enlisted Newman's editorial help in calling for a permanent place on campus to hold bonfires, a gathering place for students to pay tribute to Penn State's athletic teams. So what Joe Mason advocated in 1907 was to be called for again by a *Collegian* reporter in cahoots with the president of the College: a Nittany Lion Shrine.

Poster announcing a "mass meeting" featuring "Prexy" Ralph Hetzel and "Bez" Coach Bezdek.

The Bronze Lions

Newman, instantly sold on the idea, had two particular lions in mind for the shrine. They had been cast in bronze by an unnamed Italian sculptor and were given to the College by an alumnus in the late 1920s, spared during the demolition of a large Pittsburgh estate. When the new Allen Street gate to campus was completed in 1930, the lions were placed atop the flanking stone pillars to "guard Main Campus entrance," in the words of the *Collegian.*

The two lions stood holding a shield in front of them and were described as standing 47 inches high on a base of 2 square feet and being "of African jungle type." But their sentimental role as replacements for the missing Ma and Pa was not enough to make students and faculty like them. They seemed out of place in their surroundings and were removed about three weeks later by the College architect, Charles Klauder, who called their initial placement on the pillars "a trial." Klauder added that "personal inspection during the seventy-fifth anniversary celebration [of Penn State] brought about the decision to remove them." Although unconfirmed, it is probable that many visiting alumni attracted to the seventy-fifth anniversary celebration also made unfavorable comparisons between the bronze lions and Ma and Pa. Perhaps the lions' three-week stay on the pillars proved to be a trial in more ways than one for the architect.

As with their alabaster cousins before them, these two bronze beasts were placed in storage by the College until "a gate to be especially designed is erected for them." How Newman came to know of their existence nearly ten years later is not known or remembered, but he probably was not aware of their checkered history with the College. Newman eventually wrote:

Bernie Newman's original idea for the Lion Shrine—until he saw it.

Bernie Newman.

> Upon investigation it has been found that the two bronze lions which were to be used for the proposed shrine are not typical Nittany Lions but Old English Lions, the type which appear on coats of arms. This idea has been abandoned and Professor Burton K. Johnstone, head of the architecture department, has submitted to his students a project for drafts of a proposed shrine of sculpted stone, instead of the bronze one as originally planned.

Except for those three weeks atop the stone pillars, the lions never served Penn State again. In 1943, Orlando Wilbert Houts got a call from a friend at the Titan Metal Company in Bellefonte. The lions were about to be melted down as scrap metal, and Houts's friend thought Orlando might want to buy the lions in order to rescue them. His friend was right, and the two bronze lions have been standing guard over some portion of the O. W. Houts store ever since, with two brief exceptions.

Their first respite, lasting several months, came when they required some recuperation and restoration following a serious fire at the old Houts store on December 4, 1954. Robert Houts, son of O.W., remembers their second disappearance as quite brief. It happened one homecoming Friday night in an unspecified year. The lions were found by police early that Sunday morning at a telephone booth a couple of miles away. Apparently, even bronze lions know to phone for a ride following a homecoming celebration.

Back at their posts (chained to their posts, actually, to prevent any further trips), one lion is now missing most of his tail, and both look a bit scruffy and tarnished, but they still stand tall. The bronze lions that stood above Penn State's gates for a mere three weeks in 1930 are still guarding O. W. Houts & Sons after more than fifty years.

Orlando Wilbur Houts.

"We are . . . O. W. Houts." One of the two "guard lions" at the O. W. Houts store.

All-American Leon Gajecki.

The Campaign for the Shrine

In the fall of 1939, Bernie Newman began his campaign for a Nittany Lion Shrine in earnest. Others writing for the *Collegian* started mentioning Newman's call for a Lion Shrine in their articles on various related stories. On November 7 it was reported that the All-College Cabinet had approved the Shrine project, pending the results of a student body survey the *Collegian* would be running in early December. On November 23, in a section of the paper entitled "Student Soapbox," Football All-American Leon Gajecki replied to the question "Should there be a Lion Shrine?" with "Yes, it's a good idea. It would be much better to carry out tradition on the campus, rather than hold pep rallies in the street." President Hetzel had chosen the right collaborator in Bernie Newman.

On Friday, December 1, the *Collegian* ran the survey questions that students could answer at the Old Main student union desk before seven o'clock that Sunday evening. The four questions were fairly straightforward:

1. Are you in favor of a Lion Shrine?
2. If so, where do you believe it should be located?
3. What do you believe should constitute the shrine?
4. If such a shrine is erected, on what occasions do you believe it should be made use of?

The response to question 1 was overwhelmingly favorable: 91 percent of the approximately 500 votes cast were affirmative. The location receiving about half the votes was in front of Old Main. Other locations mentioned in smaller percentages were the center of the Liberal Arts quadrangle, in the Mall above the Main Gate, near Rec Hall, and in the field east of White Hall. A frequent response to question 3 also contained an answer to number 4: "A Nittany Lion—with an open space nearby for a bonfire."

It appeared that the idea of a Nittany Lion Shrine had been embraced by the students, or by that group choosing to vote. It is interesting to note that the 455 "yes" votes for the Shrine represented less than 8 percent of the undergraduate student body. In addition to the

Burton K. Johnstone.

Francis E. Hyslop.

45 "no" votes, more than 5,900 students abstained on the Shrine vote by choosing not to participate.

With President Hetzel behind the idea, the *Collegian* rallying in its favor, and what student opinion there was solidly in the "yes" camp, planning for the Shrine began. Earlier in 1939, Bernie Newman had had some preliminary conversations with Burton Johnstone from Architecture and Francis Hyslop from Art that began to bear fruit. Francis E. Hyslop, Instructor of Fine Arts, would become an extremely important player in the development of the Shrine. He had written to three noted sculptors, John B. Flannagan, Heinz Warneke, and Carl Milles, to elicit their ideas for and interest in a Lion Shrine. Milles declined to participate, but by early January 1940 both Flannagan and Warneke had expressed keen interest in the project. Neither could quote a price at the time—far too many questions remained to be answered. Underlying all the interest and enthusiasm, the biggest unanswered question was not even "How much?" but rather "Who will pay?"

The Class of 1940

Early in 1940 the senior class began to take a special interest in the Shrine project, and in particular the funding of the project. The Class Gift Committee included Class President David E. Pergrin, All-College President H. Clifton McWilliams, *Collegian* Editor A. William Engel, G. Warren Elliott Jr., W. Jerome Howarth, and George E. Ritter—all members of the Lion's

Dave Pergrin.

A. William Engel.

Paw Honor Society. Under Bill Engel's leadership, the student newspaper had been an active participant in the call for the Shrine, and Engel himself had written an editorial in the fall of 1939 that did an excellent job of tying the Mascot's reemergence (thanks to Gene Wettstone) to Newman's call for a permanent Shrine. He also told the story of Joe Mason, giving proper credit to the Nittany Lion's creator.

The Senior Class Gift voting opened in late February in 1940. *Collegian* Editor Bill Engel kept his paper neutral in that round, but individuals could still write letters to the editor on any topic. In one such letter to the editor on March 1, Bernie Newman had a chance to make his last pitch for the Nittany Lion Shrine, but now it was directed only to his fellow classmates, who were about to decide on their permanent gift to Penn State. He had found acceptance for President Hetzel's idea among the students, but could he help provide the funds? He wrote: "The Nittany Lion—the best symbol of the college—could most effectively add character to such a meeting place [open-air]. A lion in bronze or stone could be not only a focus for public celebrations, but a work of sculpture of permanent value as well. Such a project would be close to the student body . . . and it is not so expensive as to be beyond the reach of the senior class fund."

Gift proposals competing for the seniors' votes included funds for completing the Old Main murals by Henry Varnum Poor, purchasing books for the library, funding observatories, contributions toward the construction of a student union building, and creation of a scholarship fund. The two gift ideas receiving the most votes in the March poll would go head-to-head in April. On March 15 it was announced that the Lion Shrine and the scholarship fund would be on the April ballot.

On April 26, 1940, the *Collegian* reported that the Lion Shrine was voted the Senior Class Gift. The vote was 243 for the Shrine and 225 for the scholarship fund—only an eighteen-vote difference. President Dave Pergrin's girlfriend at the time, Peggy Cimahosky (she became Mrs. Pergrin in 1941), is one of a small group of former students (disproportionately smaller than the original 225!) who admit to having voted for the scholarship fund, but even she adds: "Don't tell Dave!"

At the time, no one ever guessed the effect this Class Gift would have on the Penn State community. Instead of a simple gathering place for bonfires, the Lion Shrine became a powerful symbol of all that was good about Penn State, and a beacon for alumni who wished to revisit and remember an important time in their lives. The efforts of Joe Mason and Bernie Newman had been rewarded in excellent measure by the Class of 1940's vote, but there was one more person required for the creation of the Nittany Lion Shrine. Of the original two sculptors interested in the Shrine, only one now remained, for John Flannagan's health was failing and he was forced to withdraw from consideration.

That remaining sculptor would eventually be chosen for the miraculous task of transforming a 13-ton block of limestone into a cherished Penn State icon. His name was Heinz Warneke.

The arrival of the limestone block that would become the Nittany Lion Shrine.

7

Sculpting a Shrine

Heinz Warneke

Heinrich "Heinz" Johann Dietrich Warneke was born on June 30, 1895, in the small German village of Hagen bei Leeste (now Weyhe) not far from the beautiful medieval city of Bremen. He was the eldest of three sons born to Anna Ritterhof and Heinrich Warneke, who strongly encouraged his artistic talents and interests.

From his earliest years Heinz Warneke loved the out-of-doors. He was a bit of a loner, a social preference well-suited to his favorite occupation: observing the natural world, especially animals. In addition to his drawing and painting, Heinz also loved to fashion clay into the likenesses of animals he saw around him.

Following Heinz's graduation from school at age 16, his father helped him obtain an apprenticeship at Wilkins & Sons Silver Factory, located in Hemelingen (now a part of Bremen), where he learned the basics of the metalsmith profession. Warneke's biographer,

Heinz Warneke in his late twenties.

Mary Mullen Cunningham, wrote: "This intensive training with metal and metal tools would prove to be of inestimable value to him as a sculptor. It provided him with a thorough grounding in casting techniques and opened his mind to the sculptural possibilities of metal." During his two-year apprenticeship, Heinz also took evening classes in drawing and worked with clay modeling at the art school in Bremen. Those evening classes added another skill that he turned to throughout his life—the ability to capture the suggestion of movement in animal subjects.

Following his apprenticeship, Heinz decided to study what he loved best—sculpture—and took the entrance exam at the Berlin Arts and Crafts School, where admittance alone was an incredible feat. Warneke's training at the school exposed him to the masters of German sculpture and the remarkable sights Berlin had to offer in 1913.

By the time Heinz Warneke finished his association with the Berlin Arts and Crafts School and moved to the United States in the early 1920s, he was making a living as a sculptor. His studies and training had included anatomy and life-modeling, decorative sculpture, and a special emphasis in the study of plants in decorative design. He had learned to carve in wood and stone, worked extensively with brass, and because of the school's connection to crafts and industry he had also spent time working in a tool shop and a porcelain factory.

"Young Skunk Cabbage," a mahogany carving by Heinz Warneke.

"African Cow Elephant and Calf," sculpted by Warneke.

The Animals and Humans of Heinz Warneke

Heinz Warneke's work with animals received nearly unanimous critical praise, but his depiction of humans did not always fare so well. Warneke's biographer wrote:

> Marya Mannes, a reviewer for *Creative Art*, wrote glowingly of the animals but panned the figures [in Warneke's 1928 Milch Gallery exhibition], remarking that the only one she liked was *Pair of Water Carriers Walking*. About *Peasant Mother* and *Eve Repentant* she wrote: "They are solid lumps of wood, beautifully turned and finished—but there is nothing in them to arrest the eye. It seems as if Mr. Warneke were born with a complete aesthetic understanding of all the animals except his own specie."

And in late 1959, when working on his famous *African Cow Elephant and Calf* for the Philadelphia Zoo, Heinz Warneke heard criticism from the other side, the zoo staff. According to his biographer, they were startled by Warneke's seeming disinterest in "precise anatomical details."

> Upon seeing his quarter-scale model, they noted some minor inaccuracies, and offered him a list of suggestions, including the need to round the front feet of the animals. Warneke took umbrage to these quibbling suggestions and responded with a heated letter to John F. Lewis, vice president of the Fairmount Park Art Association [the sponsors of the project]: "I'm sure you . . . can understand my disappointment at having these requests for literal features entering into a creation of mine. . . . You can understand that basically I don't give a damn whether or not [elephants] have three toes or twenty, feathers on their noses or not,—I want to create a statue that will speak forever of how touching, how funny, how gorgeous motherhood is, even in such an awkward and huge beast as an elephant."

When Warneke was a student, Bruno Paul (1874–1968) was director of the Berlin Arts and Crafts School. An architect, draftsman, and designer, the influential Paul was a member of the German Werkbund (work association), which promoted collaboration among art, industry, and crafts.

Postwar inflation drove Heinz Warneke from Berlin in 1923. He lived first in St. Louis when he arrived in the United States. He had friends in that city, which also was home for a thriving community of German immigrants. Although burdened with every artist's plight—having to earn a living in a world where art is valued and supported by only a tiny percentage of the population—Warneke did fairly well. He learned English, became acclimated to the peculiarities of America, and earned "his daily bread primarily through commissions for commercial, architectural, and portrait sculpture."

An exhibit at the St. Louis Public Library in December 1923 brought Warneke his first American attention for one of his lifelong strengths as a sculptor—his work with animals. A reviewer for the *St. Louis Post-Dispatch* pronounced the works "extraordinary." His biographer wrote: "Warneke's animals were different. They were not symbols of courage or power, but rather reflected the sculptor's personal feelings, attitudes, and observations." The animals Heinz Warneke created the rest of his life would remain personal—his own vision of what made the animal unique and worth capturing in stone or brass or wood.

In St. Louis, Heinz met the other love of his life—Jessie Gilroy Hall. Married to Purina Mills executive Edward T. Hall, Jessie was one of Warneke's first benefactors in St. Louis. They met when Purina hired Warneke to model some animal statuettes to be manufactured and distributed as prizes. Heinz created a mantle and a fountain for the Hall home and received Jessie's help as an English tutor and a guide to the St. Louis arts community, which she knew well as both patron and painter. Following her divorce from Hall, Heinz and Jessie were married in March 1927. Throughout his life, Heinz relied on the emotional and practical support Jessie had to offer. In her important role as research assistant, secretary, and promoter, Jessie transformed his thoughts into words so that Heinz would be free to transform his ideas into art.

When the Warnekes left St. Louis, they settled first in Paris and later in New York, in order to be more involved with the art world. Heinz's reputation continued to grow through museum shows and juried exhibits. Although most of the reviews were favorable, Heinz Warneke was developing a reputation as a specialist in animal sculpture, a reputation he wanted to keep in perspective. He did not want his other work to go unappreciated, but he was also quite happy about the praise his animal sculptures were receiving.

Penn State Fine Arts Instructor Francis Hyslop had been following Heinz Warneke's career for years. He was certain that the sculptor's talents made him ideally suited for the creation of a Nittany Lion Shrine, yet it wasn't simply Warneke's gift for creating animals that gave Hyslop confidence in his recommendation of the sculptor. It was Hyslop's belief that Heinz Warneke was the right artist to carry out something that had been suggested by the presence of Henry Varnum Poor working on his mural in Old Main and recommended by Poor himself: Hyslop wanted to have the Nittany Lion Shrine created on campus right before the eyes of the Penn State community and the community at large.

Henry Varnum Poor pauses during work on the Old Main murals.

Abraham Lincoln dedicating the land-grant university concept, realized by Penn State University, in Poor's Old Main murals.

The Committee and the Commission

Following the close vote, Senior Class President Dave Pergrin announced the appointment of a committee to plan the Shrine. In addition to Pergrin in an ex officio role, the members were A. O. Morse, assistant to President Hetzel; Russell E. Clark (Class of 1919), bursar; George L. Donovan (Class of 1935), assistant manager of the Student Union; and Francis E. Hyslop Jr. Owing to an administrative oversight, the committee's appointment was not official until

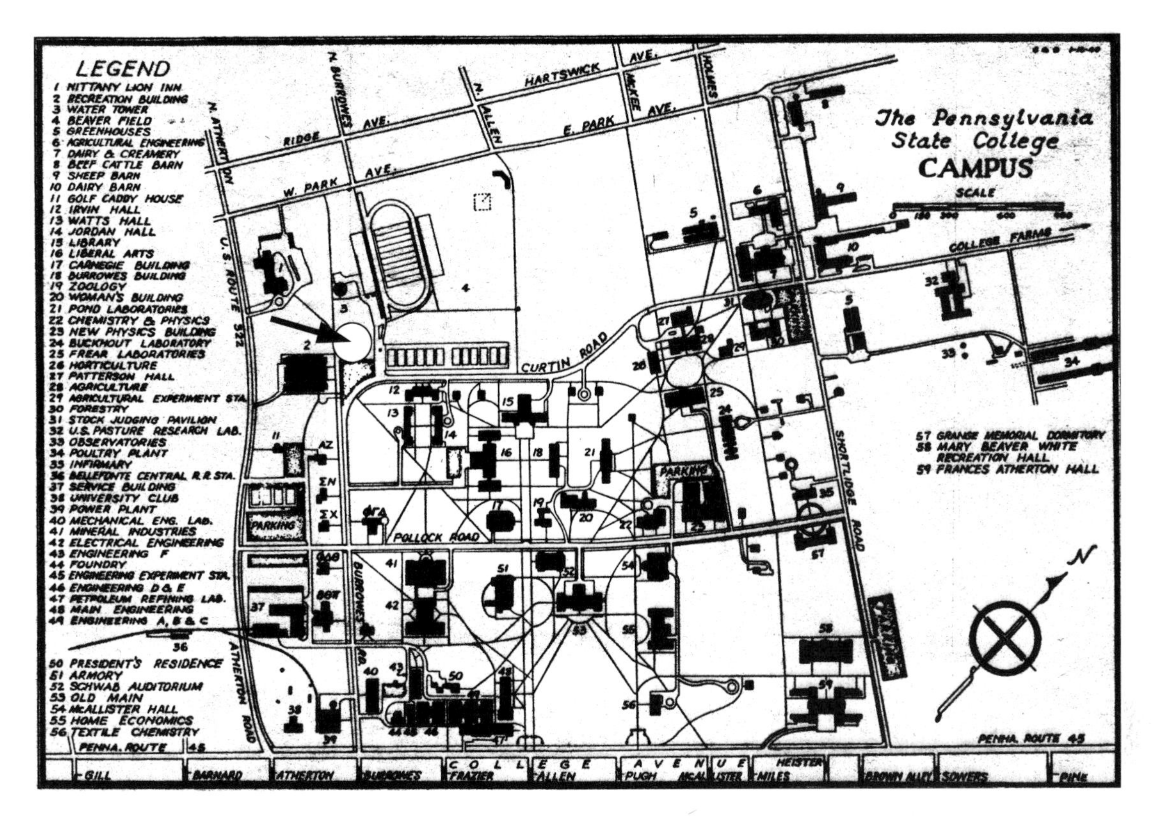

Map showing the site chosen for the Nittany Lion sculpture.

February 1941, so it was a slower start than had been anticipated. Once the committee was informed of its official status, however, the work proceeded quickly. Heinz Warneke, who had already submitted photos of Shrine sketches, was invited to Penn State in March to learn more about the committee's tentative plans and to visit potential sites on campus.

The leading contender for the location of the Shrine had shifted from the student-preferred Old Main Lawn to a small rise in front of the Water Tower (now the Biomechanics Laboratory), between Rec Hall and Beaver Field at the top of Burrowes Road. The committee members believed that a shrine to the Nittany Lion would be well suited to that section of the campus already dedicated to athletics. Although it was never mentioned specifically, someone on the Shrine Committee must have also realized that the nearby Nittany Lion Inn, already a favorite with alumni after ten years of operation, might ensure a regular stream of Shrine visitors.

Among the many people who still had to approve the Shrine Committee's suggested site were a slew of architects and the Board of Trustees. George W. Ebert, superintendent of grounds and buildings, would also be involved in the decision; he was worried about the effects that proposed additional wings to Rec Hall and the expanding of Beaver Field's main gate might have on the site. As students learned of the proposed location, most expressed their

An aerial view of Beaver Field.

agreement on the logic of the choice, but the Shrine Committee was probably most gratified when the only remaining sculptor on their "short list" heartily approved of the committee's preference during his March visit.

With a home and a studio in two locations, Heinz Warneke had been dividing his time between New York City and East Haddam, Connecticut, for a number of years, but he had just given up his New York studio when he was contacted regarding the Penn State commission. He was also dividing his creative energy between his treasured private studio work and income-producing commissions, a difficult tightrope for any artist to walk. The Penn State Nittany Lion Shrine was a commission that Warneke would never regret accepting.

Unlike some projects in Warneke's career that went awry through a mismatch of artistic vision and a funding committee's opinion, the Shrine project was smooth from the start. Francis Hyslop deserves much of the credit for paving the way, through his work on the Shrine Committee and by alerting the Penn State community about what was going to happen, how important and wonderful it would be, and what an honor it was to have a sculptor of Heinz

Warneke's stature producing the Shrine. Hyslop emphasized the uniqueness of having the Shrine sculpted on campus, and Heinz Warneke deserves much credit for complying with that request. It would become one of Warneke's most treasured memories of his work on the Nittany Lion.

When Warneke returned home in March, he spent additional time observing mountain lions and pumas at New York zoos for guidance on manner and movement. By late April he was back at Penn State with plaster casts of the six plasticine Nittany Lion models he had conceived, in six different poses. Warneke's enthusiasm for the project was evident and received well by the committee, as were the models. The committee unanimously selected the first of the six models Warneke had created—and Warneke's favorite as well: the pose Penn State has come to know so well that it is difficult to imagine it has not always existed.

Heinz Warneke was officially designated as the Shrine's sculptor, and the time had finally arrived to talk about money. Warneke believed that executing the design the Shrine Committee had selected would cost between $6,000 and $8,000. Some of the costs were directly associated with the work being performed on site. The senior class had raised $5,340 for their gift, and Warneke agreed to create the Nittany Lion Shrine for the amount available. The contract called for the sculptor to provide his own materials as part of the commission price, which was the usual custom in the profession. The Nittany Lion would become priceless, of course, but even when it was still an idea rather than an icon—$5,340 *and* he has to buy the limestone?—it seemed like an incredibly good deal for the College. It was.

Warneke was not a sculptor because it was the best way to make a living in America. He was creating three-dimensional art because "for as long back as he can remember he had an intense delight in touching objects. And anyone who has seen him now touching various materials realizes at once how fundamental is this joy in the feel of things." Heinz Warneke was a sculptor from the tips of his fingers down to his very soul. He wanted to create the Nittany Lion for the same reasons Penn State had adopted it as a mascot—to imbue it with meaning and strength beyond its physical form, to give it eternal life.

On July 29, 1941, A. O. Morse had good news for his committee, which he shared in an interoffice correspondence letter:

> Following Mr. Warneke's second visit, our committee recommended to the Board of Trustees that one of Mr. Warneke's models, the one showing the lion crouching, be accepted and that Mr. Warneke be commissioned to sculpture this lion in stone for the water tower site.
>
> This recommendation was referred to the Trustee Committee on Architecture and that committee, after viewing the models, approved the recommendation provided Mr. Cret, the college Architect, would also approve. Mr. Cret approved the model at once. . . .
>
> As soon as President Hetzel decided that everyone was in substantial agreement, we sent Mr. Warneke a contract. He signed it and returned it yesterday. . . .

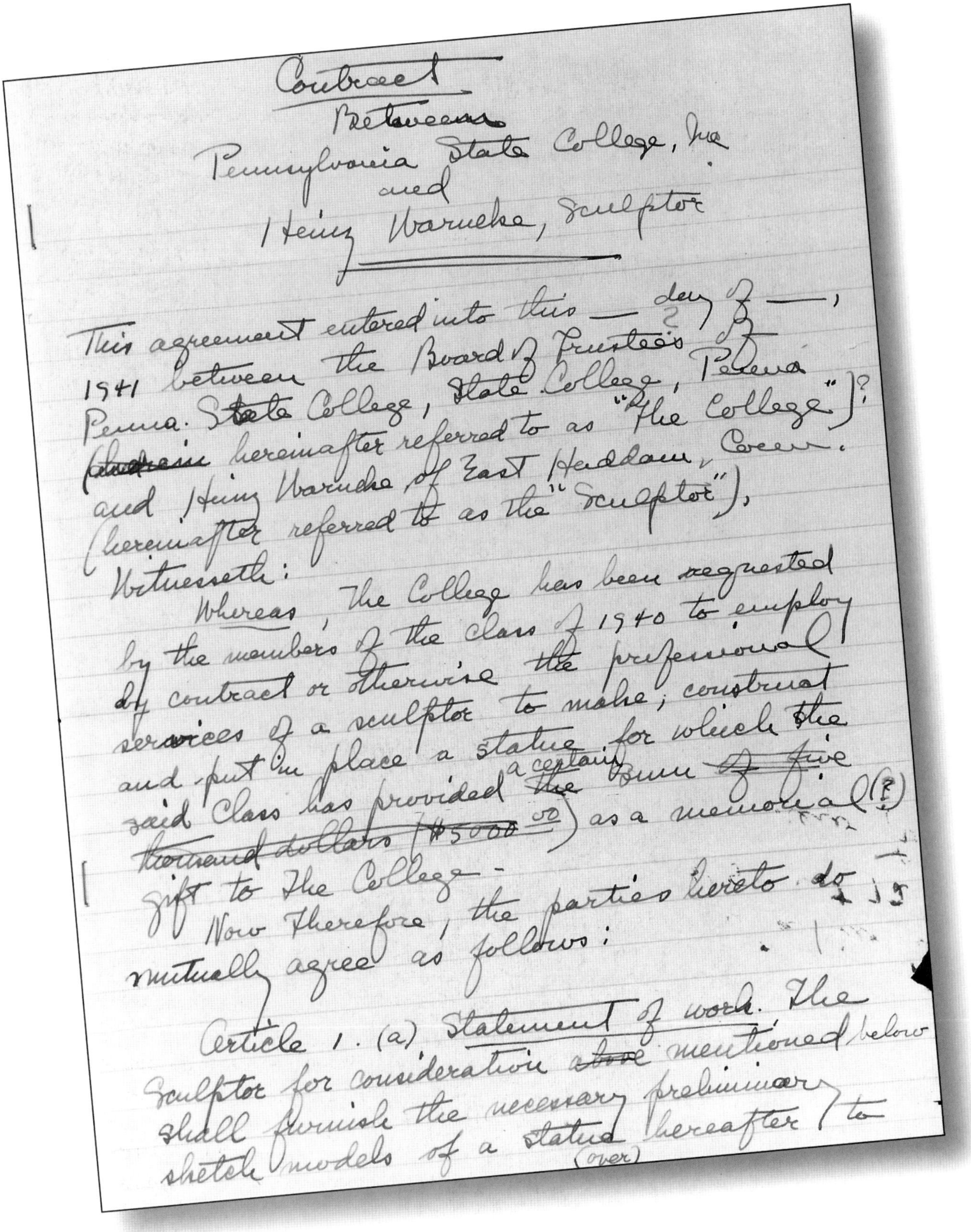

Contract
Between
Pennsylvania State College, Inc.
and
Heinz Warneke, Sculptor

This agreement entered into this — day of —, ? 1941 between the Board of Trustees of Penna. State College, State College, Penna. hereinafter referred to as "The College"); ? and Heinz Warneke of East Haddam, Conn. (hereinafter referred to as the "Sculptor"),

Witnesseth:

Whereas, The College has been requested by the members of the class of 1940 to employ by contract or otherwise the professional services of a sculptor to make, construct and put in place a statue for which the said Class has provided a certain ~~the~~ sum ~~of five thousand dollars~~ ($5000.00) as a memorial (?) gift to The College.

Now Therefore, the parties hereto do mutually agree as follows:

Article 1. (a) Statement of work. The Sculptor for consideration ~~above~~ mentioned below shall furnish the necessary preliminary sketch models of a statue hereafter to (over)

The first page of Penn State's contract with Heinz Warneke.

> I understand [Mr. Warneke] has begun a full size model of the lion. This he plans to bring to State College in September in order that we may see it in place before the foundation is begun. With the full size model there we can get final agreement as to the exact site and the height of the foundation. I understand Mr. Warneke does not want to order the stone until he has seen the model in position. While the stone is being delivered, the College Department of Grounds and Buildings will put in the foundation.

The Contract

The contract made that summer of 1941 between The Pennsylvania State College and Heinz Warneke, Sculptor, states:

> The sculptor for consideration mentioned below shall furnish a statue of "The Nittany Lion" in stone and of such proportions as shall be mutually agreed, and shall install said statue on the campus of the College within two years of the above date.
>
> The College shall provide a foundation for the lion and shall pay the sculptor the sum of five thousand three hundred and seventy-five dollars ($5,375.00) for all services rendered under this contract. . . .

In the three months since Warneke had visited campus, an alumnus had donated an additional $35. The sculptor was to receive $1,375 immediately with the acceptance of the model; $2,200 when the full-size model was completed; and $1,800 when "the work is finally completed and installed to the satisfaction of the College."

But Heinz Warneke began working on the model even before he had received the contract.

Creating Public Art

Late in August 1941, Heinz Warneke sent to the Shrine Committee photographs showing two months' progress on the full-size model. Warneke and his assistant, Ted Barbarossa, first built a wood armature in the fairly exact shape of the lion—a wood skeleton of sorts. They next applied over the entire wood frame a pliable clay that Warneke shaped and formed into the Nittany Lion from nose to tail. More clay was added for shaping features and details. At the end of each day, the work in progress was covered with oilcloth to prevent the clay from drying out. In September, Warneke cast the model in plaster and finished the details with his chisels and files.

Warneke shipped the 600-pound plaster model to Penn State to help guide the laying of the foundation and to aid in planning the surrounding landscaping. Then the model was retired to the second-floor lobby of Old Main to hibernate for the winter. It was too late in the year for the outside work to begin, even if the limestone had been on hand, but Warneke's desire to order the stone only after the model had been examined on site, combined with wartime

The wood “skeleton” of the Shrine’s model.

The plaster model at Warneke’s studio, awaiting its trip to State College.

restrictions on limestone, guaranteed that the carving would not begin until halfway through the next year.

In June 1942, Heinz Warneke arrived to begin work just ahead of his 13-ton limestone block. The plaster model was transported back to the site and would sit next to the huge stone all through the summer as its twin miraculously emerged.

Warneke described the process, the reasoning behind some of his decisions, and his reactions to working at Penn State in an article in *Art Digest* published a few months after he finished the Lion:

> In the case of the Nittany Lion it was the aim of the Art Department at Pennsylvania State College to have the carving take place on the campus in full view of the student body—approximately seven thousand young men and women. In as much as several committees had to be consulted and pleased, among others the College Board of Trustees, the Penna. State Board of Architecture and Landscaping, and a committee from the Class of 1940—the donors—it was necessary to present several small sketches in plaster to afford a selection, and finally a full-sized model for approval. This feature of the commission made it impracticable for me to employ the taille directe [direct cutting or carving] method which I prefer, but I am convinced that the students, and even the faculty, acquired a better understanding of the usual procedure in the making of the statue through watching the pointing-up process.*
>
> A platform was set up between the football stadium and the gymnasium. . . . As soon as we arrived with the plaster model, (some nine feet long), the questions began, for of course many of the students thought it was the statue itself, and it was understood that they were free to ask any pertinent questions; that was part of the program. Then the thirteen-ton limestone block from Indiana was unloaded with all the usual science and paraphernalia, involving beams, leverage, and derricks. This installation caused much speculation.
>
> To expedite the work of pointing up and roughing out, I brought along one of our best stone-carvers, Joseph Garatti; otherwise I should still be out there chopping away in the snow. Together we measured up the points, placed our nails and made the little plaster cones. At this point the mathematicians and engineers came to the fore, tantalized, apparently, by our calculations and somewhat cavalier use of the calipers.
>
> The students and townspeople were delighted by the growing forest of "warts," though some of the more sensitive ones were horrified to see "the lovely lion being spoiled." But when the lion's face and flanks began to emerge from the stone

* The *Oxford Dictionary of Art* defines pointing as "a method of creating an exact copy of a statue or of enlarging a model into a full-size sculpture by taking a series of measured points on the original and transferring them by means of mechanical aids to the copy or enlargement." First developed in the first century B.C. in a simple form, it was used in the copying of public Greek statues for people's homes. More sophisticated techniques were developed during the Renaissance and perfected during the late nineteenth century.

Joseph Garatti roughs out the lion.

The famous face emerges.

The Shrine begins to take a familiar shape.

under our strokes, it was truly moving to observe the change in the quality of the questions. . . .

For a while I had to leave Mr. Garatti alone with the roughing out, and when I returned to stay on and definitely finish the job, I was thunderstruck by his progress. It then came out that Mr. Garatti was a bashful man, to whom all these strangers with their questions were completely upsetting, so he never stopped his air-compressor from morning until night.

There was a graduation during this period and hundreds of parents came to see the Lion and to be photographed with sons or daughters beside the statue. The parents in many cases had never seen a like work in process, so that the educational influence may well be said to have spread far beyond the limits of the college campus. In the evenings while the dances were going on in the gymnasium, I often talked to the parents and other visitors who also had questions to ask, and I became interested

Warneke finishes his masterpiece with a pedicure.

> and touched to see that all statuary had taken on an actuality for them. To tell the truth, I am convinced that many a statue in Pennsylvania, hitherto not even observed, is now noticed and appreciated for whatever worth it may have.

Judging by the sculptor's own report, it seemed that the creating of public art had achieved just the effect Francis Hyslop had been seeking.

Dedication of the Shrine

The Nittany Lion Shrine was completed before the first home football game with Bucknell on October 3, 1942. Heinz Warneke, with the help of Joseph Garatti's skills (and a strong preference for working instead of talking), had created the statue in less than four months.

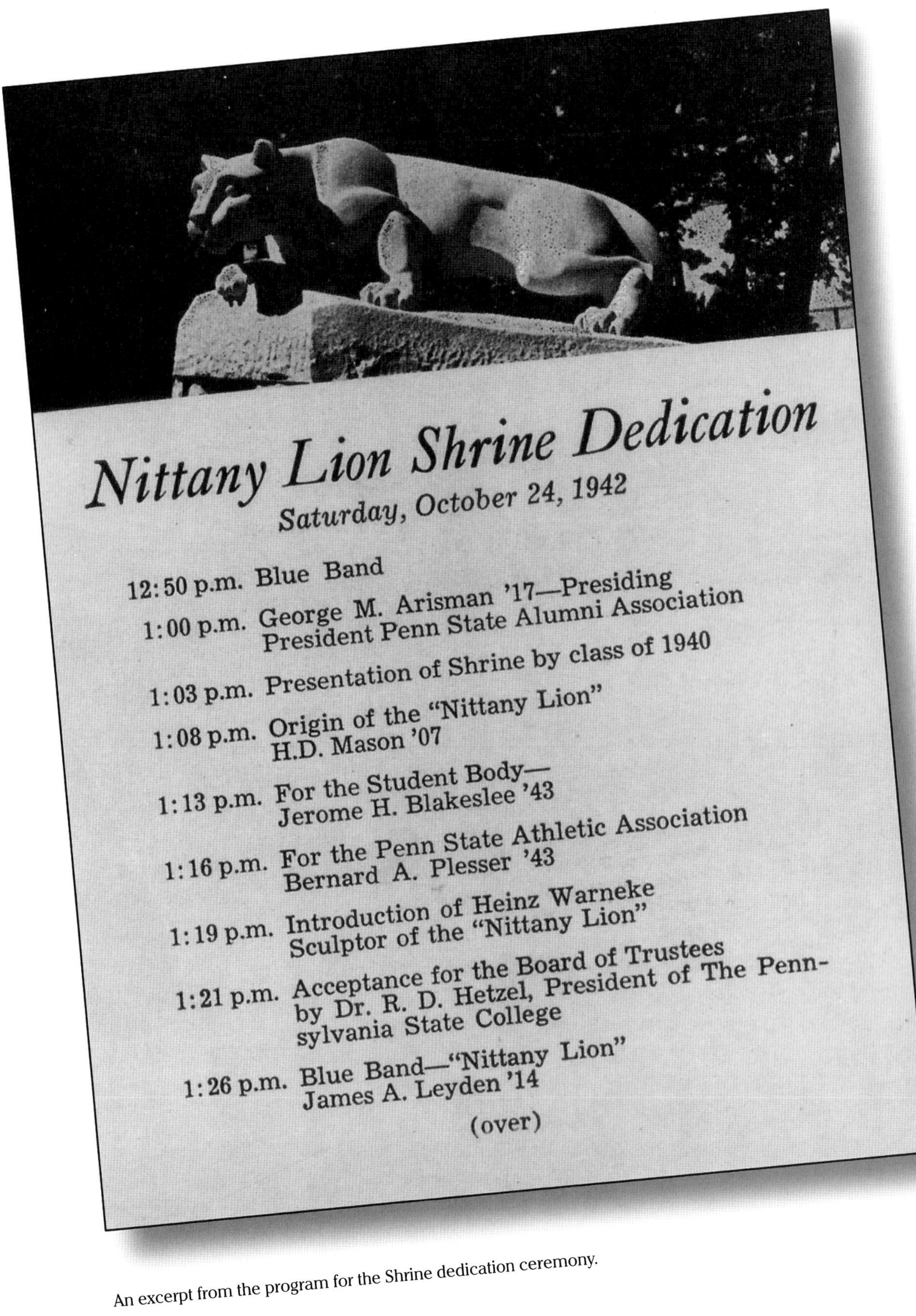
Nittany Lion Shrine Dedication

Saturday, October 24, 1942

12:50 p.m. Blue Band

1:00 p.m. George M. Arisman '17—Presiding
President Penn State Alumni Association

1:03 p.m. Presentation of Shrine by class of 1940

1:08 p.m. Origin of the "Nittany Lion"
H.D. Mason '07

1:13 p.m. For the Student Body—
Jerome H. Blakeslee '43

1:16 p.m. For the Penn State Athletic Association
Bernard A. Plesser '43

1:19 p.m. Introduction of Heinz Warneke
Sculptor of the "Nittany Lion"

1:21 p.m. Acceptance for the Board of Trustees
by Dr. R. D. Hetzel, President of The Pennsylvania State College

1:26 p.m. Blue Band—"Nittany Lion"
James A. Leyden '14

(over)

An excerpt from the program for the Shrine dedication ceremony.

The dedication took place during Homecoming Weekend on Saturday, October 24, in a thirty-minute ceremony. Dave Pergrin had his hands full elsewhere. He was about to be promoted to Captain and Executive Officer of the First Training Battalion at Fort Belvoir, Virginia, and could not attend the ceremony. Leading the Class of 1940 would seem like a picnic a few short years later when Colonel Pergrin commanded the celebrated 291st Combat Engineer Battalion. Their fame was earned under fire at the Battle of the Bulge and while building the first bridge over the Rhine, which allowed the Allied troops to enter Germany.

Bill Engel was the only representative of the Class of 1940 Gift Committee to attend the dedication. He began his remarks with a brief history of the events leading up to its creation, including the rioting that had prompted the initial discussions with President Hetzel, and then he shared his hope for the future:

> Now we have the completed shrine. And in such times as these, it is fitting that some object can be looked upon as a symbol not only of those carefree days of pre-game rioting, but also the focal point for modern-day student pep rallies, mass meetings and celebrations of victory. The class of '40 trusts that this Nittany Lion Shrine will do much toward instilling and maintaining that old Penn State spirit. And we feel sure that this statuary will prove of value far in excess of the money put into it. On behalf of the Class of 1940 and its gift committee . . . I wish to present the Nittany Lion Shrine to the College.

The Shrine dedication ceremony had to go on without Class of 1940 President Dave Pergrin. He was occupied elsewhere.

Bill Engel then introduced a very special guest—Joe Mason—who was on hand to "tell the real story of just how the idea [of the Nittany Lion] was conceived."

H. D. "Joe" Mason speaking at the Dedication, a day when boasts and wishes came true.

In top coat and hat, Mason rose to the mike with his hands behind him as if he were about to recite a poem remembered from grade school. He began:

> Old Man Lion is not accustomed to this loud speaker business. . . . My subject is, "The Origin of the Nittany Lion," which in truth, I cannot give you, as Old Man Lion was in charge over yonder on Mt. Nittany long before Columbus discovered America—and likely fifty thousand years before that, according to some geologists. Darwin's "Origin of Species" does not give us the exact date, and hence I will briefly tell you how our own Nittany Mountain Lion got his start.

The Nittany Lion Shrine: " . . . May its beauty and power be a constant inspiration to all of us."

Mason recounted the boast at Princeton and Penn State's victory later that day: "Well, Lady Luck was with us that afternoon on the baseball field. . . ." He continued with his recollection of the editorial in *The Lemon* in 1907 that had called for "a real College emblem for Penn State . . . the Nittany Mountain Lion":

> It must have been a very potent editorial, as it took just 33 years to get results—as finally the Class of 1940 voted the funds for the erection of this magnificent work of art, which we see today. . . .
>
> Finally came into full flower the realization of all our dreams, when Sculptor Heinz Warneke, created with his genius of heart, head and hand this living, breathing image in stone. We see before us the real Nittany Mountain Lion—alert, resourceful, unafraid, unconquerable, an inspiration to every loyal son and daughter of Old Penn State for generations to come.

Almost anyone else in Joe Mason's shoes that day would have had difficulty *not* swelling to the size of the Lion Shrine, but Joe remained modest and self-effacing. If the average alumnus feels pride when looking at that magnificent sculpture, how must the man who called for its creation have felt?

Bernard A. Plesser (Class of 1943), President of the Student Athletic Association, expressed his appreciation this way:

> As long as songs, traditions, and sports have existed at Penn State, our winnings and losses in athletic contests have been offered up to . . . a Nittany Lion. . . . Until recently, that lion was merely an illusion that existed in a different form in each Penn Stater's mind. Some of us pictured a shaggy-maned African Lion; many of us were more than surprised when a mountain lion skin was used as our mascot at the athletic events. Thanks to the Class of 1940, a solid counterpart of our college legend was made possible; thanks to Mr. Warneke, we have a likeness that satisfies the most vivid imagination; a likeness that speaks of readiness, alertness and cunning. This . . . is what we can all hail as THE Nittany Lion. Here . . . is a legend and a tradition to which we can pledge our allegiance, a legend which we can cherish dear; and a legend which we call "The Symbol of Our Best."

And President Ralph Hetzel, who was unable to attend the dedication, sent a written message accepting the Shrine for the Board of Trustees. It said, "President J. Franklin Shields has authorized me to accept the Nittany Lion Shrine on behalf of the trustees and to express sincere gratitude to the Class of 1940 for this beautiful and significant gift to the College. May its beauty and power be a constant inspiration to all of us to be ever loyal to the highest ideals of Penn State. . . ."

Bill Engel, Class of 1940, admires the Nittany Lion Shrine marker acknowledging the Class Gift.

The sculptor was absent that day as well, but his presence on campus would be forever felt through his Nittany Lion. He sent a letter of regret and best wishes, adding: "Please tell the students that I hope The Lion Roars them to victory after victory."

After an absence of nearly two decades, Heinz Warneke would visit Penn State three times in the last decade of his life—once to check on his Lion while working in Altoona on another commission, once to receive a special recognition, and once to serve as a veterinary surgeon for a limestone lion who had lost his ear.

High Jinks and Pilgrimages

Visiting the Shrine

It is impossible to gauge accurately just how many people have stroked the Lion's noble head or sat astride its powerful back, but the Shrine has silently witnessed a true "lion's share" of devotion since its creation. The stream of visitors long ago crossed the hundreds of thousands mark to the millions mark, and many are now repeat visitors, returning with their own children and their children's children.

The custom of having one's picture taken with the Lion Shrine began before Heinz Warneke even finished and has continued unabated since the dedication. Even after Beaver Field hosted its last football game in 1959, the custom continued, as it does after the Bryce Jordan Center supplanted Rec Hall's role as Penn State's primary indoor athletic venue. The Shrine was originally to be located at the center of Penn State's athletic world, a place of frenzied activity where thousands could gather to celebrate. Now the Lion stands guard over one

The Shrine has been the object of awe by young and old.

Candid shots near the Shrine are often identifiable only by dating the fashions worn by the participants.

of the most serene corners of Penn State's University Park campus.

The visitors come quietly and steadily in groups of two, three, four, or more, often armed with cameras. She comes with her parents on that very first visit before she enrolls. He may show it to a high school friend the first year, an out-of-town date in year two, or a visiting aunt or uncle during his junior year. Both return with their grandparents on graduation Saturday, and a few years later they bring their spouses to pay tribute to this Lion who has somehow come to represent four years of work and play—four of the most important years of their lives. They eventually bring young children who climb and laugh, and the more safety-conscious who cling and ask to get down. Suddenly, it seems, it has been twenty-five years since they were students. On the next visit, they are accompanied by a young

Standard graduation day poses at the Shrine.

For better or for worse, bound by Lion Pride.

Shrine photos are almost always accompanied by big smiles and happy faces, like these on the Duskin family, 1991.

Remember, "the Nittany Lion has never been beaten in a fair fight," so, opposing teams, look out!

son or daughter who is considering attending Penn State. As Joe Paterno, Penn State's head football coach for more than thirty years and a remarkable symbol himself, put it:

> The Lion has been a symbol to students and alumni as well as to our athletes—a majestic symbol. He has a lot of character, patience, and determination, and in many ways he reflects the ruggedness of our location. Finally, I think he almost appears to be a father figure looking over all his children, the ones he is taking care of and the ones who come back to say hello.

The Nittany Lion Shrine has been photographed from every possible angle during every type of weather Centre County has to offer. The Lion looks just as good in a steady rain as he does beneath a blue October sky. No amount of snow covering him has ever made him look silly, nor have any of the poses people have come up with through the years. He has been photographed with cats, dogs, and goats. He has posed with beauty queens, campus leaders, and heroes. Penn State presidents and national leaders have paid tribute and recorded their visits for posterity. On a few occasions, photographers have even snapped pictures of the Lion with a visitor wearing a very, shall we say, "natural" costume.*

* Known photographs of Lion visitors wearing as little as the Lion include *Playboy* magazine's "Girls of the Big Ten," the Sachs twins, and State College photographer Bill Coleman's "Lady in the Red Shoes."

“He has a lot of character, patience, and determination”: Joe Paterno on the Nittany Lion, using words others might use to describe the coaching legend himself.

Penn State presidents visit the Shrine. This photo shows President Hetzel and his wife paying their respects.

Visitors from near and far have paid homage. Former British Prime Minister Clement Atlee is on the right.

The Lion watches over the campus even on the snowiest days.

Painting the Lion Orange

Not every Shrine visitor comes bearing a camera. Some bring paint cans and brushes and do their visiting late in the night before Penn State home football games. The orange paint of Syracuse is probably the best-known attempt of another school's fans to "discolor" the Lion and thereby besmirch Penn State's athletic character.

Sue Paterno tells how she used that tradition to her own advantage one night more than thirty years ago:

> In 1966, the first year Joe was head coach, the team was struggling a bit and our fans were well-dressed, provincial and lacked emotion. I turned to the statue to help us rally support from the students. Sandra Welsh and Nancy Radakovich agreed to help me pull off a daring plan: we were going to cover the statue in orange tempera (water-based) paint. This would lead everyone to believe that Syracuse fans, the team we were playing Saturday, had done it and our students would rally behind their mascot and team. We pulled it off and escaped; however, later that night, some Syracuse

To prevent graffiti and damage, guarding the Shrine has become a time-honored tradition. These members of Alpha Chi Rho took their turn standing guard.

A rare moment of rest for Joe and Sue Paterno.

fans were caught by the police for dumping oil-based paint on the Lion. Joe and the other husbands were working Friday morning when someone told them that three people had been arrested for painting the Lion. After putting two and two together, they assumed we had been the vandals and had been arrested. Fortunately, we were all home with our children. The plan worked and even though we lost the game 12–10, two things happened: we had the highest home attendance of that year and every year after that there is a vigil to guard the Lion from any unruly fans who visit Penn State.

The Syracuse and Pitt faithful were sometimes successful in their "attacks" on the Lion, but far more often they were foiled by a staunch contingent of athletes or fraternity brothers or

Graffiti has been one way of registering support for an opposing team—not a popular choice at University Park.

a group of friends willing to sleep in the cold with at least one eye open. The University police also make a practice of being extra wary during Penn State's home games. That combined vigilance has kept most of the football weekend mischief to a minimum. In its first three decades, the Lion's worst moments were more humiliating than permanently damaging—the stroke of a paintbrush creating inappropriate words on a cherished surface, words whose misguided inspiration is now long forgotten.

Although there has always been concern about the damage most paints can cause, especially when repeated over time, the first act of real physical violence toward the Shrine instantly raised concern at Penn State to a higher level. Sometime during final exam week in the fall term of 1978, someone took a very heavy object and knocked off the Lion's right ear. That cruel blow put into motion the plans for Heinz Warneke's last visit to his Lion.

Warneke visits his beloved lion for the first time in nearly twenty years.

The Sculptor Visits

Heinz Warneke had been concerned about vandalism to the Lion for some time. He had been hearing the reports about painting and graffiti, so when he began planning his last large public sculpture—the bronze mountain lion outside Altoona High School—he recommended not using limestone, the initial choice of those funding the Altoona project. Warneke advised the Altoonans to go to bronze and pointed out why the model they chose would be relatively

Heinrich "Heinz" Warneke

Biographical Particulars

Born: June 30, 1895, Weyhe, Germany.
Father: Heinrich Warneke, freight manager for the government railroad.
Mother: Anna Ritterhof.
Early education: In grammar and country schools in Weyhe.
College: Attended Bremen City Art School (Städtische Kunstgewerbeschule), 1911–13, while apprenticed to a metalsmith; attended school of the Government Arts and Crafts Museum, generally known as the Berlin Kunstgewerbeschule (Berlin Arts and Crafts School), 1913–15 and 1919–23.
Marriage: To Jessie Gilroy Hall in March 1927.
Children: Four stepchildren from Jessie's first marriage to Edward T. Hall.
Career: Sculptor, using every imaginable material, beginning in about 1914 while still a student in Berlin. Spent war years in Bucharest, Romania, overseeing the design and creation of war memorials. Based in St. Louis, 1923–27, and in Paris, 1927–32; divided between The Mowings (home/studio) in East Haddam, Connecticut, and New York City, 1932–42; The Mowings and Washington, D.C., 1942–70; and at The Mowings, 1970–83. Taught sculpture at the Corcoran School of Art and George Washington University between 1942 and 1970.
A sampling of well-known works in Pennsylvania and the region: *Young Skunk Cabbage*, 1944, mahogany, 20 x 14½ x 11 in. (at Palmer Museum of Art at Penn State); *African Cow Elephant and Calf*, 1959–62, granite, including self-base: 11 ft. 4 in. x 12 ft. 2 in. x 7 ft. 3⅝ in., located at the Philadelphia Zoo; *Mountain Lion*, 1969–72, bronze, 5 ft. 4 in. h. x 9 ft. 6 in. w., located in the mall between the Altoona Public Library and the Altoona Area Senior High School at Sixth Avenue and 17th Street; extensive decorative sculpture (bosses, capitals), including *The Last Supper* tympanum for the south transept portal of the Washington National Cathedral, 1951–73; and, of course, Penn State's Nittany Lion Shrine.
Died: August 16, 1983, of a heart attack, in Madison, Connecticut.

difficult to damage, "even with a sledgehammer." Ironically, a sledgehammer was the most likely suspect in the removal of the Lion Shrine's ear a half-dozen years later. Heinz Warneke, saddened by the attack on his Lion, began to make plans to conduct the repairs himself, although he was by then in his eighties and doing very little traveling.

Over the years, the Nittany Lion Shrine and Penn State had become quite special to Warneke. Long before his 1972 visit to the campus, where he was delighted to see how well the Lion was holding up, Warneke had remained in contact with Penn State, largely through his friendship with Francis Hyslop.

In 1948, Warneke created the original model for the small Nittany Lion replicas still sold through the Penn State Alumni Association, after he and Penn State first suffered through several years of unauthorized and unsatisfactory reproductions. He also designed the two lion heads on the Class of 1903 Memorial Gate at Atherton Street and Pollock Road, which were carved in limestone by the Carl Furst Company of Bedford, Indiana, in 1952.

In 1968, Warneke approved the creation of the ten one-quarter-scale Nittany Lion Shrine "cubs" that were cast in plastic and placed at the Mont Alto, Hazleton, Schuylkill, DuBois,

Some extra lives for Penn State's favorite cat. Mini-shrines are located at all the Commonwealth campuses.

Altoona, Wilkes-Barre, McKeesport, York, and Ogontz campuses and at the Behrend College. Eventually all of Penn State's campuses would have a Nittany Lion Shrine replica.

Heinz Warneke was invited to return to Penn State for a very special occasion in 1975. He was named an honorary alumnus of the University by the Penn State Alumni Association, an honor given to "persons not otherwise qualified for alumni status who have made outstanding contributions toward the welfare of Penn State or have significantly enhanced its reputation and prestige."

Prominent visitors receive their own miniature versions of the Shrine. Here U.S. President Dwight D. Eisenhower displays the replica presented to him by the Alumni Association at a Centennial ceremony in 1955.

Jessie and Heinz Warneke thoroughly enjoyed the royal treatment Penn State extended to them as guests of honor that November weekend. In addition to being feted at a special Alumni Association Council dinner hosted by Penn State President John Oswald (also an honorary alumnus, as is Joe Paterno, to name two of Warneke's distinguished associates), Warneke was recognized at halftime at the Penn State–North Carolina State football game that Saturday. Embraced by the Nittany Lion Mascot and wearing a Nittany Lion tie, Heinz Warneke stood beaming before the largest crowd he had ever seen. More than 60,000 Penn State fans applauded wildly for the man who had created their beloved Nittany Lion Shrine. It was a highly public moment for a somewhat private man, but a moment Warneke would treasure the rest of his life. It is little wonder that he wanted to oversee the repairs to the Lion himself.

As masterfully as a skilled surgeon, the artist repairs his Lion.

The vandalism of November 1978 brought Heinz Warneke back for his final visit. Warneke and his daughter were greeted at the airport on July 11, 1979, by Bill and Eloise Engel. Bill Engel was certain that the frail-looking, elderly sculptor would want to go directly to the Nittany Lion Inn after his trip, but Warneke asked to go directly to the Shrine. The Engels watched as the sculptor walked up to the Nittany Lion and gently stroked the remnants of the broken ear while tears began to flow down his face.

Warneke used plastilina (oil-based clay) to model and carve the first "version" of the replacement ear right on the Lion's head. Joined by John Cook, an internationally known sculptor of medals and Professor of Art at Penn State, the two then formed a mold over the plastilina model in three sections, which when removed and joined together would be used to form the plaster model. The plaster version was then used as a guide for carving the actual ear in limestone to match the original. A little more than forty-eight hours after he had arrived, Heinz Warneke had a plaster ear wrapped in his shirt for his trip home. "I feel good now. I feel good. I think I can smile," he said.

Between the vandalism in November 1978 and the actual replacement of the ear in September 1979, there was a lot of talk about moving the Nittany Lion Shrine to a better-protected site. During one conversation between Bill Engel and Heinz Warneke, before the

Nittany Lion Shrine sculptor Heinz Warneke receives the fans' roar of approval at Beaver Stadium, 1975.

sculptor's visit, Warneke suggested making a bronze replica of the Lion for the current outdoor site and moving the original limestone Lion indoors.

Warneke's first choice for the new location was the Museum of Art on campus. When Bill Engel mentioned to Warneke that the bronze replica alone would cost anywhere from $12,000 to $15,000, the sculptor suggested: "We could obtain the money easily by making a dozen coeds 'pass the baskets' at the opening football game in September." In a memo reporting the conversation, Engel couldn't resist adding, "How about that!"

The actual carving of the limestone replacement ear was done by Vincenzo Palumbo, a nationally recognized stone carver who had spent most of his adult life working at Washington National Cathedral and was one of the last stone carvers in America. Warneke had worked closely with Palumbo over many years at the Cathedral. At the time Palumbo did the Lion's ear in 1979, he was president of the stone carvers' union, which had only five remaining members and no apprentices. In early September 1979, Palumbo traveled to Penn State to make the final adjustments and attach the replacement ear, which over time blended in quite well with the one on the left. Warneke declined to charge for his portion of the repair costs, but had he submitted even a conservative invoice the total costs of replacing the ear would have exceeded the costs of the entire sculpture in 1942.

Heinz Warneke never got back to campus to see the finished work. He died on August 16, 1983, at the age of 88. At Penn State University a wreath was placed on the Shrine in memory of its creator, and President Bryce Jordan had flowers sent to the graveside services in East Haddam, Connecticut, near the home the Warnekes had cherished for more than fifty years. Carl Zigrosser of the Philadelphia Museum of Art once wrote about Warneke:

> He has that spiritual innocence, that childlike simplicity that makes him brother to the birds and animals. In all his work there is purity of feeling, an emotional timbre that forever rings true. His devotion to his craft, his sense of beauty, his integrity as an artist, the genuineness of his plastic ideas all combine to make him one of the most distinguished sculptors of our time.

Penn State will always possess a living testament to that spiritual innocence and purity of feeling in the form of the Nittany Lion.

A Spare Lion

Vincenzo Palumbo made two additional visits to Penn State following his ear replacement trip in 1979. The first took place in June 1984, to repair a small nick in the right ear caused by two students the previous December. Unlike the vandals from five years earlier, these two were caught, and this time the damage was less evident.

A picture of sartorial elegance with a little help from a student.

Duplicating an icon, just in case, 1988.

The Lion Shrine undergoes a plastic mold procedure to assist in future repairs.

The Nittany Lion Shrine, the most famous Penn State Class Gift.

Palumbo also performed some "cleaning up" of the Shrine, the kind only a stone carver or sculptor could do. Warneke's idea of a second Lion was about to become reality, but not quite as he had envisioned. The University had decided instead to make a mold of the Lion as insurance against future vandalism and wanted Palumbo to put the Lion's body in the best possible shape before the mold maker began. The mold maker, Cesare Contini, started his work in 1985, but the plastic piece mold process he used would require so many separate pieces to form a complete mold for the large and complicated Lion that work was soon suspended.

Three years later John Philips, a mold maker and sculptor from Philadelphia, arrived at Penn State to make a mold of the Lion. With the assistance of Thom McGovern, Associate Professor of Art and head of the Sculpture Program at Penn State, Philips used a flexible mold process that involved painting the entire Lion with a liquid urethane. After the liquid became a flexible solid, it could be slipped off the Shrine in five large pieces. A case mold of plaster was then formed over the urethane mold and used to make an exact duplicate of the Nittany Lion in plaster. In an undisclosed storage building on Penn State's University Park campus sits a full-size Nittany Lion, just in case his limestone cousin needs some reconstructive surgery someday.

Warneke's associate, master stone carver Vincenzo Palumbo, works on repairing the Lion's ear a second time, 1994.

Vincenzo Palumbo's most recent trip to Penn State was to reconnect a second replacement of the poor Lion's somewhat picked-on right ear in the summer of 1994. The plaster ear Warneke had constructed in 1979 again served as Palumbo's model for carving the replacement out of matching limestone before returning to its home in the University Archives.

In the fall of 1992, the fiftieth anniversary of the dedication of the Lion Shrine finally gave David Pergrin a chance to officially represent the Class of 1940. His class had not only raised the money for the Shrine's creation back in 1940, but also paid for everything regarding the Shrine since its construction—the improved landscaping, the repairs, and the plaster model. Heinz Warneke was always grateful to the Class of 1940 for their continued care of the Lion Shrine.

Bill Engel was the only person participating in the anniversary celebration on October 17, 1992, who had also been present at the original dedication. Fifty years earlier he had said: "We feel sure that this statuary will prove of value far in excess of the money put into it." Engel's words from that day in 1942 proved to be an incredible understatement. No monetary price can ever represent the value of that limestone sculpture to Penn State.

Bernie Newman, Bill Engel, and Dave Pergrin all express amazement when they look back on the Senior Class Gift of 1940. Sure it was a good idea, but no one had any notion of how remarkable that idea would become in the hands of the sculptor, Heinz Warneke. Out of a 13-ton block of limestone, Warneke created a Shrine that gave permanent substance to something that Joe Mason pulled from thin air one cold April morning in 1904—a symbol for Dear Old State: the Nittany Lion.

9

The Men in the Suit, 1939–1969

The Lion, the Coach, and the Wardrobe

When Carl Schott, Dean of the School of Physical Education and Athletics, selected Gene Wettstone to bring back the Nittany Lion Mascot in 1939, he knew exactly what he was doing. Wettstone had been on the job for only a year, but Schott could already see that he was just what the floundering gymnastics program at Penn State needed—a dedicated coach and tireless promoter. Three decades later, Penn State Athletic Director Ed Czekaj said, "If Gene Wettstone had been born fifty years earlier, nobody would have heard of P. T. Barnum. The man is a human dynamo."

Who could be better suited than Penn State's own version of P. T. Barnum to handle the reintroduction of a Lion? No one but Eugene Wettstone, Penn State's own Circus impresario. Wettstone was Penn State's first full-time gymnastics coach, and publicizing his sport was a

"We'd do all sorts of spectacular stuff, way up in the rafters, without safety nets. We were out of our minds!" —Gene Wettstone, on the Circus

never-ending passion. The Penn State Circus was, in essence, an opportunity to showcase the skills of Penn State's gymnasts (and other student athletes) in an atmosphere of fun and lunacy. Coach Wettstone even "hired" a publicist named Busby Butterfinger to handle the press. The *Collegian* gave Butterfinger (a.k.a. Bill Engel!) some space for a few columns as the big event approached:

> Here I am folks and just itching to come out from under that tight wire . . . to rattle off some bits of stuff about "the Greatest Show on Earth," coming to Wreck Hall, April 22. I know it ain't in the College appropriation but they better start moving over one wall of Wreckreation Hall to accommodate that huge crowd that's gonna come to the All-Collitch Circus. I can even go so far as to predict that we're gonna be asked to do repeat performances during the summer to oblige the folks that stop here on the way to the World's Fair. There's been plenty of the fairer sex . . . floating around at the Monday and Wednesday evening practice sessions, which shows that interest has spread. Maybe some of them are trying to influence me to vote for them for the Circus Queen.

The first Circus, held on Saturday, April 22, 1939, was a huge success with the audience and a delight for the performers. Wettstone remembers his circuses fondly, especially the amazing feats the students performed. "We'd do all sorts of spectacular stuff, 'way up in the rafters, without safety nets. We were out of our minds." The circuses did exactly what

This Circus promotion uses a sign above the caged Nittany Lion asking the "studes" to show Penn State Spirit to help the poor Lion get back in step.

Wettstone wanted them to do: entertain and draw an audience to the gymnastic meets. Penn State standout and three-time Olympic gymnast Frank Cumiskey once remarked: "You know, I can remember the days when I could stand on the floor and count the people in the stands." Under Coach Wettstone, those days were long forgotten as the gymnasts of Penn State gained world prominence and Rec Hall was filled for every meet.

Sometime in the early autumn of 1939, at the behest of Carl Schott, Gene Wettstone traveled to New York City to have a new Nittany Lion suit made. Schott wanted the Lion to begin appearing at football games once again, while Wettstone had a few ideas for a "lion act" for next year's Circus. Wettstone doesn't recall traveling to New York with the idea that he, personally, would serve as the Nittany Lion but, since he was the one being measured and fitted—"if the Lion suit fits, the coach wears it." That fall of 1939, Coach Wettstone became the third Lion Mascot in a far more suitable suit for a lion who hails from Mount Nittany.

Fall 1939 is a somewhat murky period in Lion Mascot history. Apparently, the Lion's duties were shared by three different men. In addition to Wettstone, some Class of 1940 alumni

Gene Wettstone, gymnastics coach extraordinaire.

remember Donald "Wacky" Newberry cavorting in the suit. George Terwilliger performed too, but he remembers wearing the older version of the Lion's outfit. Terwilliger was one of the few gymnasts Wettstone chose to be the Mascot. The coach was appreciative of their athletic abilities, but he wanted to preserve his gymnasts' energies for the upcoming season.

Gene Wettstone would be involved with the selection and "training" of the Lions until the mid-1960s. He remembers the selection process as being fairly simple. He made candidates run across the gym, he watched them jump, and then he popped the big question: "What would you do if you were a lion?"

It was actually a double-edged question. Wettstone was looking for lion-like behavior in the Mascot audition, but he also wanted to find out the kind of skits or antics the candidate might perform as the Lion.

From the very start of the modern Mascot era, skit humor was a large part of the Nittany Lion's entrance

Donald "Wacky" Newberry.

George Terwilliger (the one on the left).

onto Beaver Field. Wettstone remembers Lions arriving in a hydrogen balloon, on horseback, in a horse-drawn chariot, driving a Cadillac, sitting atop a hand-carried sedan chair, and appearing in an outhouse, but in 1939, even with three Lions available (and two versions of the suit?), the Mascot managed not to arrive at the Pitt game at all. Apparently, one of the three Lions had been a bit too exuberant at the previous outing. The *Penn State Collegian* reported: "The piercing growl of the Pitt Panther will echo unchallenged through the Nittany Valley Saturday afternoon as far as noted animal rival, the Nittany Lion, is concerned. Still suffering from alterations, the 'king' will not show up on the new Beaver jungle."

The 1940s

George Terwilliger's two-year Mascot stint was followed by Tom Kelly's, and Robert Ritzmann, Penn State's longest reigning Nittany Lion, followed Kelly. Just as Franklin Roosevelt would be elected to his fourth term in those turbulent times, Robert Ritzmann would serve four years as the Nittany Lion Mascot—two of them after he graduated from Penn State. A State

Tom Kelly.

Robert Ritzmann on the porch of his "den."

College native (he left at the age of two months and returned as a freshman), Ritzmann was a member of the track team in the fall of 1942, when he pulled a ligament early in the season and was "put out of commission," as he recalled it. Not long after the injury, he saw an ad in the *Collegian* that asked anyone interested in being the Lion Mascot to see Coach Wettstone at Rec Hall for a tryout.

> I looked up Gene, who asked me if I could ride a unicycle—No! Then, he asked if I could climb a rope with my bare hands—Had the greatest difficulty with that in gym class! Well, could I do handstands—Couldn't do anything which involved getting my feet

above my head: really wasn't much of a gymnast! Well then, could I prepare an entertaining skit to do before the crowd every week. Said I was a comical engineer and I thought my crazy fraternity brothers could help me with that. He said, "O.K. you're on; no one else has applied, but you have to come up every Friday afternoon to rehearse Saturday's game's skit." I said "O.K." and that was it. The War Years had scarcities in many ways.

Ritzmann earned far more than mere accolades as the Nittany Lion—he even secured the affections of his future wife thanks to his role as the Mascot. Ritzmann says:

> During the War Years, Penn State combatted its ever decreasing enrollment by encouraging female enrollment and shortly ran out of dorm space. The College took to housing sophomore women in roominghouses in State College formerly rented to male students. In the fall of 1943 the roominghouse next to the Sigma Phi Alpha fraternity house was converted to a female student dormitory. The coed in the room directly across the side yard from my window, Barbara J. Kilbury, got my attention and asked about that lion's head gaping at her from the window sill. I was only too glad to explain, and soon had invited the entire roominghouse over for a party at the Sigma Phi Alpha house. Romance bloomed.

Miss Kilbury was the attraction that brought Ritzmann back to Penn State for the first home football game in the fall of 1944. Ensign Ritzmann was on a weekend pass from his new job at the Naval Research Laboratory in Washington, D.C.—the Navy had hired, inducted, and commissioned the entire spring 1944 class of chemical engineers. "Needless to say, the regular Navy didn't much like us. Of the twelve guys hired, ten of us had fiancées at Penn State and all we thought of was how to get a three-day pass to go back to State College."

When Ritzmann noticed the Lion was absent at the home opener in the fall of 1944, he looked for Wettstone after the game to ask why. Wettstone replied that they had decided to go without the Lion because of the scarcity of men on campus due to the war. Ritzmann volunteered to be the Lion at home games if he didn't have to rehearse the skits on Friday afternoons, and Wettstone agreed.

Ritzmann and Barbara Kilbury became engaged in December 1944 and married in June 1945. In the fall of 1945, after the war's end and a quick discharge from the Navy, Ritzmann started a graduate degree at Penn State. The three-time Mascot immediately sought out Coach Wettstone and offered to serve one more year. Wettstone replied: "By this time you know what I want, so you might as well. If only you could ride a unicycle, climb a rope, and do handstands, but the soldiers aren't quite back yet so you might as well stay on. Just continue praying for touchdowns, doing pushups for every point, and a funny skit at each game."

After serving his four shifts, Bob Ritzmann probably had more tales of weight loss and woe than any Lion before or after. He tells one that combines both elements:

Even the male cheerleaders seemed to agree that Ritzmann had a bad case of lion's breath.

> I hitchhiked to away games on Saturday morning by holding the Lion head under my arm and thumbing cars down with a big rubber thumb. I always got rides immediately and seldom missed the opening of an away game. [Once] at a Maryland homecoming game in College Park at which Penn State was trouncing Maryland, I had wandered around to the Maryland stands and looked out the side of my mouth only to see about a dozen Maryland fans jumping the fence hollering "Let's get him!" They picked me up and started to cart me off the field when about thirty campus policemen appeared and I was dropped on the ground with a big thud. I raced across the field to the Penn State stands, where Gene Wettstone said, "Take off that Lion suit." I replied, "I can't! I've got nothing on underneath but a J-strap." (It got awfully hot in that suit!) He covered me with his raincoat, and I ran off the field with the football team at the end of the game.

Ritzmann recalls an additional stunt from the early 1940s that probably contributed to the somewhat sorry look of the Mascot's suit in those days.

> [It] involved sneaking up on me from behind. . . . Someone, usually a co-ed, grabbed my tail and pulled on it. After a few jousts of this the tail came off, and I had to carry

A jaunty Lion dances to the music of the band.

> it around in my hands or over my shoulder the rest of the game. If I could catch up with the co-ed, I would flail at her with the tail, but after it was all over I'd put my arms around her and give her a big kiss. They all agreed that I had a bad case of Lion's breath. This earned me many guffaws and cat calls from the stands. Barbara got pretty good at sewing the tail back on, but not so tight that it wouldn't come off at the next game.

The night in 1943 when the CBS radio program "Vox Pop" was about to broadcast live from Rec Hall, Ritzmann was home studying. It was the custom of the show's master of ceremonies to present the hosting college with a surprise gift. Word got to Ritzmann that he was needed

Staged photograph following the "Vox Pop" presentation of the lion cub to Penn State. *Left to right:* Football Coach Bob Higgins, Park Johnson, the cub (in the interest of sequential accuracy), Aldo Cenci, and Warren Hall.

at Rec Hall—the surprise gift was to be a lion cub, and the radio program wanted to have the Mascot accept it. By the time the Lion arrived, the cub had already been presented to someone from the animal husbandry department, "much to their consternation."

A small newspaper clipping from a few days later completes the story of why Penn State never had a live lion mascot:

> A homesick baby lion went back to his mother today in Central Park Zoo, New York City. After spending three days on the Pennsylvania State College campus as mascot of the Nittany Lion athletic teams, the cub was shipped back home "to ma" when he failed to take sufficient nourishment from an eye-dropper and nursing bottle. Dr. J. F. Shigley, college veterinarian, decided it was best to send the animal back, and two veterinarians carefully caged the lion mascot and put him on the train back to New York.

Ritzmann's long-running role finally came to an end in the spring of 1946. Peter Bates shared the role during Ritzmann's last year. Ritzmann's vivid memories and wonderful stories about those times demonstrate once more that the Nittany Lion Mascot has always been a treasured contributor to Penn State's school spirit and a lifelong joy to the man inside its suit.

Bates and Ritzmann were relieved by Clark William Sharon, the last independent Lion before the Mascot became affiliated with the cheerleading squad. Sharon was a member of Delta Sigma Pi, the same fraternity to which earlier Lion George Terwilliger had belonged. Sharon's successor was Wendell O. Lomady, and Michael Kurowski would follow Lomady to close out the decade.

Special Stunts from Lomady and Bonsall

Lion Mascot Wendell O. Lomady's wonderfully musical name was not sufficient to protect him from being called "Fuzzy." Bill Bonsall, Head Cheerleader during the 1948–49 school year, remembers fondly the stunts he and "Fuzzy" cooked up for the Lion's entrances. They must have been quite spectacular, because even Coach Wettstone, who had witnessed decades of such shenanigans, recalled the stunts Lomady and Bonsall concocted as quite remarkable.

Bonsall (*left*) and Lomady (*in the suit*) performing a halftime routine.

Bonsall remembers with a rueful chuckle one that got away. It almost happened at that year's game with the University of Pennsylvania. Bonsall had secured a helicopter to hover over the field at the start of the game and directly above the automobile holding perennial U.S. presidential candidate, and Penn's president at the time, Harold Stassen. At the right moment, Lion Lomady would descend a rope ladder and land in the car seat next to Stassen. But Penn's athletic director saw the show being stolen by Penn State before the game ever started and nixed the plan. With less than two hours to go before game time, Lomady and Bonsall needed a new stunt, so they headed into the city to find what they could. That day, they rode onto the Quakers' field on a bicycle built for two: William Penn in front, the Nittany Lion in back.

Bonsall was the brains behind the outhouse stunt that Coach Wettstone also remembered fondly. Penn State's Hat Societies helped carry off some of the more complicated entrances. They had been responsible for the giant drum out of which Lomady had burst earlier in the season, but the outhouse stunt was even more elaborate. It was a work of magic, surprise, and slapstick all rolled into one. The outhouse structure was built so it could be easily reassembled,

Bill Bonsall performing without his mascot buddy.

and then was pulled apart to await its cue on Saturday. Just before the game was to start, a group of "carpenters" headed out to the middle of Beaver Field carrying boards and tools and began building a small structure. One of the carpenters was "Fuzzy" Lomady dressed in his street clothes. The Lion's suit and one additional item of clothing were taped out of sight in the small peaked roof he carried along with his hammer and nails.

As the building took shape, the audience giggles soon made it apparent that they had recognized the emerging structure—this was quite a comedown from chariots and Cadillacs! One of the carpenters slipped inside the nearly completed structure to help attach the door, while the rest continued to pound nails on the outside to ready the structure for its important halftime "mission." Few, if any, in the audience noticed that the inside man never came out during the hustle and bustle that went on to complete the outhouse. The carpenters attached their tools to their belts, inspected their work with pride, and shook hands all around. They hoisted the structure to their shoulders to carry it off the field, leaving behind a very shocked Nittany Lion sitting on a wooden bench with a giant pair of white boxer shorts around his ankles. The crowd roared its approval and then screamed with delight—until they laughed so hard they cried as Mascot Lomady attempted time after time to depart hastily from the scene of his embarrassment only to fall flat on his face, tripped up by his boxers.

Bill Bonsall summed up the goals of the stunts quite simply: "We needed to present the Lion in a different manner every week, and we needed to create a situation where the Lion wasn't seen or recognized until—BOOMBA—he was right there in the middle of the field." Bill Bonsall had been busy pleasing crowds in 1948—as an Olympic gymnast in the Summer Games in London—long before the football season arrived.

Nearly fifty years later, Bonsall remembers those days fondly and makes a special point of citing the incredible influence of Coach Gene Wettstone on collegiate gymnastics. Everyone who mentions Wettstone, in letters, articles, and interviews, speaks his name with a certain awe. And it is not the unapproachable awe of a man admired from afar, but the acknowledgment of the great and personal influence he has had on so many lives. The coach who began the Lion Mascot's second era and promoted Penn State's school spirit so effectively for thirty-eight years through gymnastics will be forever linked with the Nittany Lion.

Boomba! Wendell Lomady arrives.

Webster's defines frivology as "the act of behaving frivolously or trifling." The Nittany Lion traditionally behaves with a sense of whimsy and fun, so each one is a master of frivology.

The Lion has always had his share of female admirers.

The 1950s

John Waters opened the new decade with one year of Lion service, giving way in 1951 to Alex Gregal, a forestry major, who managed to serve three years—one shy of the record set by Bob Ritzmann. Gregal even received a special "S" (for "State," a letter awarded for athletic achievement) in recognition of his longevity and accomplishments.

One of Gregal's accomplishments was putting up with the condition of the Lion's suit. It was in horrible shape and no one could recall when it had been last replaced. Repairs were becoming necessary following every outing, as pieces of the Mascot were being left behind everywhere. The final blow came in 1952, when for the last two games of the season Penn State was represented by "a lion in sheep's clothing"—a local furrier used an old coat made

Mascot John Waters on the left, c. 1950.

Lion Alex Gregal and his friends, c. 1951.

from Asiatic sheep fur to patch the Mascot's skin in order to limp through to the season's close. A campus fund-raising campaign netted the $600 needed to replace Gregal's raggedy sheep-patched Lion suit—which was actually made of rabbit fur, a fact not readily shared with Penn State's opposing mascots.

Alfred P. Klimcke was the Lion Mascot from 1954 through 1957, the second three-year man in succession, and William P. Hillgartner covered the next year with a little help from John Behler, before Behler took over the role in 1958 to close out the decade. The All-College Cabinet had discussed creating a permanent fund to replace the Lion's suit every three years, starting with the purchase back in 1952, but by the time Behler became the Nittany Lion he was wearing a quite ratty six-year-old Lion suit, and money had to be raised for a new one once again. "Every time I take the head off, I wind up with cuts from the wire on my forehead and ears," Behler explained just before the 1958 campaign for the suit began its effort to raise $1,000.

Mascot William Hillgartner with Frothy and a seemingly stubborn mule, c. 1958.

Jack Behler had the distinction of being the last Lion Mascot to wear a suit of animal skin, and he still has the paws he once wore. Fortunately, despite the retiring of the warmer suits, the "Lion Game Day Diet" stories easily jumped over to the modern, synthetic suit era. Behler also claimed the largest single-day weight loss: 20 pounds. He left that game in an ambulance.

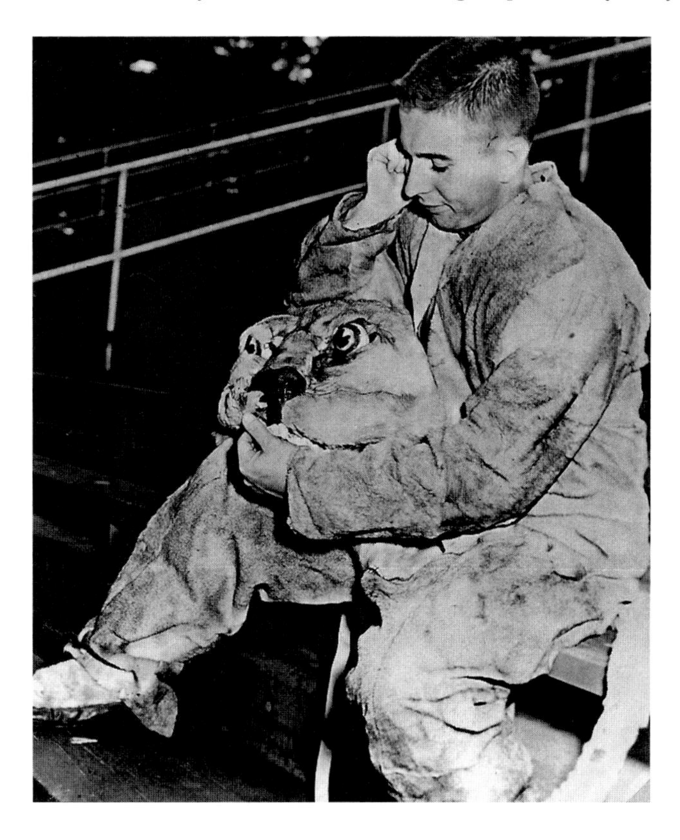

Jack Behler contemplates the sad condition of the Lion Suit.

Penn State's football program was growing and attracting national attention under Coach Charles "Rip" Engle during the 1950s. It was the period when Penn State rose to become the most consistently powerful college football team in the East. It was also the time when some of the antics and skits used to entertain the crowds during the pre-game warm-ups and at halftime were called into question. The cheerleaders lost their cannon, and for a while the Nittany Lion lost his props. The more elaborate skits soon appeared only at pep rallies. The football field became a more serious place.

"Frothy," the irreverent jester mascot of the student humor magazine *Froth*, had caused trouble once too often, according to the administration, and during Behler's stint as the Lion was banned from the football field. "Frothy is a tremendous help to me," Behler said. "What can I do without him but stand around on the field looking like a tradition." Poor Jack Behler's suit was falling apart, his props had been taken away, and he had lost his Mascot friend. One wouldn't expect him to look back on his Mascot days as rosy, but he does. He got the new suit, thought up new things to do on the field, and recovered from the loss of "Frothy" by spending more time with the cheerleaders.

Today, whenever talk turns to Penn State and mention is made of Behler's former role as the Nittany Lion Mascot, people are always delighted and impressed. His wife and one of their seven children once considered making buttons that read "Ask me for my autograph. My Dad was the Nittany Lion" because people's responses would be

Lion Behler pokes fun at the West Virginia Mountaineers.

Rip Engle took the football program to new heights.

The "Triumvirate of Pep": The Lion, Frothy, and the Cheerleader.

so much fun to witness. In a loving tribute to her husband, Marianne Behler wrote: "Jack Behler is Penn State, and I think Penn State represents much of what is still good and all right with the world. I'm sure this sounds a little corny. Not even his children know how through Penn State he was shaped to become the great father and leader he is. Everyone who truly knows him admires him for everything he stands for, everything that is so Penn State."

The Quiet Start of Something Big

John Waters was the twelfth Lion Mascot when former Brown University Coach Rip Engle faced his opening season as Penn State's football coach in 1950. That autumn, Waters roamed a football field that had one other new face from Brown pacing the sidelines. Rip Engle had talked his successful senior quarterback into deferring his law school plans to serve as his assistant coach at the Pennsylvania State College. The new assistant coach was barely a year older than many of the players, but he was a determined young man. No one, not even that new assistant coach himself, could have predicted that half a century later Joe Paterno would still be pacing those sidelines for Penn State.

A coaching reputation based on football victories and bowl trips might be enough for many schools, but Joe Paterno became college football's most outstanding coach because of the things he did in addition to winning football games. His players graduated and were successes in life after college in whatever field they chose. A commitment to the academic side of college life would always be more important to Coach Paterno than any football play or game or season. Watch Joe Paterno at the conclusion of a hard-fought bowl victory, and you will see a happy man, but watch him talking about the importance of Penn State's libraries, for instance, and you can see absolute joy.

Before the end of the twentieth century, Penn State will recognize the Paterno family's commitment and devotion to the University Libraries by naming the new library addition at University Park in their honor. Joe Paterno's standards of academic and athletic excellence, and the exposure Penn State has received through his work, have helped make the Nittany Lion one of the most positive and recognizable University symbols in the United States.

Joe Paterno as a quarterback at Brown University in 1949. Most Penn State fans can hardly remember the time before he arrived.

Oregon cheerleaders Nancy Coffen and Bunny Dean rub behind the Nittany Lion's ears during a lull in the Liberty Bowl activities—or were they attempting to bury the atrocious-looking suit worn by Jack Lesyk?

The 1960s

Even the first name remained the same as Jack Lesyk followed his fraternity brother Jack Behler as Mascot for the 1960–61 academic year. Lesyk's first memory of the suit was its incredible weight at the audition. He had heard that men who wore glasses were automatically disqualified for the role, so Lesyk's audition was only the first of many occasions that year where the new Mascot misjudged distances on the gym floor or football field without his much-needed spectacles. Lesyk was certain that his height helped him get the role. Contrary to the days of Leon Skinner's 6-foot frame filling out the suit, Lesyk's 5 feet, 5½ inches were far better suited to what had become a much smaller costume by the late 1950s.

Jack Lesyk's scariest moment as Mascot was discovering that the Army mascot, a real mule, didn't much care for humans in lion suits and had no fear of Pennsylvania's king of beasts. The Nittany Lion's only sanctuary that fateful game was discovering that mules don't climb stadium stairs willingly, even when in hot pursuit of their enemy.

In those days, the Nittany Lion Mascots were often helpful in providing their own replacements by encouraging a fraternity brother to apply and that was exactly how Lesyk found

Dr. Jekyll (Paul Seltzer) and Mr. Hyde, as depicted in a Beaver Stadium Pictorial.

himself at the audition. Sometimes the next Lion even got a little practice the year before his audition, by subbing for his brother Mascot. Jeff Knorr was another Theta Xi fraternity member who saw some Nittany Lion experience during Lesyk's year, but he elected not to apply for the Mascot job in the spring of 1961.

Jack Lesyk was followed by a mystery Lion—the unknown mascot. Lesyk doesn't remember who replaced him, and Paul Seltzer doesn't remember who preceded him. The head cheerleader at the time doesn't remember, either. Unfortunately, no one ever kept an official Lion Mascot record or list, especially after the Mascot became such a regular fixture. Several individuals may have known who each Lion was *when* he was the Lion, but constructing a historical record of *all* previous Lions proved quite difficult. Often the only record available is a single mention of a Mascot's name in a newspaper article or *La Vie* caption. Even a page-by-page perusal of every issue of the *Daily Collegian* that academic year does not provide an answer.

Paul Seltzer may not recall who immediately preceded him, but he does remember being the Lion—and enjoying it. A Beta Theta Pi, he knew Gene Wettstone's son, also a Beta. When

Trading Mascot secrets—the West Virginia Mountaineer and Paul Seltzer.

Seltzer didn't make the cheerleading squad, Wettstone offered him the Mascot position. In addition to the fun parts, Mascot Seltzer found himself getting lectured occasionally for "behavior unbecoming a lion" (or perhaps those *were* the fun parts?). One Gator Bowl incident found the Mascot getting a little too frisky with Miss America—he pretended to bite her "on the seat." Another habit that got him in trouble was his love of tackling. At one game, the Nittany Lion tackled a referee, and after one Penn State loss to Navy at home in 1964, Seltzer delivered the latest hit that quarterback Roger Staubach ever received. The Mascot sacked the opposing quarterback off-campus several hours after the game! Despite his occasional lapses in tackling judgment, Paul Seltzer served ably from 1962 through the spring of 1965.

In an interesting turn of events, the Lion Mascot that followed Seltzer was also unknown, but this time by choice. He wanted to perform anonymously. This mystery Lion vowed he would hide his identity "unless he successfully made an over-the-head shot at a basketball game." Two years later Marty Serota's identity was finally revealed. He never made that shot, but he thought fans should know who that "masked lion" had been before he graduated. Another spin to the story had Serota going public because the *Collegian* was about to divulge his identity.

Serota managed to serve two years without ever getting caught headless. Although Lion push-ups have been a long-running Penn State football tradition, some credit Serota with initiating the push-ups for every point on the scoreboard tradition that dominated the Mascot's performance for many years.

The anonymous Lion, Marty Serota. He didn't reveal his identity until a *Daily Collegian* article forced him to.

Serota unveiled.

The Mascot twirls his baton.

Danny Kohlhepp and Dave Lacey were the next two Lions, both serving double terms. Kohlhepp and Lacey each experienced something during one of their Mascot years that no Lion had yet experienced. They were the respective Nittany Lions for Penn State's back-to-back undefeated and untied football seasons in 1968 and 1969. The last such season had been 1912, a decade before the first Lion Mascot, Androcles's old friend, Dick Hoffman.

Lacey closed out the decade and went one year into the 1970s, calling his time in the suit "the best job I ever had . . . really a lot of fun." In a 1970 interview Lacey felt a need to justify his role as the Lion and put in a plug for the importance of school spirit. Despite the previous two years of undefeated football, it was not the easiest time to be the school mascot on any college campus:

Lion Danny Kohlhepp and the Penn State Cheerleaders.

Although the occasional human body part peaks out (see nose in mouth!), the suit masks the man, thereby setting the Lion free to perform without inhibition.

> I try to please myself and do what the students and alums like. I feel that if I don't let myself down I won't let them down. . . . There was a time when I thought the cheerleaders didn't help the team. But now I think I accomplish something. We keep the crowd going, and I know that's important to the teams. . . . If more people laughed, got along, slapped each other on the back, a lot of our problems might be solved. If I can do that, if I can make people laugh and forget about their trouble for a little while, then maybe I have [helped] solve some of these problems.

Mascott Dave Lacey revs up the crowd at a Penn State football game.

10

The Men in the Suit, 1970 to the Present

The 1970s

David Brazet followed Dave Lacey in 1971 and was himself replaced by Jim Schaude. Schaude had been the "alternate" Lion when he received the call to step up to the Mascot's role. "When I first came to Penn State, I tried to think of a way I could contribute to the school and still have some fun. . . . I decided the Nittany Lion job would be perfect."

Bob Welsh became the Lion in 1973 for two years of service. During the first year, his alternate, Sam Mirachi, actually got to perform at a couple of football games—a rare treat for the largely unrecognized "backup" mascots. (Today, the alternate or backup to the Lion Mascot is chosen from the cheerleading squad.) In an unusual twist of fate, Mirachi may be the only Lion ever to have gained weight during a football game. Feigning a faint following a Pitt touchdown, Mirachi fell into a puddle of water and found that a wet Lion weighs far more than a dry one.

Judy Windsor and Lion Dave Brazet as they appeared on a 1971 *Town & Gown* cover. The Lion's mane seems to have grown, just like the rest of the hair in the 1960s.

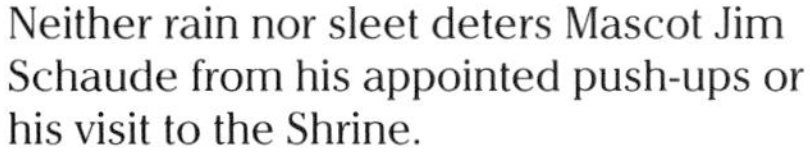

Neither rain nor sleet deters Mascot Jim Schaude from his appointed push-ups or his visit to the Shrine.

All the Nittany Lions receive a lot of attention, but Bob Welsh's personality as the Mascot seemed particularly magnetic. In addition to his larger-than-life antics on the athletic fields and courts, Welsh also developed a following in the philanthropic community. This Lion was as likely to be found at a State College charity function as in Beaver Stadium. In recognition of his community service, Bob Welsh received the first annual Barash Award for Human Service in 1975. The award was established by the family of the late Sy Barash to recognize a full-time member of the faculty, staff, or student body of the University who had "contributed most, apart from regular duties, to human causes, public service activities and organizations, or the welfare of fellow humans."

Once described by a Cotton Bowl official as the best mascot in the entire nation, Welsh "cavorts from kickoff to the final gun as if the outcome of the game depended solely on his enthusiasm." Welsh described his philosophy: "I feel that my main purpose is to stimulate that crowd for Penn State, and we're going to win if I have to tie the opposition's shoelaces together."

Welsh discovered what most Mascots have known and attempted to explain, that there was something liberating about putting on that suit and disappearing into that head. Just like his famous pre-game phone booth entrance, one minute Bob Welsh was a student, the 142-pound wrestler on Penn State's team, and then—Shazam—Lion Mascot. He's directing the Blue Band, running into the stands to wake up a quiet section, dancing with the cheerleaders, and doing those cumulative push-ups. When Penn State beat Virginia 62–14 in 1973, that added up to more than 300 push-ups. Welsh's fraternity had an interesting post-game ritual that must have delighted the Mascot on days when Penn State won big: he had to do an additional 100 push-ups while his fraternity brothers sang the fight song, "Hail to the Lion."

Following Bob Welsh was not going to be easy for the next Mascot. Fortunately, the next Mascot didn't have time to think about it. Injured at wrestling practice, Welsh asked his fraternity brother Andy Bailey if he would sub for him at the send-off pep rally for the 1975 Cotton Bowl. Bailey squeezed into the little suit and had a ball. He couldn't stop thinking about how much fun it had been, so he went to the spring tryout. When Bailey's name was announced as the new Mascot, he recalled, "I was stunned. In exhilaration I threw down my coat, and then promptly

Top: In spite of his grueling schedule, Mascot Bob Welsh found time for his visit to the Shrine.

Middle and bottom: Welsh, the 142-pound wrestler—and then (Shazam!) Lion Mascot.

Lion Andy Bailey and his fan club surround the Shrine.

tripped over it to get forward to shake hands. I couldn't imagine the thoughts going through onlookers' minds as they saw me falling all over my own feet. It wouldn't be the last time."

Bob Welsh had ordered a new Lion suit before departing, so his successor would start the year with a fresh look. But whoever designed the new head must not have been attending Penn State games with any regularity. Sure, there had always been a bit of mane fringing the Nittany Lion's head, but this new mane was a radical departure from the Pennsylvania mountain lion look. As alumnus Albert Buono (Class of 1932) put it, "The Lion's head was 'Africanus' instead of 'Mount Nittanicus.' "

The retro hairstyle was quite a shock to the fans, as well as to the new Lion. *Collegian* reporter Cathy Cipolla wrote: "The Nittany Lion seemed strange too. He still clowned around the way the old mascot did, but he has a different face—with a fierce expression and big sharp teeth. He's lost that lovable sheepish look." Bailey recalls: "She was right! At the opening game against Temple at Franklin Field, more toddlers cried when their parents motioned me over to them than ever before or after! Moreover, I can vividly remember a woman who screamed at the hotel when she saw me start to enter the elevator she was riding."

The new head lasted one more game until it was forever banned. There would be no sharp teeth or frightening expressions or hairy manes for the Nittany Lion, ever again.

Mascot Bailey with his littlest fans.

Andy Bailey's "Lion Game Day Diet" story was the 10 pounds lost during one of those summery September outings at Beaver Stadium. His favorite Lion skit was performed at the 1976 North Carolina State game.

> Right before the players charged onto the field, a group of young men dressed up as NC State students carried a large wooden crate onto the field. On both sides of the box were the words "Danger—NC State Wolfpack." As they were walking away from the crate the P.A. announcer said, "Ladies and gentlemen, somehow N.C. State University has sent their Wolfpack to Beaver Stadium. Please stay away from the crate!" I ran over to the crate, inspected it, and just as I began to peek inside, I was pulled into the crate by my scarf with the spring-latched door closing behind me. As I was in the crate, the P.A. system was filled with the familiar sound of the Lion. The crate was rocking back and forth. When the sound stopped, I emerged from the crate with four German Shepherd puppies—representing the Wolfpack—on leashes. The fans' response was a collective "Awwwwww" with subsequent applause.

Andy Bailey was the Lion for the very special event of honoring Nittany Lion sculptor Heinz Warneke, on November 8, 1975. He recalled:

> Prior to the game, [the Warnekes] attended a brunch at the President's mansion. I was always invited to these pre-game brunches and was looking forward to meeting Heinz and his wife. What an honor! Unfortunately, when he and his wife first laid eyes on me at this affair, they almost ran out of the room in fear. I had never seen anyone react quite the way they did to the Lion and felt really awful about it. At the half-time of the game, John Oswald introduced Heinz to the fans. I ran up to Heinz just about

the time John finished his introduction. When he saw me, he had a much different countenance than he had during the brunch. He was all smiles. He placed his left arm around me and we both waved to the crowd. It was a great honor to be a part of that, and I think about it when I see the Nittany Lion Shrine.

Bailey had five guiding principles for his Lion behavior, on and off the field:

> First, tailor your activities to what is happening on the field and try to be as close to the action as possible; second, appear tireless and keep in perpetual motion; third, constantly look for opportunities to excite or to entertain the crowd; fourth, demonstrate class whenever [wearing] the suit; and fifth, never say no to any invitation to a worthy cause.

Bailey voiced the feelings of all former Mascots in the conclusion of his brief memoir:

> My two-plus years as the Lion were without question some of the most enjoyable and memorable years of my life. I consider myself to be very lucky to have had the opportunity to represent Penn State as the Lion Mascot. My hope is that all future generations of Mascots maintain the reputation and unique personality of the Lion and that the traditions that were established well before my time will remain. And speaking of maintaining traditions—hey, Penn State, how about giving me an opportunity to be an Assistant Coach of the Nittany Lion? I will work for free—tickets, that is!

Cliff Fiscus took over the reins from Andy Bailey in 1977. He recalls that his interest in becoming the Lion nearly became an obsession. He was so nervous after the tryouts that "I started hearing things, I actually heard the phone ringing when it wasn't." When the call finally came telling Fiscus he

Lion Cliff Fiscus in an unusual studio shot.

had been chosen as the Lion, he was speechless. His mother's reaction a short while later was to burst into tears, dry them, and then start sewing Cliff's little brother his own Lion suit.

Spontaneity was the Fiscus key to successful performing. His favorite part of being the Lion was making people laugh, and his fondest memory was the reaction of the children he met at the Special Olympics at Penn State. He had an especially hard time remaining dry-eyed during the playing of the "Star-Spangled Banner" at that event.

Norm

It is difficult to single out any one Nittany Lion Mascot from among the wonderful, caring men who have worn the suit, entertained the crowds, and had such a positive effect on so many people, but if the Mascots started a Hall of Fame, they would pick Norm Constantine as the first member.

Norm Constantine dreamt of playing football for Penn State, but in his freshman year he realized that his athletic ability would not allow for that leap from the high school game to the college game. Instead, he began to watch the Mascot and started a new dream. Constantine won the Mascot role in his junior year by out-auditioning sixty other candidates, and soon after that he began his daily regimen of 600 push-ups (not all at one time!).

Norm Constantine was an exceptional Lion, for all the traditional Mascot reasons—and for something more. Like many Mascots, he was fun and funny. He allowed that suit to release any inhibitions he may have had as a young man so he could carry the crowds to new heights of school spirit,

In addition to football, the Nittany Lion is also a strong presence at both men's and women's basketball games.

but he also expanded the role of the Nittany Lion as far as he could. "One thing I want to do while I'm the Lion," he said, "is to show up at more of the less popular sports."

> I'm the mascot for *all* the teams, no matter how small, and it's my responsibility to support them all. Like, for example, this week I went to a girls fencing match. There were maybe 15 spectators there, at the most, and they couldn't believe that the Lion would come to something like that. It's a great morale booster for the team and the people watching.

Nittany Lion Norm Constantine strikes a familiar pose.

Many Nittany Lion Mascots find themselves in an important social service role while they are wearing the suit. They become important crowd-pleasers at the fund-raising events that are so critical to the success of many social service agencies. Norm Constantine knew how to work the crowd and deliver an excited audience, whether it was a football game, a wrestling meet, or a dinner, but he also knew how to touch individual lives. He had a rare ability to spend a few moments with people at games and events where the shake of a paw or the glance of an eye could convince those he met that the Nittany Lion Mascot actually cared for them. Norm did care.

His love of working with children was well known long before his Mascot years, but the Lion suit added a new dimension. One of his dormitory neighbors reported: "If Norm doesn't have anything else to do, he'll slip into his Lion costume and take to the streets downtown, shaking hands with kids, making people smile. He's totally involved in his role. . . . The happier Norm can make you, the happier he is."

Norm Constantine made extra time for people with disabilities. He always greeted the folks in the wheelchair section before the game began and tried hard to imagine their lives. Once,

Mascot Constantine visits with a young friend during a charity event.

he spent an entire day as a wheelchair-using Lion, "to publicize the difficulties the people with physical disadvantages had performing daily tasks that most of us took for granted."

In 1980, Norm Constantine earned his bachelor of science degree in recreation and parks, with an emphasis on therapeutic recreation for the mentally retarded and physically handicapped. Throughout his college years he worked in group homes for the retarded and the disabled and spent summers working at Easter Seals camps. Along the way he learned sign language and taught martial arts to people in wheelchairs. Norm Constantine was constantly striving to reach and help people.

Following graduation, Constantine took a job as a recreational therapist for the United Cerebral Palsy Association of Philadelphia. He also became area coordinator for the Special Olympics and was active with the Delaware Valley Wheelchair Sports Association. But he was most proud of his role as originator and coordinator of the Philadelphia Community Adapted Games Festival. His goal for the Festival was "to create an atmosphere where the disabled and the able-bodied could interact, play, and learn about themselves and each other—an atmosphere where differences would vanish and acceptance might begin."

Norm Constantine elected to serve people's needs both in and out of the Lion Mascot suit, but he was especially generous to those who needed him most. Early in the morning of October 17, 1981, just one month after the Adapted Games Festival, Constantine left a friend's party and was about to get into his car. A still-unidentified driver traveling down the street sideswiped the two cars parked behind his and then hit Norm. He was thrown 35 feet. Norm Constantine's head injuries kept him in a coma for the next seven months and in a wheelchair for the rest of his short life. He would never walk or speak again, but his will to survive would provide a constant inspiration to all who have faced the insurmountable. The young man who had cared for so many would now require constant care to get through each day. The Mascot who could communicate so easily to thousands of people at once now needed to point to letters on an alphabet board to form his words.

Norm Constantine returned to Beaver Stadium one last time following his accident. It was for the West Virginia game in 1989. During halftime, while the Blue Band played "Hail to the Lion," people stood and cheered as Norm accepted $15,000 raised in his name by "Back the Lions" for the creation of a scholarship for the Lion Mascots.

> When the helicopter approached and circled the stadium, an unbelievable hush fell over the crowd—a very unique occurrence for the eighty-thousand-plus passionate Penn State fans in attendance on that or any other football Saturday. When Norman actually came onto the field that day . . . 80,000 plus individuals came together, on their feet, with tears in their eyes and lumps in their throats, celebrating together the devotion and love for Penn State that Norm exhibited. Norman, as both the Nittany Lion Mascot and as an individual, represented the University as well as anybody could.

Norm Constantine died on July 18, 1990, the same month and year that the Americans with Disabilities Act was signed into law. The epitaph on his gravestone reads:

> The Lion is, beyond dispute,
> Allow'd the majestic brute;
> His valour and his generous mind
> Prove him superior of his kind.
>
> The lion is laid down
> beside the lamb.

In 1995, Harriet May Savitz's biography *Remembering Norm: A Victim's Story* was published. In her moving tribute, Norm Constantine's life is defined and celebrated through the positive effect he had on so many of the lives he touched. The Norm Constantine Scholarship Fund for the Nittany Lion Mascots surpassed $100,000 in September 1995, and Norm's devoted parents, Cy and Eleanor Constantine, accepted the continuing memorial to their son in a moving ceremony at Beaver Stadium.

Debbie Slavin, in the Suit, is the first woman to try out for the Mascot's role.

The 1980s

The decade of the 1980s opened with the first woman candidate for the Mascot position. Debbie Slavin said, "I don't look at the Nittany Lion as a male/female position. I look at it as a job to do. I would just want to do it because I thought I was the best person for it, not for any other reasons."

Someday the Mascot gender barrier may be broken, but the position has remained the province of men throughout the 1980s and well into the 1990s, most serving two-year terms. Roy Scott followed Norm Constantine, and Scott was followed by David Dailey, who had lived in State College from the age of 2 and remembered watching Lion Mascots from age 5 on. "I'm quiet and controlled without the suit," Dailey said at the time, "but when I get it on, I just let loose."

> Once I realized no one knew who I was underneath the suit I could go out and go crazy, ham it up. . . . It's almost as though I have a split personality now. . . . I'm filling awfully big shoes; I'm following awfully good lions. And every time I put the suit on I've got to remember I'm representing the University. I hope I can keep up the traditions.

Roy Scott hears the good news—he will be the next Lion Mascot!

Ever versatile, ever musical, the Nittany Lion is everywhere.

Perennial cheerleaders Henry Blankenbiller and Lee Fencil, both Class of 1928, led the team onto the field at the 1982 Penn State–Temple game. Lion Dave Dailey joins them.

Dailey's "daily" exercise program consisted of 300 to 400 push-ups, running two to three miles, and lifting weights—all that in addition to workouts with the cheerleading squad. Robert Sterling took his turn as the Mascot following Dailey and remembers Lady Lion basketball most fondly. Without a long history of Lion appearances at their games, the Lady Lions and their fans were especially appreciative of the Mascot's support. During Sterling's tenure, Andy Bailey also made one last "reappearance" in the suit. The football team was about to be sent off to the 1985 Orange Bowl contest against Oklahoma when Sterling became ill and Bailey stepped in to save the day at the Harrisburg Airport pep rally.

Rob Sterling rouses the crowd in his continuing role as "Cowbell Man."

Life After Being the Lion

Even the Penn State Blue Band enjoyed Rob Sterling's regular presence at the women's basketball games—they gave Sterling a small cowbell to serve as the Mascot's very own musical instrument. Little did the band members suspect that a serious habit would be set in motion with that innocent gift. Sterling's use of the cowbell at basketball games ended when he took off the Suit for the final time, or so he thought.

Rob Sterling was always an antsy guy, but he was having a great deal of trouble at Penn State football games in particular. The man who once could roam the stands at will in the guise of a Lion and rouse the crowd anytime he felt like it was having a hard time sitting still and simply cheering. He needed something extra to recapture that old excitement, and he found it at the Rutgers game in 1991. Way up in the middle of the sky, the newly completed section of stands at Beaver Stadium was just begging for something raucous, and Sterling happened to be sitting there with twenty-nine of his friends.

That game saw the initial transformation of the former Nittany Lion Mascot into his popular incarnation, "Cowbell Man," and the crowds went wild. So popular has Cowbell Man become at football games that the athletic department asked Sterling if he wouldn't mind taking his instrument and enthusiasm to basketball games at the Bryce Jordan Center. Is it only a coincidence that both the men's and women's basketball teams had remarkable seasons in 1995–96—the first year of his return to the court?

In real life, Penn State's Cowbell Man sells veterinary pharmaceuticals for a living, including one product that actually has a picture of a lion on the package: a de-wormer!

Mascot Rob Sterling in the typical blanket trajectory position—soaring.

Doug Skinner joined the Nittany Lion Mascot ranks in 1986. After his first football season, Skinner commented: "I really enjoy my privacy. I was always the kind to stay in the background, and I never liked to be the center of attention, and now I am. But I don't look at it as Doug being the center of attention, but the lion. I like being unknown. It's like Clark Kent."

During his first summer as the Lion, Skinner had a chance to attend Mascot summer camp. Instead of beating up on each other, the seventy Mascots in attendance worked on prearranging the matchups they would face during the upcoming season. "What we usually do is say, 'Okay, you come down to my end and let me get the best of you, and I'll come down to your end and you get the best of me.' Most of the time it works. You don't want to embarrass the other mascot because it shines on your school." It still boiled down to planning out the skits and gimmicks ahead of time, but this way the other mascot knew the part he should play as well.

Skinner also addressed the Mascot legacy on that day in the late autumn of his first Lion year: "Every lion . . . wants to leave [people] thinking you're the best. You want to do everything [the other Lions] did well, and you also want to put in a new wrinkle that people will remember, something that you started." It is that accumulating list of "prior Lions' skills," with an original trick added every year, that makes each new Mascot's role a greater challenge than the last.

Peter Garland took over from Doug Skinner in 1988. Upon learning he had been chosen, he gave his reason for wanting to be the Nittany Lion: "I love Penn State, and this is a way for me to give something back to the school that has given so much to me."

Mascot Pete Garland performing at both football and basketball games.

Lion Doug Skinner appeals to a higher power for baskets.

Raising the flag for Penn State's teams.

The 1990s

Todd Shilkret, the first 1990s Mascot, once said, "The Lion is the most recognized symbol of Penn State, so everything that the Lion does must project the University." It seems the Nittany Lion Mascots have grown increasingly aware of the powerful image they portray and its effect on how Penn State is perceived. Fortunately for all Penn Staters, that awareness has not stopped the Mascots from delivering the fun that fans have come to expect.

Gene Wettstone is one of a number of Penn State faithful who claim that from 1991 through 1993 the Nittany Lion was exceedingly adept at delivering fun. "Tim Durant was the greatest Lion I ever saw," says Wettstone. Because the only Lions Wettstone had never seen perform were Hoffman and Skinner, from the 1920s, his praise for Durant is high indeed.

Tim Durant's goal for a football Saturday was "to get the stadium rockin!" When he put on the suit, he said, "I become a different person. I like hamming it up for the fans, and I get shivers down my spine." Durant kept fit as the Lion by lifting weights and doing push-ups—a good thing, since he had to do 516 in the 1991 Cincinnati game. In 1992 alone Mascot Durant made more than 250 appearances in the suit. "Almost every day I have to remind myself that I am a student first and the Lion second."

Ricky Williams followed Tim Durant in 1993 and served through the spring of 1995. The Mascot's role is not an easy one, but Williams is one more Lion in a long, long line who acknowledges how much the experience has meant in his life and how important the Mascot is in the lives of others. In a *Town & Gown* interview Williams said: "At my first football game, the crowd was passing me up through the stands and I got dropped . . . right down on the seats. A little while later, I'm thinking, 'Why do I put myself through this?' But every time I see a kid smile, it's worth it."

Williams believed that improvisation was crucial to his approach to being the Lion: "Most other teams' mascots come to the games with all their moves pre-planned. I just do what comes to my mind. It doesn't matter how much you prepare, because you never know what can happen at a game. Whenever I put on the suit, I feel like I'm a completely different person—I'm the Lion! If my friends scream 'Ricky' during a game, I don't think they're talking to me. The suit acts as kind of an alter ego." Ricky Williams was the first African American student to be the Nittany Lion Mascot.

Brad Cornali followed Ricky Williams for a one-year hitch from the spring of 1995 until the Blue-White game of 1996. Cornali holds the distinction of being the first Lion Mascot to have benefited from a full scholarship thanks to the Norm Constantine Fund. He was also the first Lion to emerge from the ROTC program. Cornali summed up the rules for being the Lion quite simply: Observe the traditions and don't do anything to embarrass the University. He was surprised by the latitude the Lion is given in interpreting the Mascot role, but he appreciated the creativity that required from him. "I have always been a showboat. I like to be in the spotlight. . . . I have always been kind of crazy and off the wall [and] from my freshman year, friends were saying I'd make a great Lion."

Mascot Tim Durant, named by Gene Wettstone as the "best Lion ever."

Lion Ricky Williams with President and Mrs. Joab Thomas at the Alumni Association's 125th Anniversary Gala, where Williams was made a lifetime member of the Association.

The traditions and rules for the Nittany Lion Mascot *are* very simple. The reigning traditions in the 1990s include ear-rubbing, Lion-passing from fan to fan, push-ups, and an ever-changing assortment of on-field antics with the cheerleaders, the Blue Band, and the fans. The Lion's overarching goals are to entertain and to gather every ounce of school spirit from the Penn State crowd so it can be used to deliver thunderbolts of support for Penn State's athletic teams. The few "rules" or guidelines the Mascot follows are:

- Practice with the cheerleaders at two practices a week
- When in uniform, keep the head on whenever possible and remain silent
- Appear at football and basketball games, other sports' NCAA and Big 10 tournaments, and other sports/events as schedule allows
- Maintain a 2.5 grade point average
- Represent the University in the best possible manner

Nannette Sheaffer, Cheerleading Advisor and head of the Mascot Search Committee, knows well that the toughest part about being the Nittany Lion is not necessarily the required creativity: "The demand on [the Mascot's] time is terrible, terrible. It takes a special person to be the Nittany Lion." Cornali agreed that the schedule was the biggest challenge, but added, "Why wouldn't you want to be the Nittany Lion?"

The fact that the Lion gets no special parking privileges may come as a surprise to Penn State fans, but the Mascot's biggest challenge often comes from the split-second timing it takes to go from class to event to class without the benefit of a legal place to park. If ever a Penn State "official" deserved a floating permit, the Lion probably ranks the highest in need.

PENN STATE
44
LIONS

Staying Lean

In addition to the traditional weight loss caused by the suit, Brad Cornali's typical football game-day schedule reveals the second major reason some Lions are so lean:

8:00 A.M.	Get up and skip breakfast (!)
9:30 to 11:00 A.M.	President's Tailgate and Alumni Association Tailgate and Bookstore Appearance
11:00 A.M.	Warm-up on field (skip lunch!)
12 noon to 4:00 P.M.	Football game (Think of the calories expended here!)
4:00 to 4:30 P.M.	(May consider light dinner if time)
4:30 to 7:00 P.M.	Travel to next event and perform, e.g., volleyball game
7:00 P.M.	Home (Eat!)

The ever-popular crowd pass finds Mascot Brad Cornali traveling up toward the rim of Beaver Stadium.

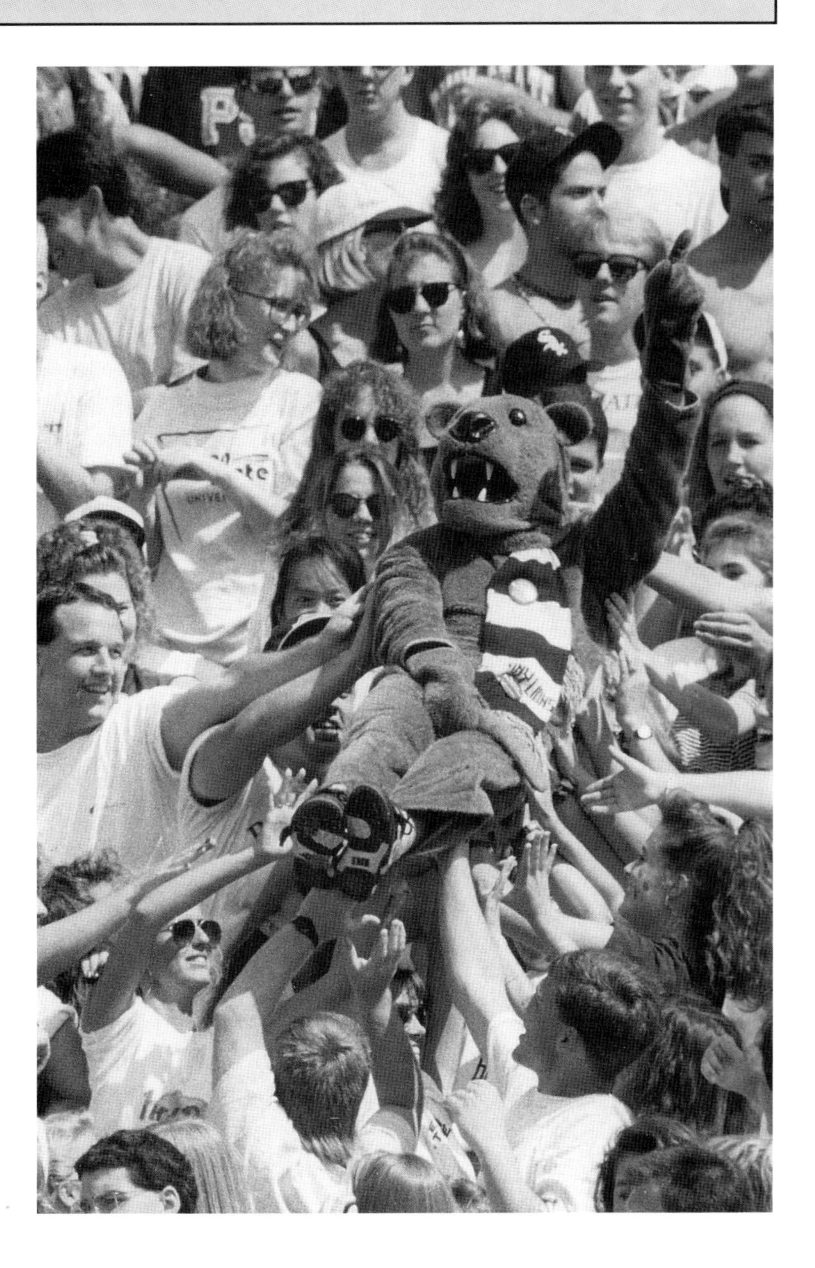

Clap those hands and make some noise, Penn State!

In one of the last basketball games played at Rec Hall, Lion Cornali proves just as adept at coming down.

As with all his predecessors, and despite the grueling schedule, Brad Cornali had no regrets about being the Nittany Lion. He danced and spoofed and tumbled his way into the hearts of Penn State fans everywhere. One of Brad Cornali's last official acts as the Nittany Lion was a bittersweet one. He helped choose the person who would take his place in the Suit.

The Audition

When the call goes out for a new Mascot in the spring, there is usually no shortage of applicants for the job, despite the grueling schedule, the threat of hundreds of push-ups, and the occasional botched blanket toss. The number of candidates who attended the initial informational meeting had been easily topping 50 for years, often approaching 100 applicants for most of the 1990s, but the spring of 1996 saw a dramatic decline in Lion aspirants to less than two dozen. Perhaps the Mascot's reputation for hard work had finally become a deterrent, or perhaps it was the popularity of Brad Cornali's humorous dance pieces. Watching Mascots perform can create a classic approach-avoidance situation: "My, that looks like fun. I want to do that myself" versus "My, that looks like fun. I could never do that."

When the applicants gathered one evening in early April 1996 to hear what being the Nittany Lion Mascot was all about, Nannette Sheaffer was politely frank. She explained that it was a tough job with a difficult schedule and that everything the Lion did reflected on the University. It was a huge responsibility. Brad Cornali spoke next and was blunt about the work, the importance of the image, but also the glory. Everyone attending could see what being the Lion meant to Cornali. There was an unstated pride in the way he stood, even out of the Suit. His tone in protecting the Mascot image was like that of a big brother letting the neighborhood kids know that they would have to deal with him if the Lion's image was tarnished. Even with the tough talk, everyone present filled out the Mascot application. All had passed the first test: the Lion Mascot cannot scare too easily.

The applications were scrutinized by the selection committee and whittled down to the ten who were invited to interview for the position. The same committee, which included the Cheerleading Advisor, the Cheerleading Coach, other coaches and members of the athletic administration, and two community representatives, as well as the outgoing Lion in an ex officio role, conducted the interviews. They had all the appearances of classic job interviews, except for those extraordinary questions that might tip off an observer that this was no ordinary job.

Questions were asked about physical fitness (those pesky push-ups!), the lyrics of a certain Alma Mater, favorite sports, recent Penn State athletic events attended, and the applicant's schedule for the school year. "What would you do if taunted or attacked by an opposing team's fans?" was a great open-ended question that measured how applicants perceived the Lion's role, how quickly they thought on their feet, and how creative they were in solving problems.

Probably the best question of all was easy to ask and incredibly difficult to answer: "What would be most important to you in your role as the Mascot: tradition or innovation?" And the question least likely to occur at any other job interview in the world required the applicant to choose which he or she thought would be the best role model for the Lion Mascot: the personality of a certain public television purple dinosaur, or the personality of a gang of sewer-dwelling adolescent reptiles fond of martial arts and pizza.

Nine of the ten selected candidates chose to follow through with the interviews late that Wednesday afternoon. At the conclusion of the interview sessions, four names were chosen to advance to the next round: an audition in the Mascot's suit. The four finalists were delighted to find their names posted in Rec Hall that Thursday. They were one step closer to something they all had been dreaming about for months, and some had been thinking about this moment for years.

Nancy Barrett was an accounting major leaning toward a minor in exercise and sports science and about to close out her sophomore year. In preparation for her interview, she had studied up on Nittany Lion Mascot history at the University archives and worked out diligently for six months in preparation for the tryout. Barrett was waiting with a gleam in her eye for the one-armed push-up question she knew was coming. The committee declined to witness a demonstration during the interview, but Barrett would have a chance to do fifty push-ups

Nancy Barrett was one of the four finalists for the 1996–97 Mascot role, the first woman to make the final cut. In addition to doing one-arm push-ups, Barrett competes as a pentathlete in her spare time.

that Sunday. For the first time in Mascot history a woman had become a true contender for the Mascot's role, and Nancy Barrett was more than ready to take the final step.

Scott Gaston was a civil engineering major ready to begin his senior year, and he wanted to spend it as the Lion. On his application, Gaston offered his skills at stilt-walking and guitar playing as two possible improvements he might make in the Lion's routines—all applicants had to answer that immodest question. Gaston called the Nittany Lion "the extra teammate in the big game" and "the most honorable position that can be bestowed upon a Penn State student."

Greg Santucci was ready to graduate with a degree in exercise science that May but would stay in school an extra year if selected as the Lion. He had been working as a personal trainer, taught ballroom dancing, and had served as Morale Captain at Penn State's 1996 IFC Dance Marathon—three specialized skills he thought might come in quite handy for a Nittany Lion Mascot.

Nick Indeglio was no stranger to Lion territory. The special education major had spent a semester in the suit at the Delaware County Campus of Penn State as a freshman and had been backup Lion to Brad Cornali throughout 1995–96, his sophomore year. Indeglio was one of Penn State's outstanding cheerleaders and a rousing presence at all the sporting events he attended.

The Saturday night following their mid-week interviews, the four Lion finalists were given an opportunity to suit up at a Penn State gymnastics meet at Rec Hall. Because he had spent some time in the suit already, Indeglio took only five minutes in the suit, so he could remember the feeling of restricted vision that special head delivers to its wearer. The other three candidates worked the crowd and got to feel firsthand the power the Lion suit delivers. But no specific judging took place that night. The appearances were meant only to make the candidates feel comfortable in the suit and to see how the suit fit them.

On Sunday, April 14, 1996, after a few hours of cheerleader tryouts in Rec Hall's South Gym, it was Nittany Lion time. A coin flip determined that Barrett would start, but the audience was not told who was performing. The four finalists had each been given two minutes to perform a prepared skit to music of their choosing. They were being judged on personality, creativity, how they looked in the suit, and gymnastic abilities. The prepared skit would be followed by a 30-second impromptu session using a prop pulled from a large gym bag. The tryout concluded with the fifty one-arm push-ups.

The first Nittany Lion came out dressed in a tuxedo jacket (with top hat no less), playing a baritone sax, and accompanied by a trio of musicians. At the end of her brief sax intro, the sounds of "Putting on the Ritz" floated up and Barrett's Lion Mascot began to strut "his" stuff. Twirling the top hat on a cane, leaping into the air, and closing with a round-off into a split, Nancy Barrett delivered an excellent routine.

Barrett chose the mop and pail from the prop bag for her 30 seconds of impromptu performance. In addition to some traditional uses, she also cleaned the Lion's teeth and armpits, to the accompaniment of audience laughter. Barrett ended with fifty convincing one-arm push-ups, alternating between arms every ten repetitions, and still had the strength to wave to the audience with the other arm.

Scott Gaston came next, perched atop a pair of atrocious baby-blue platform shoes (circa 1975) and danced the opening number of "Saturday Night Fever" in classic disco style. His whole wardrobe had come from Goodwill—someone had actually worn those clothes two decades earlier! The shoes were the only exception, having belonged to a friend. Not falling from those shoes was probably an impressive enough accomplishment, but Gaston danced his way through the entire two minutes. He too selected the mop (without bucket) for the impromptu skit, and moved the routine between janitor and air guitarist extraordinaire. He finally climbed down from the shoes to perform his fifty single-limb push-ups.

Greg Santucci came third and must have brought at least fifty supporters, who cheered when he hit the floor. Santucci opened with a tribute to tradition, a slow-motion Lion transformation from prone cat to majestic Mascot to the theme from *2001: A Space Odyssey*, and then took the Lion somewhere he had probably never been: ballroom dancing. Santucci's impromptu sketch was the inspired approach, attack, and proud domination of a very unusual Lion enemy: a small picnic cooler.

Final candidate Nick Indeglio appeared wearing a Hawaiian shirt and traveling on a skateboard to the sound of "Wipe Out"—and promptly did wipe out, tumbling into a forward roll. He leaped to his feet as the music shifted to "Shout," and executed a perfect backflip followed by a series of handsprings. Indeglio was all over the floor, running, leaping, twirling

PENN STATE
PS
BLUE BAND

with Penn State's featured twirler, and rescuing a bound cheerleader by entering a phone booth and bursting forth as Superlion. Indeglio admits that Superman is an admired character—all that power used only for good, kind of like the Nittany Lion.

"And the 1996 Nittany Lion is—Nick Indeglio!"

The Lion auditions had come a long way from Gene Wettstone asking someone to run across the gym and back, but it is still the undefined "something" that seems to win the Mascot his part. Barry Jones, Athletic Department Publications Coordinator and head of the Lion selection process from 1977 to 1993, has said: "Certain people just rise to the top, and from there we pick the new Lion. The tryouts are so rigorous because we're talking about such an important position. The person is constantly in the limelight. He *is* Penn State."

The announcements for cheerleader were made first that April evening, and Nick Indeglio was called up front, giving a moment's hope to the other three candidates. The judges had decided to keep Indeglio's application process for the two positions separate issues, but a moment later the suspense was over. Nick Indeglio would be a cheerleader for only five minutes because his next offer was the one he had been dreaming about for two years. "When they say 'and the 1996 Nittany Lion is . . . ,' " he reports, "your heart stops and you just wait. When you actually hear your name, you have to say it over to yourself, play it over in your head a couple of times until you actually believe it."

Nick Indeglio is doing a great job honoring the noble traditions of the Lion lineage while putting his own mark on the Mascot history. As so many have before him, the latest Mascot is having the time of his life, but Nick knows something this wonderful can't last forever. Somewhere in the Commonwealth on a Penn State campus is a young man or a young woman daydreaming about the day when Nick hangs up the suit to pursue the goals of his adult life. It may be a long-held daydream or a suddenly formed wish. It may be a tribute to a former Lion Mascot hero, or it may be the absolute knowledge that he or she was *meant* to wear that suit. Whatever the motivation for that dream, one more Penn State student's wish will come true one day soon, and another name will be added to the roster of special people who have worn the suit of the Nittany Lion Mascot.

Mascot Indeglio doing
his version of "the wave."

The Tale Goes On

It has been nearly a century since Joe Mason first said, "Well, up at Penn State we have Mount Nittany right on our campus, where rules the Nittany Mountain Lion, who has never been beaten in a fair fight. So, Princeton Tiger, look out!" It has been more than five decades since the Lion Shrine called for by Joe Mason and sponsored by the Class of 1940 was turned into a magnificent reality by sculptor Heinz Warneke. The history of the Nittany Lion encompasses much of the history of Penn State University.

It has only been a day or two since the Nittany Lion Mascot last appeared somewhere and delighted a group or crowd with his antics. It may have been an athletic competition or a school visit or a benefit dinner, but the people there had something to smile about. It has only been a few hours since the latest visitor stood silently before the Nittany Lion Shrine for a moment of quiet reflection. The strength of the Nittany Lion is the strength of those collected moments of joy and reflection.

The Nittany Lion is one of the most recognized of all college or university symbols in the United States, and that recognition is incredibly positive. But a symbol has no special or absolute value unless the institution it represents has value. Thus, this book is also a selective anecdotal record of some of the reasons Penn State is a great university. From its original land-grant mission to its remarkable school spirit, Penn State has always focused on its people—the students, the faculty and staff, its neighbors, and its alumni. Without that Mascot inside, the

Nittany Lion is only a worn cloth suit. Before Heinz Warneke came along, the Shrine was only a large lump of undefined limestone. And before Joe Mason, Penn State was simply "Dear Old State."

This tale is a tribute to all the people who have helped make Penn State what it is today and thereby bestow on the Nittany Lion its symbolic value. Think of it as the first chapter in a continuing saga.

The Original Nittany Lion. (Photo by Greg Grieco)

Mount Nittany—inspiration for many legends.

Henry Shoemaker at his writing desk. (Courtesy Historical Collections / Labor Archives, Penn State University)

The Nittany Lion Shrine, photographed shortly after its completion.

“I’m ready for my close-up, Mr. DeMille.”

The Nittany Lion Shrine looking over its domain.

On guard in winter.

If it could only talk, the stories it could tell!

The Nittany Lion Shrine in the shadows.

“Phantom” of the Nittany Lion Shrine, 1988. (Courtesy Thom McGovern)

Nittany Lion Mascot Nick Indeglio poses with his stuffed "cousin." A new photo tradition is born. (Photo by Dick Ackley)

Mascot tradition: Push-ups for points.

The Nittany Lion Mascot in a rare studio shot (1970s).

Mascot gymnastics always gets a Perfect 10.

The Mascot roar.

The Nittany Lion Mascot and the Nittany Lion Shrine, Penn State's two most recognizable symbols (1958).

A Nittany Lion Mascot tradition: Being passed through the crowd.

A Nittany Lion Mascot staple: Dance a little dance, any style will do. (Photo by Pat Little)

Goal: Motivate the team to a victory. Method: By pumping the crowd into a frenzy.

One of the tougher Mascot roles!

The Nittany Lion Mascot Scholarship Fund goes over the top: halftime presentation, September 1995. Back-the-Lions raised more than $100,000 in Norm Constantine's name to support a full-time scholarship for the "Man in the Suit." (Courtesy Bodkin Photo Services)

Nittany Lion Mascot duties go beyond athletics to Alumni functions, University events, and special occasions. *Left to right:* Then Alumni Association Director Peter Weiler, Lion Brad Cornali, and University President Graham Spanier, September 1995. (Courtesy Bodkin Photo Services)

Nittany Lion Shrine visitors include hundreds of students, thousands of alumni, and countless numbers of friends each year. Pictured here are DrueAnne Schreyer and Kelly, Buddy, and Rodney Frazier, family members of former Board of Trustees President William Schreyer. (Courtesy DrueAnne Schreyer)

Nittany Lion protectors come in all shapes and sizes.

The Nittany Lion Inn.

The Nittany Lion Red Geranium. (Courtesy Richard Craig)

Nittany Lion Miscellany

Not every fascinating fact and detail regarding the Nittany Lion lends itself to appearing in a story. We include here some additional particulars related to Penn State's famous symbol, as well as a sampling of the many items and organizations that have shared its name.

Licensing

The plethora of Lion memorabilia and souvenirs are closely regulated by the University's Licensing Program. The Licensing Program Office "is responsible for overseeing the federal registration and the use of the University's indicia, consisting of various names, trademarks, and symbols." Use of the symbols and designations is expressly forbidden without written permission. "It is the University's policy to charge a royalty for use of University indicia on merchandise. The revenues that are generated through the Licensing Program have in the past been channeled into various scholarship funds for the benefit of University students [currently returning 7.5 percent of the price of every item sold, with 86 percent of those funds going to scholarship funds and the remainder being used for administrative costs]. Included in this program are the names, trademarks, and symbols for the Nittany Lion(s), The Nittany Lion Inn, the Lion logo[s], and the Nittany Lion statue." Licensing regulations include restrictions on the type of paw prints and lion caricatures that may be used, as well as how the mascot and the statue are portrayed:

PENNSYLVANIA STATE UNIVERSITY

NITTANY LIONS

Top: The classic Shrine Logo; *middle*: "The Pride of the Lions," the newest logo; and, *bottom*: the earlier, "chipmunk" version.

The Nittany Lion

"Reproduction of the registered image of the classic Nittany Lion statue should only be made from good quality, camera-ready artwork, available from the Licensing Program Office. Artwork is available for both the full-bodied Lion and the Lion's head. Reproductions should be facing the same direction as the original artwork."

The Nittany Lion Logo

Since its development in 1982 and introduction in 1983, Penn State's Lion Logotype was a side-view stylized rendering of the Nittany Lion's head. Nicknamed the "chipmunk" lion for its resemblance to a slightly smaller mammal, the Lion Logo received a new look on August 3, 1996, when a "proud and determined" Lion image was introduced at a press conference at Beaver Stadium. One would be foolish to mention, at least within earshot, that this latest Lion resembles anything other than what it is—one determined-looking mascot. The new logotypes were developed to give manufacturers and retailers the ability to market additional Penn State products creatively. "We are attempting to respond to suggestions that we provide an identity program that is less formal than those presently available. Our intention wasn't to replace any of the existing graphic representations of Penn State but to supplement them in a fashion that might increase the appeal to the various publics our licensees serve."

The Nittany Lion Mascot

"The image of the Nittany Lion mascot may be used on merchandise provided that the rendition, or designs including the rendition, are reviewed and approved by the Licensing Program Office before they are used on merchandise. Any reproduction or illustration of the Lion mascot should include the trademark symbol. Licensees may obtain a photograph of the Nittany Lion mascot by submitting a request in writing to the Licensing Program Office."

Paw Prints

The paw prints "may be used in designs provided that they are rendered as *three*-toed or *five*-toed paw prints. The *four*-toed paw print is registered property of Clemson University and is not available for use by other universities. All designs featuring paw prints in conjunction with University indicia must be approved. . . ."

Lion Caricatures

"Any . . . caricatures that represent Penn State in any way must be approved by the Licensing Office . . . before that design is applied to the product. This is the case regardless of whether or not other Penn State indicia are included with the lion caricature. Some lion caricatures are copyrighted by the original artist and may not be used without permission. Licensees who wish to reproduce *any* copyrighted item must provide the Licensing Office . . . with a signed release from the owner of the copyright pending approval for manufacturing. Approval for any Penn State lion caricature also will require adherence to the following criteria:

a. Do not show fangs, claws, or any features that portray the lion as vicious or ferocious.
b. Do not depict the lion as bloody or gory.
c. Do not depict the lion with a mane (a Penn State lion is a mountain lion, not an African lion).
d. Do not use realistic cat artwork to represent the Nittany Lion."

Lion Ambassadors

The Lion Ambassadors (the Student Alumni Corps) began in 1981 and is supported by the Alumni Association. Their mission is "to promote the Pennsylvania State University, its interests and goals among future and current students, alumni and friends, and to instill in them the value of a lifelong relationship with the University." Ambassadors membership is open to all full-time students with a minimum 2.5 grade point average and at least third-semester

Cover of the Lion Ambassadors promotional brochure.

standing. Ambassadors' activities include campus tours, acting as student liaison for new students, assisting in minority recruitment offices, appearing at career days and Penn State Alumni Club functions, and other opportunities for sharing their "enthusiasm and commitment to Penn State."

Lion's Coats

Inaugurated at Penn State in 1926, these white denim coats were used as a canvas to collect autographs, drawings, and good wishes from one's fellow students. The purpose of the coats was to provide seniors with special recognition as part of the Move-Up Day celebrations. The coats were designed to be similar to beer jackets used at Princeton and Cornell Universities. They remained in vogue through the mid-1950s, at which point student support waned and the custom was discontinued.

Lion's Paw

This senior honor society was established at Penn State in 1908 with the primary purpose of uniting undergraduate leaders in service to the University. "Lion's Paw is self-perpetuating. To each retiring chapter is accorded the privilege of naming those seniors it deems best able and most willing to serve selflessly and with clear conscience the best interests of the University-at-large. Members are traditionally chosen for their leadership potential and/or because of the positions of responsibility they hold. . . . Lion's Paw endeavors quietly and democratically to advance those causes in which it believes and to oppose with equal

In addition to helping save Mount Nittany, Lion's Paw members raised funds to create the two bronze paw sculptures that reside in front of the Palmer Museum of Art.

vigor those proposals which it considers to be contrary to the best interests of students, faculty, and administration. Membership . . . is based primarily on character, dedication, and achievement. . . ."

Lion's Paw Alumni Association

This lifetime extension for Lion's Paw members was formed in 1909 "to promote the welfare and best interests and to maintain and perpetuate the traditions" of Penn State University. The Lion's Paw Alumni have been especially active in support of the Nittan y Lion legend and symbol in a variety of ways. Their long-term commitment to protecting Mount Nittany through land purchase led to the formation of the Mount Nittany Conservancy. The Association was also the sponsor of the two bronze lion's paw sculptures placed in front of the Palmer Museum of Art in 1993. The Lion's Paw Medal, established in 1965 by the Lion's Paw Alumni Association, "honors any person who has contributed notable service to the University. . . ." Recipients of the award include John Henry Frizzell, Joseph V. Paterno, Ridge Riley, Eugene Wettstone, Julia Gregg Brill, Margaret Tschan Riley, Mimi Barash Coppersmith, Kenneth and Grace Holderman, Frank Gullo, and Helen Dickerson Wise.

THE LION'S TALE

Published by the Women of The Pennsylvania State College

Volume I — DECEMBER, 1924 — Number 1

CHRISTMAS PARTY PLANS COMPLETED

The Old English Christmas party, which is to be held in McAllister Hall next Wednesday evening, December 17th, was introduced at Penn State in 1919. Upon that occasion this form of Christmas celebration met with such universal approval that the girls decided to make the affair a yearly event.

For the celebration McAllister Hall dining room is transformed into an Old English Manor, decorated with spruce and lighted only with candles. The rough pine tables, the costumes, and the entertainment by the jesters, carolers, and dancers give a mediaeval Yuletide atmosphere.

The Lord and Lady of the Manor chosen from the Senior class, have invited as guests at their table a Lord and Lady from each class, the Cardinal and the Poet. In front of the Lord's table, which is placed on a platform at one end of the room, is the table reserved for the guests and faculty. Around the three walls are tables occupied by the friars, nuns, hunters and peasants, also invited to the Manor for the Yuletide feast. These characters are represented by the student body who dress in appropriate costumes. During the feast the dancers, jesters, and carolers entertain the assembly.

The dancers are being trained by Miss Haidt, physical director, and the carolers by Mr. Richmond. Candelabras and steins used on the tables are secured from the fraternity houses, while the trumpet used by the Herald is loaned by Mr. Thompson, bandmaster. Spruce for decoration is supplied by Mr. Anderson, of the Forestry Department. Costumes are secured from costume-designing houses in Pittsburgh and Philadelphia.

At the beginning of the feast the boar's head is carried in by the Herald and placed on the table in front of the Lord of the Manor. It is roasted with a baked apple in its mouth, and surrounded with mashed potatoes, decorations, and candles. Around its head is placed a holly wreath.

Marie Heindel '26, is in charge of arrangements for the Christmas party, with the following committee chairmen cooperating: Invitation, Caroline Hahman; Lord's Table, Hilda Mayes; Entertainment, Alice Heffner; Table Decorations, Margaret Leitch; Costumes, Martha Lindemuth; Property Manager, Louise Hurlbrink.

DEAN CHARLOTTE E. RAY

GREETINGS FROM MISS RAY

This is to say "Good-morning" to all our alumnae recent and remote. If you belong to the recent group you know the long-felt desire for a paper among the girls of Penn State. If you are in the earlier group you have the gratitude of all the girls now present for establishing the fact that girls may carry a full college course without injury to mind or body. We count you among the "founders strong and great," and in your name we still "raise the song." What Erasmus, Mary Lyon, Alice Freeman Palmer, and others have accomplished for the education of women in general, you have accomplished for the girls of Penn State in particular. You have our undying gratitude.

Do you know that the Alumnae Club of this town was influential in bringing to realization our hopes for this little paper? Their support both literary and financial had much to do with making possible this first issue of THE LION'S TALE. We hope that thru these pages you will renew acquaintance with your friends of college days and will also give to those of us who remain any advice that may be helpful to the girls of your Alma Mater.

Sincerely yours,
CHARLOTTE E. RAY

December 8, 1924

Y. W. C. A. PROMINENT IN GIRLS' ACTIVITIES

Enthusiasm is always a necessary factor for any successful endeavor. The Y. W. C. A. cabinet has felt this necessity and, for that reason, has considered it a great privilege and benefit to join with the W. S. G. A. and W. A. A. in an annual camping trip just before the opening of school, in order to make plans for the coming year. This year a most successful one was held in the mountains at Lamar Gap and every one came back to college filled with enthusiasm for the coming year. Upon arrival in State College, a very helpful surprise was found in the person of Mrs. Kitchen. "Bea" as the Y girls have learned to call her, has been a wonderful factor in keeping alive our enthusiasm for Y Work. Mr. Kitchen, Penn State's new Y. M. C. A. secretary, and "Bea" have been instrumental in bringing about a closer union and co-operation between the two cabinets.

The religious meetings this year have been most interesting and the new plan of having a meeting only every other week, with the singing of hymns after dinner on Sundays, has worked out well. One of the first meetings was a discussion of the conference at Eaglesmere this summer. Several weeks later Betty Walker, national secretary, visited Penn State, and gave a very inspiring talk on the purpose which the delegates of Eaglesmere had adopted.

As has been done in the past, the annual Christmas party for the rural Sunday School children will be held in the Armory. Marion Stevens is in charge of this affair, which promises to be very successful. Also, the usual Japanese sale was held in MacAllister Hall from December 9th to 12th.

Twice during the Fall members of the cabinet have gone to conferences at other colleges with representatives from the Y. M. C. A. Cabinet. The first of these was a conference at Susquehanna held December 3rd and 4th, and the other a Bible study conference, held at Gettysburg over the week-end of December 5th.

The two cabinets have also enjoyed some fine times together. On October 31st, they spent a pleasant evening in the Y Hut. "Bea" and "Kitchen" were there to keep things going, so there was not one dull moment from the starting of the first game—that of learning the names of the guests—until the grand march when the judges

(Continued on third page)

Volume 1, page 1, of *The Lion's Tale.*

Lion's Tale

The Lion's Tale was a student newspaper published quarterly from December 1924 through December 1926. Its purpose was to "meet a long-felt need for a girls' newspaper." Supported by the Women's Student Government Association, the Young Women's Christian Association, and the Alumnae Club, the goal of the newspaper was "to promote girls' activities in varied fields such as student government, sports, dramatics, music, science, and scholarship. . . ." It was followed in 1937 by *The Co-Edition*.

Mount Nittany Conservancy

In 1945 the Lion's Paw Alumni purchased 525 acres on Mount Nittany when it appeared that this traditional landmark was about to be "shorn of its timber and foliage by lumber men." Bill Ulerich, Class of 1931 and then editor of the *Centre Daily Times*, "was proofreading his newspaper when he read that 525 acres on the campus crest were to be sold for lumbering. As a student and resident, he admired the magnificent Mt. Nittany from campus and town. . . . Ulerich immediately called fellow Lion's Paw Alumni. They acted quickly to save those

Mount Nittany.

525 acres. They agreed to buy the land on behalf of the Lion's Paw Alumni Association, and then raised the now mere, but then huge $2,000 from members."

It was not the first attack on Mount Nittany's natural beauty in Penn State's history. In the early 1920s, there was a strong movement afoot to form a gigantic "S" on the side of Mount Nittany facing Penn State using stone or concrete. Colonel Theodore Boal, who had purchased the land "to preserve untouched the natural beauty and grandeur of Mt. Nittany," was opposed to such a plan, but he became a supporter when the plan shifted to creating an "S" by planting trees instead. Even the use of a "natural" "S" was criticized by some who saw any alteration of Mount Nittany as a defacement rather than a celebration of Penn State. American Literature Professor Fred Lewis Pattee, for whom the Main Library at University Park was named, was one person who spoke out against the plan:

> The making of a huge letter "S" on the side of Mount Nittany, though it be done with evergreen trees, is to me a thing of doubtful expediency. No one will question, I think, my loyalty to the College or my interest in any student project, that will add to her glory or her influence. My position in this matter is dictated solely by my love for Penn State and her environment.
>
> The mountain is the most distinctive single object in our landscape, a dignified and impressive mass against our Shingletown and beyond. . . . It has a melodious name that more and more is becoming a unique Penn State possession. To make a huge letter on the front of it like a hideous scar on a human face is to turn it into a sensational object and to take away much of its poetry. It becomes not the sentinel of the extreme flank of the range overlooking the magnificent valley, but it is turned into a mere billboard. Why should not some rich and enterprising class in coming days plant its numerals on Bald Top to be imitated by other classes until the series extended to Shingletown and beyond? It would be a sensational sight and certainly provoke comment. A rich Dartmouth class might have the letter D painted on the cheek of the Old Man of the Mountain in Franconia Notch. That would be college loyalty all must admit. Colorado College could plant a colossal "C" on Pike's Peak, and the University of Buffalo might hang a B equal in size to the college loyalty over the Niagara Falls. Most states have laws against defacing natural scenery with advertising or anything else and such a law should apply here. It is a cheap idea and unworthy of Penn State. Before it is put into effect the alumni should be consulted and all who love our eastern sky-line should have a vote.

Fortunately for Mount Nittany and Penn State, the enthusiasm for the "S" faded in the face of arguments like Pattee's.

In 1981, Lion's Paw looked toward a permanent, long-term solution when they formed the Mount Nittany Conservancy, an incorporated nonprofit organization that opened the protection of Mount Nittany to the larger Penn State community. Able to receive tax-deductible contributions from all of Mount Nittany's friends, the Conservancy uses funds "to purchase and preserve land on the mountain. . . . The Conservancy's goal is to own all available land from the 1,300-foot elevation to the 2,200-foot crest."

Mount Nittany Society

Membership in the Mount Nittany Society is the honor accorded those whose cumulative giving to Penn State has reached or exceeded $100,000. The Society's members are the leaders in raising funds for scholarships and fellowships, among other categories of giving. Inducted at an annual awards ceremony, members receive the Mount Nittany Society medallion designed by Professor of Art Emeritus John Cook. It depicts the landmark Mount Nittany within a circle that symbolizes the ties that bind the Society's members together. A laurel branch at the top portrays Pennsylvania's state flower, the mountain laurel, and at the bottom of the circle is a seed, representing the potential for growth.

The Mount Nittany Society medallion.

Nita-Nee Club / Kappa Alpha Theta

Established in 1922 as the first women's social club, the purpose of the Nita-Nee Club was to coordinate activities for women and to provide opportunities for social interaction previously unavailable to women. In 1931, the club became the sixtieth chapter of Kappa Alpha Theta sorority. The sorority was the first Greek letter organization established for women in the United States. Penn State's chapter was named Beta Phi.

Kappa Alpha Theta Sorority, 1964.

An early view of Nittany Halls.

Nittany Halls

The barracks-like dormitories known as Nittany Halls were built in 1947–48 to house the ever-increasing number of returning World War II veterans. They were constructed east of Pollock Circle (downwind from the poultry barns) and named for students killed in World War II. Between 1949 and 1950 the residents were kept informed by way of a residence hall publication entitled *Lionews*. Nittany Halls were replaced in phases during the early 1980s by the Nittany Apartments.

"The Nittany Lion" Song

This song did much to popularize the Lion Mascot. James Leyden wrote both the words and the music in 1914:

> Every college has a legend, passed on from year to year,
> To which they pledge allegiance, and always cherish dear.
> But of all the honored idols, there's but one that stands the test,
> It's the stately Nittany Lion, the symbol of our best.

The music and words for James Leyden's "The Nittany Lion."

Chorus:
Hail to the Lion, loyal and true.
Hail Alma Mater, with your white and blue.
Penn State forever, molder of men.
Fight for her honor—fight—and victory again.

There's Pittsburgh with its Panther, and Penn her Red and Blue.
Dartmouth with its Indian, and Yale her Bulldog too.
There's Princeton with its Tiger, and Cornell with its Bear,
But speaking now of victory, we'll get the Lion's share.

And now that Penn State is in the Big Ten, there is an appropriate (and anonymously penned) additional verse:

Indiana has its Hoosiers, Purdue its gold and black.
The Wildcats from Northwestern, and Spartans on Attack.
Ohio State has its Buckeyes, up North, the Wolverines.
But the Mighty Nittany Lions, the Best they've ever seen.

Nittany Lion Club

Composed of Penn State alumni and friends of Intercollegiate Athletics, the Nittany Lion Club was established in 1961 "to create greater interest in and financial support for Penn State's varsity athletic program. Members of the Nittany Lion Club make possible grants-in-aid and operational support for more than five hundred student-athletes, representing the entire twenty-nine sport program." Annual contributions approached $5 million in 1994. The Club members keep themselves informed about athletic activities and issues through their monthly newsletter, which began publication in October 1980.

Nittany Lion Inn

Opened on May 5, 1931, with seventy-five rooms, the Nittany Lion Inn was constructed and managed by L. G. Treadway Services Corporation. Highlighted by its Dutch colonial style architecture with gabled wing ends and a mansard roof with dormers, the Inn is painted white with a Penn State blue trim. It was managed by Treadway until 1947, when Penn State took over its operations. Renovated a number of times over the years, the most recent work, which expanded the Inn's room capacity to 262 and increased its ballroom, meeting room, and restaurant facilities, was completed between 1992 and 1994. For many alumni, homecoming weekend at the Nittany Lion Inn is as important a part of Penn State tradition as the football game itself.

The Nittany Lion Inn.

Nittany Lion Mascots

The "Men in the Suit":

Richard Hoffman	1921?–1923
Leon Skinner	1927
Eugene Wettstone	1939
Donald Newberry	1939?
George Terwilliger	1939–1940
Tom Kelly	1941?–1942
Robert Ritzmann	1942–1946
Peter Bates	1945–1946
Clark Sharon	1946?–1947
Wendell Lomady	1947–1949
Michael Kurowski	1949–1950
John Waters	1950–1951
Alex Gregal	1951–1954
Alfred Klimcke	1954–1957
William Hillgartner	1957–1958
John Behler	1957–1960
Jack Lesyk	1960–1961
? ? ?	1961–1962
Paul Seltzer	1962–1965
Martin Serota	1965–1967
Danny Kohlhepp	1967–1969
David Lacey	1969–1971
David Brazet	1971–1972
James Schaude	1972–1973
Robert Welsh	1973–1975
Andrew Bailey	1975–1977
Cliff Fiscus	1977–1978
Norman Constantine	1978–1980
Roy Scott	1980–1982
David Dailey	1982–1984
Robert Sterling	1984–1986
Doug Skinner	1986–1988
Peter Garland	1988–1990
Todd Shilkret	1990–1991
Tim Durant	1991–1993
Richard Williams	1993–1995
Brad Cornali	1995–1996
Nick Indeglio	1996–

Nittany Lion Orchid

Harrison T. Meserole, former Professor of English and orchid hobbyist, grew a new variety of orchid and gave it the name "Penn State, Variety Nittany Lion." This "burnished gold flower with a red velvet center (the blossom does evoke the Nittany Lion's tawny coat!)" got an Award of Merit from the American Orchid Society in 1974. Meserole explained: "I've had it in mind for some time to name an orchid after Penn State when I got one good enough. This plant was sent to me as a two-inch seedling over five years ago by a breeder named Hans Gubler. . . . He hadn't named it and was agreeable to my doing so." Contrary to rumors, the orchid does not roar, nor does it do push-ups.

Nittany Lion Red Geranium

This red zonal geranium was developed by Richard Craig and Darrell E. Walker at the Flower Breeding Research Lab, Department of Horticulture, College of Agriculture, at Penn State in 1964. The first commercial geranium created to be grown from a seed, it won both a gold certificate and a silver trophy at the International Geranium Society exhibit in New York in 1964.

Craig and Walker also earned a "Special Recommendation for Horticultural Achievement" from All-America Selections.

Nittany Lion Suit

Originally made from real animal skin (sometimes even rabbit), Mascots' Lion suits have demonstrated as much variety as the men inside them. For many years, Clearfield Furs & Taxidermy was responsible for maintaining the suit. More recently, the cloth suit is made and repaired by tailor Mieko DeAngelo of State College. "It takes five yards of fake fur, a huge cone of thread—stronger than the stuff used for everyday garments—and lots of patience," according to DeAngelo. Inside the Lion's head is a football helmet—a little extra protection from the occasional fan who unintentionally drops the Lion on his head.

Mieko DeAngelo, Nittany Lion tailor.

Nittany Name

Over the years the Nittany name has been attached to far more than the Lion—in fact, nearly every type of business or service imaginable. Remember Nittany News and the Nittany Lodge? How about the Nittany Theatre? The Nittany name has an inherent positive value, as evidenced by all who elect to make it part of the name of their organization or business. A small Nittany sampler of State College area businesses and organizations includes: Nita-Nee Kennel Club,

One of the many businesses to use the Nittany name.

Even college dances evoked the name of Nittany.

Nittany Amateur Radio Club, Nittany Antique Machinery Association, Nittany Beverage Company, Nittany Construction Company, Nittany Geoscience, Nittany Grotto, Nittany Gymnastics & Dance, Nittany Hot Springs, Nittany Kickers, Nittany Line Hobbies, Nittany Mall, Nittany Office Equipment Inc., Nittany Oil Company, Nittany Railroad Company, Nittany Valley Chiropractic, Nittany Valley Feed & Hardware, Nittany Valley Rehabilitation Hospital, and the Nittany Valley Symphony.

Another State College institution to bear the Nittany name—the Nittany Theatre—opened on July 1, 1914, as the town's second silent motion picture theater and boasted Penn State Professor of Music Hummel Fishburn as a featured piano player. Shown here on an early postcard, the theater had an interesting reputation, especially for attracting student demonstrations and boycotts protesting the prices of admission and peanuts. Increasingly the peanuts were not for patron consumption but for hurling at the screen (or the poor piano player) at the slightest provocation. The Nittany was renovated in 1929 to accommodate sound motion pictures, and once more in 1973 when it was renamed the Garden Theatre. The Garden closed its doors in 1986, and the old Nittany Theatre now houses a clothing store at 114 South Allen Street.

"Old Nittany," The Poem

This poem from the 1908 *La Vie* serves as Penn State's first declaration of the Lion as Penn State's mascot, the first solid evidence that Joe Mason's call for the Nittany Lion as the guardian spirit for Penn State had been answered by his fellow students:

We stood amid the rain that day
    As sullen as the weather,
That drove all pleasant thoughts away,
    And banished altogether
The hope to make the Indians yield
And carry victory from the field.

But when we heard our lion roar
    We felt that joy was ours,
For we had heard that sound before
    In just such dismal showers.
We took it as a sign that we
Should carry off the victory.

As when the startled pheasant hears
    The mountains tumble round his ears
And sees 'mid peaceful scenes below
    The awful avalanche plunging go,
Jarred by a foot fall from its place
And wreaking ruin on his race.

So startled by that savage sound
At a time when they were losing ground,
The Indian line prepared to meet
The disappointment of defeat.

And when we saw our giants roll
    ('Mid cheers that thundered o'er them)
And press toward the distant goal
    The tawny line before them,
And make the leather spheroid soar
Again we heard our lion roar.

Now may the lion ever stand
The mascot of our favoured band,
The hope of all that's true and great.
All hail the "King of Pennsy State."

The music and words for "Old Nittany" by James Darlington.

"Old Nittany," The Song

The words and music of this tribute to Mount Nittany and Penn State were written by James Henry Darlington in 1916:

> Upon our Alma Mater fair, the mountain blue looks down;
> The highest of them all in sight, Mt. Nittany's the crown.
>
> And so to our loved college e'en, the mountain gives its name,
> And Nittany we call her, and will ever spread her fame.
>
> > *Chorus:*
> > Then join our Litany, for dear old Nittany,
> > Like the mountain fair and strong, fair and strong;
> > For you we raise the song, our hearts to you belong;
> > Nittany! Fair Nittany.
>
> 'Mid rolling green clad highlands of the noble Keystone State,
> She shows the struggling student how to conquer and be great.
>
> Afar from city turmoil and the ocean's surf and sand,
> She leads us all to virtue, and to honor native land.
>
> > *Chorus*
>
> From Ocean to Lake Erie, from New York to Maryland,
> Come sons of Pennsylvania, a noble earnest band.
>
> The stars of heav'n look down upon two thousand maids and men,
> Who fit themselves for living, and to win with hand and pen.
>
> > *Chorus*
>
> No matter where we wander far, o'er all the whole round earth,
> We'll never forget fair Mater, or the free land of our birth.
>
> We honor all schools everywhere, from farthest East and West,
> But Nittany, our college, is the dearest and the best.
>
> > *Chorus*

Bibliographic Notes

The resources of the Penn State University Archives were utilized extensively in creating this book. General vertical files, biographical materials, and manuscript collections were especially helpful. Specific citations are provided whenever authorship or ownership credit could be established and wherever such specificity might help a reader find the original sources the authors used. Each notes section begins with information about unpublished and archival material, followed by interviews and correspondence, and concluding with the citations of published material (for example, books, magazine articles, and newspaper articles). Within those subsections, wherever possible, the notes are presented in the order in which they appear in the text.

Notes for Chapter 1

Some of the unpublished materials used in the preparation of this chapter included scrapbooks and diaries of Harrison Denning "Joe" Mason Jr. that were provided by his son Captain John D. Mason. Other scrapbooks consulted are in The Pennsylvania State University Archives at the University Park campus.

Additional Joe Mason anecdotes come from an interview the authors held with Captain Mason at his home in State College, Pennsylvania, on October 16, 1995.

The information in the box regarding the number of mining accidents Joe Mason attended is from his letter of resignation to the U.S. Bureau of Mines, dated January 31, 1916, located in one of the scrapbooks.

Published sources quoted or cited in the chapter are:

Wayland Fuller Dunaway's *History of The Pennsylvania State College* (University Park: Pennsylvania

State College, 1946) and Michael Bezilla's *Penn State: An Illustrated History* (University Park: The Pennsylvania State University Press, 1985), for the "Dear Old State" material.

Ridge Riley's *Road to Number One: A Personal Chronicle of Penn State Football* (Garden City, N.Y.: Doubleday & Company, 1977), for some of the information in the "School Spirit" section.

Also used in the preparation of this chapter were various *La Vies* (especially 1903–8), the *Penn State Alumni News* (February 1928 and November 1942), and *Town & Gown* (January 1991).

Notes for Chapter 2

The unpublished manuscript, "Mountain Lions of Susquehanna County, Pennsylvania," by Edwin L. Bell, Emeritus Professor of Biology at Albright College, was an important source for tracing the history of the Brush Lion. The Suzanne McLaren letter cited in "An Extended Visit" was written to Edwin Bell, November 5, 1986. Copies of both are in the Penn State University Archives.

Several discussions the authors held with Richard Yahner, Penn State Professor of Wildlife Conservation, in October and November 1995, and a telephone interview with Duane Schlitter, Curator of Mammals at the Carnegie Museum of Natural History, on November 20, 1995, provided much of the anecdotal material in this chapter.

Consulted for statistical information about Pennsylvania mountain lions was Leonard Pearson's *Diseases of Poultry, Part I* (Harrisburg, Pa.: Clarence M. Busch, State Printer, 1897).

Consulted for information about the restoration of the Brush Lion was Catherine Hawkes's Conservator's Report on the "Pennsylvania State University Nittany Lion, PSC 1-14562," dated May 8, 1995. Follow-up conversations with Hawkes in October 1995 and July 1996 provided additional details.

Published sources cited or quoted in the chapter are:

Don Stearns's "When Mountain Lions Roamed Susquehanna County Hills—Parts 2 and 3," *Montrose Independent*, February 10 and 17, 1966.

Samuel N. Rhoads's *Mammals of Pennsylvania and New Jersey* (Philadelphia: Privately published, 1903).

Henry W. Shoemaker's *The Pennsylvania Lion or Panther: A Narrative of Our Grandest Game Animal* (Altoona, Pa.: Altoona Tribune Company, 1914).

Penn State's student newspaper *The Free Lance** 16, November 1902.

A. B. Farquhar's *Catalogue of the Exhibits of the State of Pennsylvania and of Pennsylvanians at the World's Columbian Exposition* (Harrisburg, Pa.: Clarence M. Busch, State Printer, 1893).

Notes for Chapter 3

The letter to Henry W. Shoemaker from Richard Ernest regarding the origin of "Nittany" is dated December 31, 1914, and was made available to the authors from the papers of Henry Shoemaker by Shoemaker biographer Simon Bronner.

Some particulars regarding the post–Penn State history of Pa (or Ma) come from an interview the authors held with Ethel Noll Koch at her home in State College, Pennsylvania, on January 6, 1997; from an unpublished remembrance of her husband written by Mrs. Koch; and from an interview with Clifton Joseph Campbell at Centre Community Hospital, State College, Pennsylvania, on January 6, 1997.

* *The Free Lance* ran from April 1887 through April 1904. It was succeeded by the *State Collegian*, September 29, 1904, to June 10, 1911; renamed *The Penn State Collegian*, September 28, 1911, to May 30, 1940; and called *The Collegian* from July 3, 1943, to June 21, 1946. Since that time, Penn State's student-run newspaper has been known as *The Daily Collegian*.

Published sources cited or quoted in the chapter are:

The Lemon: A Squirt of Astringent Juice for Everybody in State College: Squirt 1, December 14, 1906; Squirt 3, January 1907; Squirt 6, March 17, 1907; Squirt 7, March 31, 1907; Squirt 8, April 13, 1907; Squirt 13, June 12, 1907.

George M. Graham's "Sunbury's 1905 Baseball Success Due to the Hitting Ability of Its Team of Aggressive Youngsters," *North American* (Philadelphia), September 2, 1905, for the description of Captain Root's (a.k.a. Joe Mason) success as leader of the championship Sunbury Cubs.

Also used in the preparation of this chapter were Michael Bezilla's *Penn State: An Illustrated History* (University Park: The Pennsylvania State University Press, 1985); *Daily Collegian,* February 18, 1956; *La Vie*, 1908; and *Penn State Alumni News*, June 1915.

Notes for Chapter 4

Unpublished materials used in the preparation of this chapter include correspondence between Richard Ernest, head of the Department of Fine and Industrial Arts at Penn State, and Henry W. Shoemaker, from December 1914 and January 1915, made available by Professor Simon Bronner of Penn State Harrisburg, author of *Popularizing Pennsylvania: Henry W. Shoemaker and the Progressive Uses of Folklore and History* (University Park: The Pennsylvania State University Press, 1996). A pre-publication excerpt from the book was also made available to the authors. The Don Yoder quote in the "Folklore or Fakelore" box is from Bronner's *Popularizing Pennsylvania*.

Additional Henry Shoemaker particulars come from an interview the authors held with Professor Bronner in his office in Middletown on August 2, 1995. Consulted for additional biographical information was Miriam Dickey's "Henry W. Shoemaker: Pennsylvania Folklorist" (master's thesis, School of Library Science, Western Reserve University, 1955).

Published sources cited or quoted in the chapter are:

Henry W. Shoemaker's *Juniata Memories: Legends Collected in Central Pennsylvania* (Philadelphia: John Joseph McVey, 1916), for the text of "Nita-nee and the Creation of Mount Nittany," quoted and retold from the legend of the same name.

The Centre Reporter (Centre Hall, Pa.) 76, March 12, 1903.

Henry W. Shoemaker's "The Legend of Penn's Cave," from *Wild Life in Western Pennsylvania* (New York: Composite Printing Company, 1903), for the Shoemaker quote regarding fictitious Indian names and for the text of the Legend of Penn's Cave.

Henry W. Shoemaker's *Penn's Cave: Pennsylvania's Grandest Cavern and Beautiful Lake Karoondinha: The History, Legends, and Description of Penn's Cave and Its Magnificent Lake in Centre County, Pennsylvania* (Altoona, Pa.: Times Tribune Company, 1930), for the quote regarding Isaac Steele's telling of the Legend of Penn's Cave.

Henry W. Shoemaker's *Pennsylvania Mountain Stories* (Reading, Pa.: Reading Times Publishing Company, 1911), for the quote found in the "Folklore or Fakelore" box.

Nicholas Scull's self-published maps entitled "To the Honourable Thomas Penn and Richard Penn Esq., True & absolute proprietaries & Governours of the Province of Pennsylvania & Counties of New Castle Kent & Sussex on Delaware, This Map of the improved part of the province of Pennsylvania is humbly dedicated by Nicholas Scull" (1759 and 1770); and map based on Scull's work entitled "A map of Pennsylvania, exhibiting not only the improved parts of the province, but also its extensive frontiers: laid down from actual surveys and chiefly from the late map of N. Scull, published in 1770; and humbly inscribed to the honourable Thomas Penn and Richard Penn Esquires, true and absolute proprietaries & Governours of the Province of Pennsylvania, and the territories thereunto belonging" (1775).

John Blair Linn's *History of Centre and Clinton Counties, Pennsylvania,* bicentennial edition (1883; reprint, Centre County Historical Society, 1975).

George P. Donehoo's *History of the Indian Villages and Place Names in Pennsylvania* (Harrisburg, Pa.: Telegraph Press, 1928).

Notes for Chapter 5

Unpublished materials used in the preparation of this chapter include the letter Joe Mason wrote to the Penn State Alumni Association dated February 24, 1921; the letter Leon Skinner wrote to Lou Bell dated November 8, 1955; and some additional autobiographical material on Richard H. Hoffman and Leon D. Skinner, all found in The Pennsylvania State University Archives.

Published sources quoted or cited in the chapter are:

Katey and Ross Lehman's "1st Nittany Lion Recalls High Spots," *Centre Daily Times,* December 16, 1959, which includes Richard (sometimes also listed as Richards) Holmes Hoffman's reminiscences of his time as the first Nittany Lion.

La Vie, 1923 and 1992; *Centre Daily Times*, January 20, 1975; and an article entitled "Under the Skin" in *The Penn Stater*, September–October 1977, provided additional information on Richard Hoffman. Hoffman's obituary appeared in *The Penn Stater*, November–December 1977.

Michael Bezilla's *Penn State: An Illustrated History* (University Park: The Pennsylvania State University Press, 1985), for information on Hugo Bezdek and the reformation of Penn State's athletics program in the 1920s.

Henry W. Shoemaker's *The Importance of Marking Historic Spots: An Address at Dedication of Marker, Nittany Furnace, Near State College, Pa.* (Altoona, Pa.: Altoona Tribune Press, 1922) is the source of his remarks on the significance of Nittany and his comments regarding the Pennsylvania heritage of the Nittany Lion. (*Note*: Shoemaker erroneously used the name "Nittany Furnace" in the follow-up publication, instead of the correct "Centre Furnace.")

Penn State Collegian, October 10, 1939, for the story about Gene Wettstone's appearance at the pep rally as the Nittany Lion.

The Lemon, Squirt 12, May 29, 1907, for Joe Mason's call for a campus memorial to the Nittany Lion.

Notes for Chapter 6

Unpublished materials used in the preparation of this chapter include records regarding the Shrine vote found among the papers of Francis E. Hyslop in the Penn State University Archives.

Some anecdotal information used in the preparation of this chapter comes from interviews the authors held with four members of the Class of 1940: Peggy Cimahosky Pergrin and David Pergrin at their home in Wallingford, Pennsylvania (August 22, 1995); A. William Engel at his home in State College, Pennsylvania (October 16, 1995); and Bernard Newman by telephone (December 13, 1995). Information regarding the bronze lions comes from a telephone interview with Robert Houts at his store (November 15, 1995).

Published sources quoted or cited in this chapter are:

Ridge Riley's *Road to Number One: A Personal Chronicle of Penn State Football* (Garden City, N.Y.: Doubleday & Company, 1977), for the bonfire story of 1914.

"Mob Damage May Mount to $2,000," *Penn State Collegian*, September 30, 1938, for the bonfire story of 1938.

"Seniors Can Lead in Preventing Further Riots, President Says," *Penn State Collegian,* October 7, 1938, which quotes Ralph D. Hetzel's remarks.

"Bronze Lions to Guard Main Campus Entrance," *Penn State Collegian*, October 21, 1930.

"College Removes Lions from Gate," *Penn State Collegian*, November 14, 1930.

Rog Alexander's "Lost Lion Statues Discovered on Farm," *Daily Collegian*, February 18, 1956, for the quotation regarding the construction of a "gate" for the bronze lions.

"Wanted Place to Have Fire, Lion Shrine Suggested as Possible Site for Rallies," *Penn State Collegian*, November 17, 1939, for Bernie Newman on the bronze lions being "Old English" rather than Nittany.

Penn State Collegian, November 7, 1939; "Student Soapbox," November 23, 1939; December 1, 1939; and "Students Favor Shrine Plan," December 5, 1939, for the series of quotations regarding the Campaign for the Shrine.

"Outstanding Sculptors Consulted by Hyslop for Shrine Erection," *Penn State Collegian*, January 9, 1940, for information on the three sculptors consulted.

Bernard Newman's "Letter to the Editor," *Penn State Collegian*, March 1, 1940.

"Scholarship Fund and Lion Shrine Lead in Senior Gift Poll," *Penn State Collegian*, March 15, 1940.

Notes for Chapter 7

Unpublished materials used in the preparation of this chapter include archival records regarding the work of the Nittany Lion Shrine Committee and Penn State's contract with sculptor Heinz Warneke. The papers of Francis E. Hyslop in the Penn State University Archives were an especially useful resource. For example, in a letter dated August 26, 1941, Warneke reported to Hyslop on the progress of the construction of the full-size model.

Additional background details come from interviews the authors held with David Pergrin at his home in Wallingford (August 22, 1995) and with A. William Engel at his home in State College (October 16, 1995), and from *First Across the Rhine: The Story of the 291st Engineer Combat Battalion,* by Colonel David E. Pergrin with Eric Hammel (New York: Atheneum, 1989).

Published sources quoted or cited in this chapter are:

Mary Mullen Cunningham's biography, *Heinz Warneke, 1895–1983: A Sculptor First and Last* (Newark: University of Delaware Press, 1994), is the source of the biographical material on Heinz Warneke, including the Marya Mannes review quoted in the box.

The Heinz Warneke letter to John F. Lewis dated March 23, 1960, quoted in the same box, is quoted by Cunningham. In the notes for this quotation Cunningham states: "Here again, I would like to stress that although these words are obviously those of Jessie Warneke, they do express the sculptor's sentiments"—a reference to Heinz's habit of having Jessie do most of the actual writing issued above his signature.

Carl Zigrosser's "Heinz Warneke: Sculptor," *Creative Art: A Magazine of Fine and Applied Art* 2 (April 1928), for the quotation regarding Warneke's delight in touching objects.

"Warneke Carves Lion Shrine for Penn State," *Art Digest* 17 (January 1, 1943), for the excerpts from Heinz Warneke's remembrances about working at Penn State.

The Oxford Dictionary of Art, edited by Ian Chilvers and Harold Osborne (New York: Oxford University Press, 1988), for the definition of pointing in a footnote.

"Remarks on the Occasion of the Dedication of the Nittany Lion Shrine," *Penn State Alumni News*, November 1942, for the Lion Shrine dedication speeches and letters by A. William Engel, Joe Mason, Bernard Plesser, Ralph D. Hetzel, and Heinz Warneke.

Notes for Chapter 8

Unpublished materials used in the preparation of this chapter include the Joe Paterno quote, from a piece on Heinz Warneke by Ann Meyer dated May 1975 and located in the Heinz Warneke Biographical File in the Penn State University Archives. The Warneke quote about coeds passing the basket is from an A. William Engel Jr. Inter-Office Correspondence memo dated May 7, 1979, Hyslop Papers, Penn State University Archives.

Sue Paterno's reminiscences regarding the Lion Shrine were provided in reply to the authors' request in August 1995.

Some of the anecdotal information used in the preparation of this chapter comes from interviews the authors held with David Pergrin at his home in Wallingford (August 22, 1995), with A. William Engel and Eloise Engel (Class of 1940) at their home in State College (October 16, 1995), and with Bernard Newman by telephone (December 13, 1995). A telephone interview with Penn State Associate Professor of Art Thom McGovern (December 13, 1995) is the source of the details on making the duplicate Nittany Lion.

Published sources quoted or cited in this chapter are:

Marge Helsel's "A 'Personal Triumph' for Warneke," *Pennsylvania Mirror*, November 2, 1975, for the Warneke sledgehammer quote.

Mary Mullen Cunningham's *Heinz Warneke, 1895–1983: A Sculptor First and Last* (Newark: University of Delaware Press, 1994), for the information regarding the carved lions in the Class of 1903 Memorial Gate and many of the details in the biographical box.

Joan A. Kurilla's "Sculptor Pleased with Lion Repair Work," *Centre Daily Times*, June 14, 1979, for the quotation about Warneke "feeling good" about the ear repair.

Jules Loh's "For Vincenzo Palumbo, Being Last Carver a Great Burden," *Centre Daily Times*, August 14, 1979, for background on Palumbo.

Francis E. Hyslop Jr.'s "A Rare Spiritual Innocence," *Penn State Alumni News*, October 1965, quotes Carl Zigrosser on Warneke.

Notes for Chapter 9

Unpublished materials used in the preparation of this chapter include the program for the Lion's Paw Award honoring Eugene Wettstone, June 5, 1976, which has the Wettstone quote about Circus performers in the rafters; and Penn State Athletic Director Ed Czekaj's words about Gene Wettstone and P. T. Barnum, from a Pennsylvania State University Department of Public Information Press Release dated January 25, 1973.

Robert Ritzmann's reminiscences about his four years as the Lion Mascot come from the authors' call for Lion Mascot memories in the May 1995 *Penn State Alumni News*. Ritzmann's letters to the authors dated July 11, 1995, and August 11, 1995, are the basis for all Ritzmann quotes, including the quoted comments of Gene Wettstone that were made directly to Ritzmann. George Terwilliger also wrote in response to the authors' request, and his letter to the authors dated July 13, 1995, is the basis for the information about him. Marianne Behler's letter to the authors dated October 27, 1995, provides the personal anecdotes regarding her husband Jack.

Additional anecdotal information used in the preparation of this chapter comes from interviews with Eugene Wettstone at his home in State College (August 26, 1995) and with A. William Engel and Eloise Engel (Class of 1940) at their home in State College (October 16, 1995), as well as from telephone interviews with William Bonsall (January 13, 1996), Paul Seltzer (September 16, 1996), and Jack Lesyk (October 2, 1996).

Published sources quoted or cited in this chapter are:

Busby Butterfinger's (A. William Engel's) "Circus'll Be Great Show, Says Busby," *Daily Collegian*, April 21, 1939.

Earle "Sandy" King's "Wettstone: His Fine Touch," *Penn State Alumni News*, October 1965, for the Frank Cumiskey quotation regarding Wettstone and gymnastics meet attendance.

Penn State Collegian, November 23, 1939, for the quote regarding the Lion's reason for missing the Penn State–Pitt game of 1939.

"Homesick Lion Sent Home to His Mama" (newspaper clipping), from a United Press release, State College, Pennsylvania, November 19, 1943, tells the story about the "Vox Pop" lion cub being sent home to its mother.

Tom Gibb's "Hail to the Lion," *Harrisburg Patriot News*, April 16, 1995, for the information about Alex Gregal's "S," Jack Behler's 20-pound game-day diet, and the Dave Lacey quote about the fun of being the Mascot.

"Lion in Sheep's Clothing Gets New Coat—Money Raised by Student Drive," *Penn State Alumni News*, December 1952.

"Funds to Be Sought for New Lion Suit," *Daily Collegian*, October 9, 1958.

"*Froth* Editors Froth over Frothy Ouster," by Alan Elms and James Winpenny, editors of *Froth*, in Letters, *Daily Collegian*, September 30, 1959, for the Jack Behler quotation regarding Frothy.

"Nittany Lion Unveiled," *Daily Collegian*, April 7, 1967, for the information regarding Marty Serota.

"Nittany Lion Takes Real Pains to Raise School Spirit," *Centre Daily Times*, October 30, 1970, for the Dave Lacey school spirit quote.

Notes for Chapter 10

Unpublished materials used in the preparation of this chapter include numerous Penn State University Department of Public Information press releases. The James Schaude quotation is from a release dated November 2, 1972; the information regarding Bob Welsh is in releases dated May 7, 1975, and November 16, 1973; the Dave Dailey quotations are from a release dated May 17, 1982; and the Doug Skinner quotations are from a release dated December 10, 1986.

Also used were Andy Bailey's "Memoirs of a Nittany Lion Mascot," written in 1995 and located in the University Archives, as well as a letter Bailey wrote to the authors dated October 22, 1995. A telephone interview with Robert Sterling (August 13, 1996) provided the genesis of Cowbell Man.

Additional anecdotal information comes from interviews the authors held with Nanette Sheaffer at her office at Penn State (July 31, 1995), Eugene Wettstone at his home in State College (August 26, 1995), Brad Cornali in the Penn State Room at Pattee Library (October 16, 1995), and Greg Santucci (April 23, 1996), Nancy Barrett (April 25, 1996), Nick Indeglio (April 25, 1996), and Scott Gaston (May 2, 1996) at the Education Library at Penn State.

Published sources quoted or cited in this chapter are:

Tom Gibb's "Hail to the Lion," *Harrisburg Patriot News*, April 16, 1995, for the information about Bob Welsh's extra push-ups, and for the Nanette Sheaffer (then Smith) quote regarding the Lion Mascot's schedule and Brad Cornali's reply.

Cathy Cipolla's "Pep Rally Didn't Rally the Crowd," *Daily Collegian*, September, 8, 1975, for the quotation about the fierce head.

"Under the Skin," *The Penn Stater*, September–October 1977, for the Cliff Fiscus quotation.

Harriet May Savitz's *Remembering Norm: A Victim's Story* (Pittsburgh: Dorrance Publishing Company, 1995), for much of the information regarding Norm Constantine. The quotations regarding Norm attending the fencing event and taking the Lion to the streets are from an unpublished interview by Linda Beamon Clyne (1978) quoted by Savitz.

Katy Koontz's "Look Out, Guys: Next Nittany Lion May Be Lioness," *Daily Collegian*, February 14, 1980, for the Debbie Slavin quotation.

Daily Collegian, March 29, 1988, quoting Peter Garland.

Erin Burke's "Mascot Projects University," *La Vie*, 1991, quoting Todd Shilkret.

Dana Greenberg's "The Face Behind the Fur," *State College Magazine*, September 1992, quoting Tim Durant.

Melody Tanti's "The Best of Town & Gown: Update," *Town & Gown,* May 1994, quoting Ricky Williams and Barry Jones.

Notes for Nittany Lion Miscellany

Much of the information in this section comes from materials published by The Pennsylvania State University.

The *Licensing Manual* (Pennsylvania State University, 1995) provided all details in the "Licensing" section except the information regarding the "Pride of the Lion" logos of 1996. The latter comes from the Penn State Department of Public Information press release entitled "Penn State Unveils New Logotypes" dated August 3, 1996.

Particulars on the Lion Ambassadors, the Lion's Paw Honor Society, the Lion's Paw Alumni Association, Kappa Alpha Theta, the Mount Nittany Conservancy, the Mount Nittany Society, Nittany Halls, Leyden's lyrics to "The Nittany Lion," the Nittany Lion Club, the Nittany Lion Inn, the Nittany Lion Orchid, the Nittany Lion Red Geranium, and Darlington's lyrics to "Old Nittany" are from various Penn State informational and promotional publications and archivist-generated information folders, all located in the Penn State University Archives. The last Mount Nittany Conservancy quotation is from a fund-raising letter written by Conservancy President Kenneth Reeves in the fall of 1995.

Published sources quoted or cited in this chapter are:

Dwight Kier's "Penn State Unveils New Sports Logos," *Centre Daily Times*, August 4, 1996, for additional information regarding the "Pride of the Lions" logos.

Daily Collegian, April 29, 1952, and May 4, 1926, for information on the custom of Lion's Coats.

La Vie 1927, for information on *The Lion's Tale* newspaper.

New York Times, March 29, 1964, and Marjory J. Sente's "Geranium U," *The Penn Stater*, July–August 1987, for additional information on the geranium.

Town & Gown, January 1976; *Penn State Alumni News,* July 1957; and *Penn State Collegian,* January 9, 1918, and January 23, 1918, for details on the Nittany Theatre in the photo caption.

"Tentative Plans Made for Placing 'S' on Mt. Nittany," *Penn State Collegian*, January 13, 1922, and "On Defacing Old Nittany," *Penn State Collegian*, Letter Box, February 21, 1922, for background on the Mount Nittany "S," and the quotation from Professor Pattee's letter in response to the plan.

Acknowledgments

This tale of the Nittany Lion is based largely on information obtained from a variety of archival sources, newspaper stories, and interviews. Some of those sources may contain inaccuracies that we pass along unwillingly and unknowingly with advance apology. We welcome from readers any information regarding our omission of important information or our commission of errors.

Much of the material used in the preparation of this book can be found in the Penn State University Archives, which is housed and maintained in the Penn State Room of the University Libraries at University Park. All photographs are archival photographs unless otherwise noted. The importance of historical archives can never be overemphasized. To all the archivists, librarians, and staff throughout Penn State's history who thought "This is probably worth keeping" and who documented what they kept—thank you so very much.

This book may list two authors, but anyone who has ever worked on a book knows that the contributors to its creation belong on a far more extensive list. We would like to begin with a universal "thank you" to everyone who played a part in the creation of this particular *Nittany Lion*. Thanks to the alumni who shared their memories, the family members of departed Lion heroes who shared their feelings, the colleagues who provided guidance, the staff members who supported this project and excused our bouts of mental preoccupation, and the loved ones who gave us the time and space to create—and to all the "Men in the Suit," who embody the spirit of what has become Penn State's most recognizable symbol: the Nittany Lion. To all of you we send this note of deepest appreciation.

Special appreciation goes to Shirley Davis, Administrative Assistant to the Dean of the University Libraries, who provided the enthusiastic push that got the project moving and the ongoing motivation that kept it from flagging. Special appreciation also goes to Nancy Cline, the former Dean of the University Libraries and now the Roy E. Larson Librarian of Harvard College, for her unwavering support and for her astute conceptualization of how to approach the project.

Thanks also go to the University Libraries administrators—Katie Clark, Sally Kalin, Bonnie MacEwan, Charles Mann, Gloriana St. Clair, and Lee Stout—who allowed the authors the time and resources to create the book. Enormous thanks are due the University Libraries faculty and staff who worked with the authors on a day-to-day basis to ensure the accuracy and quality of the book. Each deserves recognition far greater than this brief mention: Betty Arnold, Robyn Comly, Michelle Dzyak, Cindy Faries, Diane Gingerich, Pat Hermann, Jamie Jamison, Jennifer Litz, Mary Ellen Litzinger, Mila Su, Alston Turchetta, Sue Watson, and Carol Wright. Our colleagues Sandra Stelts in Rare Books and Simon Bronner, Distinguished Professor of Folklore and American Studies at Penn State Harrisburg, deserve special mention for their unique contributions.

The capturing of a tale this grand required the assistance and approval of many University administrative offices. Thanks to Budd Thalman, Ellen Perry, Barry Jones, and Nanette Sheaffer at Intercollegiate Athletics; Jean Barrett at University Licensing; Peter Weiler, Patrick Scholl, and Elizabeth Wilson of the Alumni Association; Michael Bezilla in University Relations; and the staff at University Photographics.

Our appreciation goes also to Sue Paterno, who shared her insights on the Nittany Lion and its meaning; to Ross Lehman, who served ably as an early reader; and to Mickey Bergstein, who checked the manuscript against his memory. Thanks also to Richard H. Yahner, Professor of Wildlife Conservation at Penn State; Edwin L. Bell, Emeritus Professor of Biology at Albright College; Duane A. Schlitter, Curator of Mammals at the Carnegie Museum of Natural History in Pittsburgh; and Mrs. Carol Brush Kotz, great-granddaughter of Samuel Brush, for their help in tracing the history of Penn State's "Original Nittany Lion." For their assistance in obtaining information about Pa and Ma, we offer our gratitude to Clifton "Joe" Campbell; Emilie Jansma, Curator of the Koch Collection; Carolyn Smith of the Centre County Historical Society; and Ethel Noll Koch, widow of Hubie Koch, a dedicated collector of early State College memorabilia and photographs. Thanks also to Thom McGovern, Associate Professor of Art at Penn State, for his explanations regarding sculpture molds and models; to Bill Bonsall, for the delightful memories of his antics with "Fuzzy" Lomady; to the Mount Nittany Conservancy, for its guardianship of the mountain; and to DrueAnne Schreyer, for her friendship.

We wish to recognize all at Penn State Press who contributed to this book at all stages. Special thanks to Steve Kress and Ray Liddick, designers; Janet Dietz, production manager; Peggy Hoover, manuscript editor; and the marketing staff of the Press. In particular, we wish to single out Sanford G. Thatcher, director of Penn State Press, for his support and encouragement throughout the process.

To John D. Mason, thank you for your hospitality and for the memories of your father—we could not have done this book without you. To Dave Pergrin, Bill Engel, Bernie Newman, and the entire Class of 1940, thank you for the Shrine and for your help with this book. And to all the Nittany Lions who have catapulted their way into the hearts of Penn State fans, this book salutes you. Our appreciation goes especially to these former "Men in the Suit": Andrew Bailey (Class of 1977), Jack Behler (Class of 1960), Brad Cornali (Class of 1996), Jack Lesyk (Class of 1962), Robert Ritzmann (Class of 1944 and 1946), Paul Seltzer (Class of 1965), Clark William Sharon (Class of 1948), Leon Skinner (Class of 1927, thanks to daughter Camilla Hoy), Robert Sterling (Class of 1986), George Terwilliger (Class of 1940), and to Eugene Wettstone, former Penn State Gymnastics Coach, for reviving the "Man in the Suit" tradition in 1939 after a long absence and for providing some of the best stories (and biggest laughs) we collected. Special thanks to the current Nittany Lion, Nick Indeglio, and his three fellow finalists from the audition of 1996—Nancy Barrett, Scott Gaston, and Greg Santucci. And to Cy and Eleanor Constantine, thank you for sharing the memory of your son Norm, who perfectly captured the essence of what it means to be the Nittany Lion.

Finally and most important, thanks to our families for their love, patience, support, and belief in the worthiness of this project.

Photo and Illustration Credits

Unless otherwise noted, all black-and-white photos and illustrations are courtesy of The Pennsylvania State University Archives / Penn State Room.

Dick Ackley: 35, 36, 38 (bottom); Nancy Barrett: 204; Beese Photographic Services: 217; Stacie Bird: 22, 26, 27 (top and botton), 37, 38; R. H. Breon: 159; Carnegie Library of Pittsburgh: 34; Scott Elmquist: 208; A. William Engel: 127; Tom Fedor, courtesy of the *Centre Daily Times:* 225; Greg Grieco: 38 (top), 99 (right); George H. Harrison: 137 (top); Walter Herb: 131 (lower left); Historical Collections / Labor Archives, The Pennsylvania State University: 60; Nick Indeglio: 207; Koch Collection: 49; Carol Brush Kotz: 24; *La Vie 1907:* 18; *La Vie 1908:* 52; *La Vie 1916:* 65; Pat Little: 145, 148, 191; Captain John D. Mason: 6; Thom McGovern: 146 (top and bottom); Howard P. Nuernberger: 199, 215; Palmer Museum of Art: 107 (top); David Pergrin: 123; Princeton University Archives: 3, 4 (top); A. J. Rader, courtesy of Shelley and Doug Abel: 132 (top); Rare Books Room, The Pennsylvania State University: 32, 48 (top); Dave Shelly: 132 (bottom); Rob Sterling: 193; Penn State University Licensing: xiii, 212; *Town & Gown,* 180; Zoological Society of Philadelphia: 107 (bottom).

Color photos that are not from The Pennsylvania State University Archives / Penn State Room are courtesy of Bodkin Photo Services; Dick Ackley; Richard Craig; Greg Grieco; Historical Collections / Labor Archives, Penn State University; Pat Little; Thom McGovern; and DrueAnne Schreyer and are credited in the respective captions.

Index

Page numbers in italics refer to illustrations.

About the Authors

Jackie R. Esposito graduated cum laude from St. Joseph's College, Brooklyn, New York, with a dual B.A. degree in History and Political Science. She received a master's degree, with honors, in American Political History from St. John's University, Queens, New York, and is pursuing a Ph.D. in Political Science at The Pennsylvania State University. She holds a C.A. from the Academy of Certified Archivists and serves as Vice-Chair of the Mid-Atlantic Regional Archives Conference and Chair of the College & University Archives Section of the Society of American Archivists. She is Assistant University Archivist / Senior Assistant Librarian for The Pennsylvania State University Archives, where she created and manages the University's Records Management Program and Penn State's Sports Archives.

Steven L. Herb holds a B.S. in Special Education, an M.Ed. in Early Childhood Education, and a Ph.D. in Curriculum and Instruction, all from The Pennsylvania State University, and he has a master's degree in Library Science from Clarion University of Pennsylvania. He is founder of the Children's Literature Council of Pennsylvania and the Immediate Past-President of the Association for Library Service to Children, a division of the American Library Association. At The Pennsylvania State University, he is Head of the Education Library / Associate Librarian for the University Libraries and an Affiliate Associate Professor of Education in the Language and Literacy Education program of the Department of Curriculum and Instruction.